A Critical Study of the Fictional World of R.K. Narayan

Edited by

Amandeep Rana

ATLANTIC
PUBLISHERS & DISTRIBUTORS (P) LTD

Published by

ATLANTIC

PUBLISHERS & DISTRIBUTORS (P) LTD

7/22, Ansari Road, Darya Ganj, New Delhi-110002
Phones : +91-11-40775252, 23273880, 23275880, 23280451
Fax : +91-11-23285873
Web : www.atlanticbooks.com
E-mail : orders@atlanticbooks.com

Branch Office
5, Nallathambi Street, Wallajah Road, Chennai-600002
Phones : +91-44-64611085, 32413319
E-mail : chennai@atlanticbooks.com

ISBN 978-81-269-1807-2

Printed in India at Glorious Printers, A-13, D.S.I.D.C.,
Jhilmil Industrial Area, Delhi-110095

Foreword

Writing forewords to edited books of essays by various scholars does not come naturally to me. It seems to convey that I either know everything or know nothing significant about the subject under question, for otherwise, I would have been included in the anthology itself. Since no one can know everything, one is usually in the second position. This is not such a bad position when it comes to a book on R.K. Narayan. We are talking about a writer who smiled at academic writing, one who felt that he was an observer of the vicissitudes and the ironies and humour of daily life and ordinary characters, one who felt that he didn't have anything really significant to say. Perhaps, it is this quality that makes him such a significant writer, one who seems to speak to different generations, and one who, I think, will be read for a very long time. R.K. Narayan is a writer easier to read and recommend than write about with academic seriousness, for that seems to cause serious damage to our reading experience without adding very much to its pleasure.

When Amandeep Rana invited me to the national conference on R.K. Narayan that he organized, I hadn't realized that it would result in a book, nor that I would meet scholars who felt that they had a real connect with Narayan's world. The conference was held in a town that Narayan would have recognized, one that was like the quintessential South Indian small town that was his spiritual and literary haunt, and one in which the feudal past lived with the modern present. For Narayan wrote about time and timelessness, about genetic memory and contemporary consciousness. He wrote about how we carried on in our traditional ways of life even as we accommodated the modern, the changes brought about in our material world. This was his world in which the traditional imbued the modern, the Tamil imbued the English. It was a world of continuities and contradictions, a world where humour was always in the air in this very contrariness, a world where characters almost bumbled their way through life. Narayan hold us up to scrutiny, finds us amusing and lets us drop—his novels never really end, it is just that he has been amused enough and, in his estimation, has amused us enough.

People see Malgudi everywhere, all the time. This means, as I said earlier, that Narayan appeals across generations, and across borders. There is of course an us/them, here/there, now/then dichotomy in critical positions. Is he Indian, or quaintly Indian? Is Malgudi in our part of the world or somewhere remote? Can or does Malgudi exist now or is its time over, part of a historical past? Perhaps, it is even more complex than that where some of these distinctions have porous boundaries and there is a lot of seepage and commingling and confusion—almost like the Indian English that Narayan wrote in. Is it Indian or is it English? Is it his first tongue or adopted tongue? Does it show his colonized mind or showcase the journey that educated postcolonials had to make in order to make sense of their worlds? Is he trapped in his caste sensibility or is he liberated from it? (for his novels which seem so clearly located do not show any caste distinctions in society) Is he ironic because he uses English which automatically distances him from his Indian world or is his vision ironic, regardless of the language he uses? A man who seems to be so rooted was a Tamilian in a Kannada speaking region, an English writer in India, one who wrote to be published and read abroad, but was bewildered by the western understanding of India, one who cheerfully allowed an English writer to edit and change everything he wrote, one who hunted for good South Indian coffee and curd rice on all his sojourns abroad. One remembers Walt Whitman, "Do I contradict myself?/ Very well, then I contradict myself,/ I am large, I contain multitudes." R.K. Narayan is large, he contains multitudes. You have to when you are Indian and represent even a corner of India!

This anthology of essays put together by Amandeep Rana reminds us of this. When Rana Nayar asked for "deconstructive, postcolonial, poststructuralist, eco-critical, meta-fictional, inter-textual, new-historicist and Bakhtinian reading of Narayan" in his opening remarks in the conference (the paper is contained in this book), he might not have anticipated that he would be answered immediately. This is a book of essays that looks at Narayan's works from different perspectives—from the postcolonial to the ecocritical—to the poststructuralist—to the intertextual. Several of the sixteen essays look at the notions of tradition, spirituality and philosophy; two look at education and one looks at the portrayal of children. This is a buffet where you may want to taste everything fully, even though there are so many different dishes. What more can an anthology hope to serve? Amandeep Rana set out to give us new perspectives on R.K. Narayan and I must say that the book reflects his purpose fully. Critics will always engage with Narayan's works, not only from every new perspective that comes along, but also from the same old perspectives since Narayan will speak differently to every new generation, whatever be their perspective(s).

I am glad that I agreed to write the foreword to this volume, since I got to read the essays and see the wide range of perspectives that obtain now in the reading of R.K. Narayan's works. This is a book that rewards the reader and I know that it will be an important contribution to the criticism on R.K. Narayan, and to our understanding of and approaches to Indian English literature.

GJV Prasad
Professor of English; Editor, *JSL*
Vice Chair, IACLALS,
Centre for English Studies,
School of Language Literature & Culture Studies,
Jawaharlal Nehru University, New Delhi

Preface

Indian English novel has achieved a significant position in the works of Mulk Raj Anand, Raja Rao and R.K. Narayan. Along with the other two, R.K. Narayan is regarded as the founding father of Indian fiction in English. Even though the 'brilliant trio' of Indian English novelists, as G.N. Agnihotri calls them, are basically concerned with the Indian life, there is a significant difference between their innate attitudes—contrasted with Mulk Raj Anand and Raja Rao, R.K. Narayan has kept away from addressing himself directly, openly and centrally in his novels to any political, social or economic problem of the age. Narayan is a great storyteller and the critics regard him neither a modernist nor a postmodernist, but rather, a traditional storyteller. He always has, in H.M. William's words, a good story to tell, like the bazaar story teller of immemorial tradition. He is a meticulous recorder of the ironies of life. Much of his fiction relates the unexpected disruptions and subsequent crises in the lives of his protagonists. Many of his stories are replete in irony and comedy, but they do take up important political and social issues. This particular quality facilitates him to turn many of his weaknesses into qualified virtues. His merit lies in the fact that he portrays life as it is and not as it ought to be; it is more realistic, and his stories, as Shashi Tharoor scrutinizes, have a universal appeal and are almost always absorbing; these are infused with a Hindu humanism that is ultimately Narayan's most valuable characteristic, making even his most poignant stories comedies of suffering rather than tragedies of laughter. After discovering Malgudi in his very first novel, Narayan sets it as the backdrop of all his fictional works and, thus, seems to follow Thomas Hardy's observation that it is better for a writer to know about a little bit of the world remarkably well than to know a great part of the world remarkably little; and it is perhaps for this reason that he never tries to venture beyond his fictional geographical location, which, in terms of A. Hariprasanna, is a 'dream country', in which physical features of various places, intimately known to Narayan, fuse in single detail and are rear-ranged and magnified.

R.K. Narayan is perhaps one of the most researched Indian English novelists and when we look around and review the literature available in journals and books, we find that much work has already been done on his novels and short-stories. His fictional world has been explored several times for an analysis of his characters, themes, narrative techniques, setting, irony, mythology, allegory, religion, philosophy, culture, etc. Research students and critics have always shown a keen interest in R.K. Narayan's fictional world for their Doctoral and Post Doctoral research works. In spite of all extensive research on Narayan so far, there is still a craving to explore more about this brilliant storyteller and to look at his works from a new perspective.

The present anthology, entitled *A Critical Study of the Fictional World of R.K. Narayan*, is one such attempt. The book contains sixteen research papers. It took more than a year for the compilation of this book. The genesis of this anthology took place in February 2011, when I came across a few unpublished scholarly articles on Narayan. It was then that I thought of a book, comprising a number of papers, exploring new and different dimensions in Narayan's fictional world. Many of the papers, which I had received over the past one year, were somehow not meeting my criteria of versatility towards Narayan, or say, they were dealing with Narayan in the same manner as many had done earlier. A sort of dissatisfaction remained within me as the objective of my effort was to explore Narayan's fiction in the light of modern and post-modern concepts, along with a multi-disciplinary approach. Despite several calls for papers, I could not receive many views, since the new researchers in Indian Writing in English have almost stopped working on R.K. Narayan by simply assuming that much work has already been done on his fiction. It did take a long time to collect the papers, and this anthology is a strong answer to those who think that there is little scope for research on R.K. Narayan. A considerable number of the papers in the anthology deal with post-colonial and post-modern study of Narayan's fictional world. The anthology, overall, is an attempt to re-visit the fictional world of R.K. Narayan for re-exploration and re-capturing of new themes and ideas. Many renowned and distinguished critics, in this book, have tried to venture beyond the already explored territories of Narayan's works.

The book begins with a scholarly paper entitled "R.K. Narayan's Fiction: Has the Moment of Re-Assessment Arrived?" by Prof. Rana Nayar, which is, in fact, a keynote address to a National Conference on "Re-Visiting the Fictional World of R.K. Narayan". The paper establishes Narayan as more contemporary than most of the contemporaries. The paper not only appraises the work done so far on R.K. Narayan, but also underscores certain areas where the critics have not yet concentrated. He demands a deconstructive, post-colonial, post-structuralist, eco-critical, meta-fictional, inter-textual, new-historicist and Bakhtinian reading of Narayan. The paper provides ample scope for research on Narayan.

Raju Parghi's paper is a post-colonial interpretation of the great novelist. It is an attempt to show how minutely Narayan has presented the impact of English language and British education on Indians. He has focused on how Narayan, who himself learnt the language of the colonizers first and mastered it before mastering his native tongue, resists the linguistic imperialism in India. Parghi observes that colonialism is still prevailing in India, and English language and Cricket are ruling the minds of Indians. The paper also focuses on the attack of the Western education on Indian education system and hence, firmly establishes Narayan as a post-colonial writer, a committed writer of once colonized India. Dr. Arun Kumar Mukhopadhyay, in his paper (first published in *Labyrinth*, a bi-annual literary journal Vol. 1 No. 1), has tried to find Indian roots which seem lost in the problematizing colonized education. He has critically evaluated *The English Teacher* for the analysis of this. Dr. Kishwar Zafir visits Narayan's fictional world with an eco-critical approach, which surely is a contemporary aspect and which needs further consideration.

Javaid Ahmad Lone, in his paper, sees renunciation in Narayan's *Mr. Sampath* with reference to V.S. Naipaul's interpretation of Narayan. Dr. Kavita Gopalakrishnan's paper is a study of shaking and debunking of massive structures in Narayan's fiction. Narayan's way of puncturing the structure of patriarchy in *The Dark Room*, decentering of reason and rational thinking of men in *The English Teacher* and decentering of moral value system and building of a new system based on utilitarianism have been evaluated and it has been established firmly that the cross-cultural influences break the existing cultural structures. This dimension of studying Narayan's novels is an area which still needs explorations. Prof. Bina Biswas invistigates Narayan's four novels for the theme of quest for self. Family, culture, society, religion, academic econoclasm of the West in the colonized education, Indianness, spirituality, tradition and traditional values—all have been studied for the analysis of quest for self, of various characters of Narayan. This post-colonial approach to Narayan calls for further inquiries and thus, opens new window for the researchers. Dr. C.L. Kharti's study of *The Bachelor of Arts* examines regional ambience, not in terms of topography and description of nature, but in those of customs, manners, human behaviour and relationships and goes on to examine the clash between the ideologies of the traditional and the modern, the old and the new generations.

Dhananjay Tripathi's visit to R.K. Narayan's fictional world is in context of the third space, with a flashlight on mimicry, hybridity, ambivalence, inbetweenness and cultural imprisonment. The paper shows how Narayan, despite being completely unfamiliar with the concept of the third space, unconsciously anticipated it, and how, in his several novels, the process of inbetweenness, with the cultural ambiguity and ambivalence, results in hybridity of cultures, which passes through mimicry and finally, results in the third space. The paper offers a considerable scope for the researchers to explore

Narayan's fiction, particularly, *Swami and Friends, The Bachelor of Arts, The English Teacher* and *The Guide*, and a couple of others like *The Dark Room* and *The Painter of Signs*, where the third space is the result of ambivalent relationship between man and woman. Dr. Shyam Bihari Tiwary's paper, which first appeared in *Cyber Literature*, a bi-annual journal of English studies (Vol. XV & XVI No. I & II), is an analysis of traditionalism in Malgudi in the light of religion, myth, morality, orthodoxy, sex-based relations, belief in *karma* and after-life. Yakiah Kathy's paper is an evaluative study of Narayan's novels in the light of colonial and postcolonial aspects.

Prof. Indrani Mukherji's paper is a comparative study of two novelists, writing in two different languages—R.K. Narayan and Sarat Chandra Chattopadhyay. The common themes and techniques, focusing mainly on the non-conformist attitudes and feminist concerns, have been captured. The boldness of both these novelists in portraying woman of the first half of the twentieth century has also been compared and it has been instituted that there are many wires which connect these two writers of different Indian regions and languages.

Dr. Harcharan Singh Arora's paper is an evaluative study of spirituality in major novels of R.K. Narayan. Dr. Rashmi Gupta has endeavoured to establish that Narayan's novels are the modern versions of Hindu mythological stories. Riyaz Ahmad Kumar's paper is a psychological study of children of Narayan's *Swami and Friends*. The way in which Narayan has traced the ideals, aspirations and frustrations of the children and the way in which their mind and heart encounter oppression, injustice and exploitation—all have been studied in detail.

Prof. Anand Balwant Patil, in his paper titled "Re 'visioning' Intertextualities in R.K. Narayan's Novels: Comparative-Cultural Critique", which is a speech by him as a comparatist in the aforementioned National Conference on R.K. Narayan, provides a wider scope for research on Narayan. He not only studies Narayan as a cultural comparatist, but also discusses Narayan's fiction in context of cultural representation of 'the other double', Prospero-Cannibal relationship, intertextuality, interliterariness and inter-culturalness, and with reference to the theories and ideologies expounded by Namwar Singh, Ngugi Wa Thing'O, Frantz Fanon, Edward Said, Homi K. Bhabha and others. There is much more than this and the paper is surely a valuable assistance to those who take interest in post-modern research on Narayan.

I take this opportunity to submit that undoubtedly, there is enough research on R.K. Narayan's novels and short-stories, but there are several regions in his fictional world which are still untrodden. Much has already been done, yet enough is yet to come. A re-visit to any area certainly results in new discoveries and innovations, and this anthology is a serious effort to re-visit the fictional world of R.K. Narayan, especially the unvisited quarters, with a new and modern outlook. A multi-disciplinary approach is still awaited. In this anthology, I also wanted to include a paper on the language or linguistic aspect of Narayan's works, which, unfortunately, I could not manage to get even during this long period of more than a year. The works of critics and scholars in this anthology lie somewhere between what Prof. Nayar and Prof. Patil have looked forward to in their papers. I hope, the book will be very beneficial for all those who are working on or wish to work on R.K. Narayan's fictional genius.

I whole-heartedly express my gratitude to all the contributors for sending their scholarly papers for this book. I also thank the publisher for bringing out this volume so quickly, as the book was already very late due to certain reasons as mentioned before. I dedicate this book to the spirit and the need of the reader, who wants to know a little more about Narayan in a new perspective altogether; it is this need only which has made this anthology see the light of the day.

Amandeep Rana

Contents

Foreword .... *iii*

Preface .... *vii*

1. R.K. Narayan's Fiction: Has the Moment of Re-Assessment Arrived? 1
   Rana Nayar

2. English Language and British Education: A Postcolonial Interpretation of R.K. Narayan's *The English Teacher* 11
   Raju Parghi

3. What about Our Own Roots? Problematising Education and Philosophy in R.K. Narayan's *The English Teacher* 31
   Arun Kumar Mukhopadhyay

4. Revisiting R.K. Narayan Through Eco-criticism 51
   Kishwar Zafir

5. Renunciation: An Indian Way: V.S. Naipaul's Interpretation of R.K. Narayan's Novel *Mr. Sampath* 58
   Javaid Ahmad Lone

6. Decentering the Centre: A Post-structuralist Study of R.K. Narayan's *The Dark Room, The English Teacher* and *The Guide* 66
   Kavitha Gopalakrishnan

7. Quest for Self in the Novels of R.K. Narayan 75
   Bina Biswas

8. R.K. Narayan's *The Bachelor of Arts*: Regional Ambience, Universal Appeal 89
C.L. Khatri

9. Reflection of the Third Space in the Novels of R.K. Narayan 102
Dhananjay Tripathi

10. Old Wine in New Bottles: Traditionalism in R.K. Narayan's Novels... 115
Shyam Bihari Tiwary

11. R.K. Narayan's *Swami and Friends* and *The World of Nagaraj*: A Re-Reading in Colonial and Postcolonial Contexts... 130
Yakaiah Kathy

12. R.K. Narayan and Sarat Chandra Chattopadhyay: A Study in Overlapping Landscapes of the Mind..... 142
Indrani Mukherji

13. Spiritual Syndrome in the Fictional World of R.K. Narayan 156
Harcharan Singh Arora

14. Modern Version of Hindu Mythology: A Critical Analysis of R.K. Narayan's *The Man-Eater of Malgudi* and *The Painter of Signs* 165
Rashmi Gupta

15. Portrayal of Children in the Works of R.K. Narayan 176
Riyaz Ahmad Kumar

16. Re-"visioning" Intertextualities in R.K. Narayan's Novels: Comparative-Cultural Critique 190
Anand Balwant Patil

List of Contributors 209

1

R.K. Narayan's Fiction: Has the Moment of Re-Assessment Arrived?

Rana Nayar

If I have to think of R.K. Narayan, today, I would not refer to him as a writer who belongs to another age or another era. Though he was born in 1906, which, by the standards of our fast-moving generation, would make him look like a writer from another century, or even a dinosaur, if you like, yet he certainly wasn't one. The world his characters inhabit may look somewhat like the replica of a slow-moving, 19th century Indian town or a suburb; and the simple, tastes, habits and manners of its denizens may appear to our MacDonald generation as distasteful as the *dhaba* food, R.K. Narayan is, and shall continue to remain, should I say, for a long time, a contemporary writer par excellence. If an ability to laugh at human faults and foibles is a quality of contemporary fiction, R.K. Narayan is contemporary to the core. If comedy is a tool of subversion in contemporary fiction, R.K. Narayan employs it to the hilt. If the hallmark of contemporary fiction is to turn our world upside down, and give us an inverted view of our reality, without being maliciously satirical or explicitly moral, then R.K. Narayan is far more contemporary than most of the contemporary writers we often speak or talk about. My purpose in underlining R.K. Narayan's contemporariness is merely to emphasize that though much work has been done on him already (some of which I shall also share with you as I go along), re-assessment of his work, like Althusser's project of modernity, is still incomplete, and thus far from being over.

Much before I start proposing the ways in which we may yet be able to read R.K. Narayan's fiction, I would start off by looking at some of the popular ways in which his work has been received so far. Naipaul, who is congenitally dismissive of all things Indian, had, in his characteristic churlish manner, once pooh-poohed R.K. Narayan as an "intensely Hindu" writer. He believed that Narayan's fiction was not only a direct product but also a clear endorsement of his Hindu-centric philosophy of life, something he couldn't really escape, being a devout South Indian Brahmin. While offering such a sweeping generalization, Naipaul perhaps overlooked the fact that most of his own non-fiction, too, has come in for an equally belligerent attack, on the very same grounds. My point is simple: If Naipaul couldn't shed the burden of his Hindu legacy despite the fact that his ancestors had migrated to the Caribbean Islands for over a century ago, how did he expect Narayan (who was born and brought under the shadow of Swadeshi and Swaraj, and grew up to believe in the Gandhian philosophy of non-violent struggle against the British) to escape his destiny. Anyway, I'm not trying to argue that Narayan be read as a Hindu writer (far from it!), but only suggesting that such labeling as Naipaul indulges in, often based as it is on grounds of religion, race, caste or gender, may lead us into a literary/aesthetic impasse and thus may become a ground for the rejection of a writer, but certainly not for a systematic study of his works aimed at developing critical understanding or evaluation, much less revaluation.

The process of critical evaluation of any writer is an extremely complex one. Often we turn to a writer for very personal reasons, but somewhere down the line, we begin to understand him in relation to his life, his works, his milieu, his immediate context and his relation to other writers, who have either preceded him or are likely to succeed him. All preliminary investigations into an author, if you allow me to say, do take on the form of a biographical-historical approach that aims at contextualizing an author within his space-time and moment. R.K. Narayan is no exception to this general rule. One of the earliest forays into Narayan's fiction was made by Harish Raizada, an Indian scholar, who published his book *R.K. Narayan: A Critical Study of His Works* way back in 1969. Lakshmi Holmstrom, who had spent early part of her life in Madras (where Narayan was born), and was thus familiar with the milieu of Narayan's works, later (when she chose to do her postgraduate degree from Oxford), worked on Narayan's novels for her dissertation. This dissertation was published in a book form by the Writer's Workshop in 1973, under the title *The Novels of R.K. Narayan.* To a large extent, Harish Raizada and Lakshmi Holmstrom could be said to have inaugurated the first phase of Narayan's critical evaluation. Being largely exploratory in nature, their books deal with the distinctive features of Narayan's fiction, recognize its significance and contextualize it within the wider frame of Indian English writing.

William Walsh, who published his *R.K. Narayan: A Critical Appreciation* from the University of Chicago Press in 1982, was perhaps the first European to offer a systematic and sustained critique of Narayan from outside. Walsh, who has also been Narayan's biographer, is of the view that his narrative art is both comedic and inclusive in its spirit, and is characterized by the transience and illusory nature of human action. Before Walsh came up with his assessment, Narayan had already won plaudits from some of the well-known writers of Britain and USA; though no book-length study had been undertaken on his work until then. Graham Greene (who first drew the attention of the Western world towards Narayan's fiction) considered Narayan to be more similar to Chekhov than any other Indian writer. Anthony West of *The New Yorker,* too, had noted the special quality of his realism, when he compared it to that of another Russian writer, Gogol. To an extent, R.K. Narayan's gentle humor, irony and fidelity to detail are reminiscent of the 19th century Russian realists. Comparing him to Charles Dickens, the American writer John Updike has acclaimed him "as a writer of a vanishing breed—the writer as a citizen, one who identifies completely with his subjects and has immense faith in the significance of humanity." In the recent times, Jhumpa Lahiri has placed Narayan's short fiction alongside that of the great masters such as Guy De Maupassant, O' Henry and Frank O'Connor et al. What she likes about Narayan is his ability to compress the narrative without losing the story, and his portrayal of middle-class characters with "an unyielding and unpitying vision."

For a long-time, Malgudi, the fictional South Indian town Narayan created, complete with its flora and fauna, its ecology and ambience, its sinuous alleyways and sloppy pathways, remained a subject of intellectual curiosity among his ardent readers and critics, alike. The idea of creating this town Malgudi, as Narayan had once mentioned to N. Ram and Susan Ram, came to him in form of a vision of a railway station, deriving its name from a freight train (*maalgaadi*). Often compared to Hardy's Wessex or Faulkner's Yoknapatawpha County, Malgudi remains etched on our consciousness long after we have put down a typical Narayan novel. Not only does Malgudi have its own distinctive colors, flavors and rhythms, but its own mythology and history, too. Commenting on how Narayan has successfully transformed this into an incredibly believable place, Graham Greene once said:

> Whom next shall I meet in Malgudi? That is the thought that comes to me when I close a novel of Mr. Narayan's. I do not wait for another novel. I wait to go out of my door into those loved and shabby streets and see with excitement and a certainty of pleasure a stranger approaching, past the bank, the cinema, the haircutting saloon, a stranger who will greet me I know with some unexpected and revealing phrase that will open a door on to yet another human existence.

One of the scholars of Narayan, Dr James M. Fennelly, has, in fact, carried this idea of "authenticity" of Malgudi a little too far by creating a map of Malgudi based on the fictional descriptions available in many of his novels and stories. Real or imagined or a mixture of both, Malgudi certainly doesn't embody a static world caught in a time-warp, but a dynamic social and historical reality, always in throes of change and flux. Whether or not we see it "in metonymic terms" (John Thieme's phrase), it is a microcosm of the macrocosm, which again makes Narayan into a constantly evolving, cosmopolitan Indian writer rather than a self-limiting, regional writer. Endorsing this position, Michael Pousse claims that "Malgudi is India and India is the world.... This universal appeal comes from the author's humanism." (*R.K. Narayan: A Painter of Modern India,* Lang, Peter Publishing, 1995). For close to two decades, R.K. Narayan criticism continued to operate within the traditional framework, varying from the biographical to the historical, from the psychological to the sociological; only occasionally veering off towards archetypal and/or cultural, in most of these studies, the critics focused either on Narayan's characters, characterization, themes, motifs, symbols, narrative strategies, comic spirit and/or or artistic modes. As it is not possible for me to go into the specifics of each work here (apparently, for the want of time), please allow me to mention some of the major publications in this regard. No bibliographical listing on Narayan can possibly ignore the contribution of such eminent Indian critics as P.S. Sundaram (who wrote two books on Narayan, i.e. *R.K. Narayan,* New Delhi, Arnold-Heinemann, 1973, and *R.K. Narayan as Novelist,* New Delhi, B.R., 1988), M.K. Naik (*The Ironic Vision: A Study of the Fiction of R.K. Narayan*, New Delhi, Sterling, 1983), U.P. Sinha (*Patterns of Myth and Reality: A Study in R.K. Narayan's Novels*, New Delhi, Sandarbh, 1988); Atma Ram (who edited *Perspectives on R.K. Narayan,* Ghaziabad: Vimal, 1981) and Bhagwat S. Goyal (who also edited a collection of essays titled: *R.K. Narayan: A Critical Spectrum,* Meerut, Shalabh Book House, 1983). This, I must say, is, by no means, a complete or comprehensive list (as there are some very important exclusions here), but it certainly does give us a fair idea of the whole range of issues that the Indian academics have debated on Narayan's fiction from early 1970s to late 1980s.

If I have to put it in perspective, then the re-assessment of Narayan's fiction is not a very old phenomenon, and could be said to have started in early 1990s. Ironic though it may sound, the first few attempts towards this 'reassessment' were made, not by the Indian, but the Western critics, instead. Some nativists, treating this as an attempt toward colonizing/re-colonizing Narayan or re-territorializing him within the critical space of West-dominated, post-structuralist theory, may also try and resist it. Regardless of how we choose to look at it and whether or not we feel the need to resist it, what we cannot possibly ignore is an extremely significant collection of essays titled *R.K. Narayan: Contemporary Critical Perspectives* (East Lansing, Michigan State University Press, 1993) edited by Geoffrey Kain. This particular collection of eighteen essays proved to be a trend-setter, as it opened up new frontiers and possibilities on Narayan's fiction that we couldn't have conceptualized in the earlier decades. Drawing upon the recent developments in literary theory, postcolonial, feminist and cultural studies, this particular collection expanded the parameters of Narayan criticism significantly, pointing out the complexity and subtlety of his art and also the direction his studies could possibly take in the future. Paul Brians is of the view that Narayan's exclusive emphasis on the private lives of his characters to the total exclusion of the public (even the British) is a willful neglect of colonialism or even an act of liberation from it (*Modern South Asian Literature in English*, Westport, Connecticut, Greenwood Press, 2003). Here Paul Brians is apparently offering a deconstructive, postcolonial reading of Narayan's fiction. Some contemporary critics like Homi Bhabha, Gita Rajan and Sadhana Puranik, have also read Narayan as an ambivalent, postcolonial writer, one who, caught between Western and Indian cultures, and like his protagonist Raman in *The Painter of Signs,* is positioned "between myth and modernity" (Bhabha, "Brahmin" 421). Such readings need to be re-visited and pursued further, if we have to re-interpret Narayan in the post-colonial context.

Reading Narayan's novel *The Dark Room* (1938) as both a national allegory in its indirect criticism of British rule and a religious ideological fiction, R.M. George (2003) notes that the author's Hindu nationalism "never solidifies into conscious intent and an exclusionary Brahmin nationalism is perceived only when one reads against the grain of the narrative ("Of Fictional Cities and 'Diasporic' Aesthetics", *Antipode* [Blackwell Publishing] 35 (3): 559-79). George's essay, too, opens up new theoretical possibilities for those of us who want to get into a re-assessment of Narayan's fiction. In her essay "The Magic Idyll of Antiquated India: Patriarchal Nationalism in R.K. Narayan's Fiction" (*Ariel*, Vol. 31, No. 4, October 2000, 59-75), Harveen Mann has offered yet another "against the grain" reading of Narayan's ostensibly apolitical narratives in an attempt to "re-open dominant critical views of the author to a new debate focused on the issue of nationalism and feminism." This overtly political reading of Narayan's fiction assumes great significance in view of the fact that all his life, the author not only resisted such readings but also argued stoutly against them. R.K. Narayan had a particular distaste for "polemics and tract-writing" (See his collection of essays titled *A Writer's Nightmare* and *A Story-Teller's World*, 1989) and he always favoured "an aesthetic and universalist appreciation of his works." In his essay, "The Problem of the Indian Writer", he claims to be following in the line of "all imaginative writing in India" which "has had its origin in *The Ramayana* and *The Mahabharata*," thus affirming his own commitment to reproducing in his works the India of cultural and also narrative tradition. Despite all his disclaimers and pronouncements to the contrary, I'm of this firm opinion that the process of Narayan's reassessment shall remain incomplete and even inconclusive, if we don't attempt what Said calls "contrapuntal" readings of his fiction. For only in these readings can we possibly discover a whole set of new meanings or construct a new "archaeology of knowledge" (to borrow the eloquent title of Foucault's book) that has remained unknown to us until now.

To an extent, the books that have appeared on R.K. Narayan in the latter half of 1990s and in the first decade of 21st century have done a great deal to spark off a new debate and also generate a new wave of criticism. All these critical endeavours were aimed at rehabilitating Narayan at a time when the academic interest in his writing had almost begun to show a perceptible downward trend. In this context, I would like to mention a couple of books that have contributed very significantly towards revising our critical perceptions about Narayan and his work. N. Ram and Susan Ram were the ones who took lead in this direction by publishing the first authorized biography of R.K. Narayan in 1996. S.S. Ramtake's *R.K. Narayan and His Social Perspective* (New Delhi: Atlantic Publishers, 1998), M.K. Bhatnagar's *New Insights into R.K. Narayan* (New Delhi: Atlantic, 2002), Amar Nath Prasad's *Critical Response to R.K. Narayan* (New Delhi: Sarup & Sons, 2003), Ranga Rao's *R.K. Narayan* (New Delhi: Sahitya Akademi, 2004) and Chotte Lal Khatri's *R.K. Narayan: Reflections and Re-evaluation* (New Delhi: Sarup & Sons 2008) have appeared in the past one decade or so, re-defining the frontiers of our knowledge about Narayan and re-drawing the map of critical possibilities, too.

While on this subject, I'd like to make a special mention of an essay titled "Indian Fiction Today", Anita Desai, an eminent Indian English writer, wrote way back in 1989. In this essay, Desai had pointed out the disjunction between the seamless, orthodox discourse of the realist novel in India and the contemporary national instabilities; between a "narrative of historical continuity" and "the politics of difference". Her point is that "magic idyll of antiquated India" that Narayan invokes so assiduously in his fiction is not only passé but also torn to shreds by today's strife, riots and communal commotion. Elsewhere, in a direct commentary on Narayan's fiction, Desai rues his tendency to create "the essential...India" in his writings, pointing to his neglect of the very "fissures, explosions, shatterings" that she highlights, saying, "[I]n the 50 years that Narayan has been writing his tranquil fiction, his "rootedness" has become as unique in India as it is in the West, the traditional structure of rural existence that he celebrates having given way and collapsed irrevocably.... There are many of Narayan's readers who feel that his fiction does not reflect the chaos, the drift, the angst that characterizes a society in transition and that his "rootedness" is a relic of another, pastoral era now shaken and threatened beyond recovery" (R.K. Narayan, 3). What Desai is suggesting is that Narayan's fiction fails to capture the throbbing, pulsating rhythms of everydayness of Indian life, much of which is not entirely free of virtually every conceivable form of violence that runs so close to our lives, otherwise. In a way, she is obliquely pointing out that we need to study not only the manifest but also the latent, even the repressed contents of Indian life in Narayan's fiction.

Whether or not we agree with Anita Desai's extreme views, the fact remains that her opinion does constitute the "other" end of the spectrum along which the re-assessment of Narayan's fiction must be represented. There are many other possibilities that are simply waiting to be explored. For instance, no effort seems to have been made to attempt a Bakhtinian reading of Narayan (at least I haven't come across such a reading so far), which carries his idea of the comic to its logical conclusion, by positing the entire question of East-West dialogue in wider cultural context, exploring its dialogics through the notions of polyphony, heteroglossia and carnivalesque. In the same manner, we need to explore if Narayan's sense of comic could actually be inverted and seen from the postmodern perspective of "parody and pastiche" and whether the limits of his texts could be pushed to discover how and under what conditions his "texts" become "inter-texts", too. I'm hinting towards mediating Narayan from the standpoint of "intertexuality". While proceeding along these lines, somewhere we may have to assume that the "author is now dead" (which he, incidentally, is), thus paving the way for the reader-oriented criticism in his case. This may also enable us to speculate about another related question: how far and in what different ways does Narayan's fiction become explicitly a form of self-reflexive, metafiction. It can easily be argued that he is a storyteller par excellence, and as such has explored the subterranean archives of story-telling and its wayward, complex processes. Besides, if we look at his entire corpus, we get this impression that Narayan has developed a far more mature vision in his later works than he actually possessed in his earlier works. If such is the case, then there is some point in investigating the meta-fictional aspects of his writing. In a way, all great writers are meta-fictional in the sense that they constantly cast an inward glance at what they are doing; constantly reflect on their art and artifice, thus betraying a totally different dimension from the one that we may often see on the surface. Similarly, I haven't yet seen either an eco-critical or a new historicist reading of Narayan's fiction, both of which, to my mind, would prove to be quite rewarding. Narayan's Malgudi is a true embodiment of how in our urban or semi-urban planning, we could effectively integrate and synthesize nature into culture, thus creating eco-friendly havens for ourselves that ensure both our survival and our continuation as a species.

It is quite possible that right now as I'm sharing these ideas with you, emphasizing the need to explore hitherto unexplored terrains, someone is already thinking either of a Bakhtinian or a post-modern approach, an eco-critical or a new historicist reading of Narayan, thus challenging the limits of my suggestions, deflating my complacency in the process. Well, that is what research is all about. It is a continuous process, which always seeks to re-define its contours and its critical maps, thus humbling the pride of the most rigorous of researchers among us. The moment of re-assessment I had spoken to you about with such aplomb in my title, I dare say, has been with us for close to two decades now and yet it is constantly being re-invented, thus giving us new insights into the works of this grand old man of Indian letters.

In this essay, I don't claim to have either articulated this moment or positioned it historically, constantly aware as I'm of the fact that my implication in this critical spectrum is anything but marginal. I have neither written a book on Narayan nor done extensive research on him. I'm only an ardent admirer and a casual reader of his fiction. Here, my effort was to give you an overview of the directions that Narayan criticism has either taken in the past or could possibly take in the future. If I have succeeded in mapping out the jagged edges and rough contours of this critical enterprise in a somewhat comprehensible manner, I would take it, my job is done, even if it's not all that well done.

2

English Language and British Education: A Postcolonial Interpretation of R.K. Narayan's *The English Teacher*

Raju Parghi

R.K. Narayan's one of the most critically acclaimed novels, *The English Teacher*, may well be known for its cultural interpretations and autobiographical portrayals, but it has also postcolonial elements which many scholars and critics have neglected or partially interpreted as a text, resisting the colonial power in India. As is generally known, Narayan's novels portray a real-life situation of colonial and postcolonial India, which is also an answer to those who have been influenced by E.M. Forster's *A Passage to India*. *The English Teacher* is a novel of a constant struggle between the Western influence and the national-cultural practices. The protagonist of the novel, Krishnan, is a modern Indian professional, an English teacher at Albert Mission College, while his wife Sushila is a typical South Indian woman, who even feels uncomfortable eating with a fork. Husband and wife share an ambivalent relationship, where Krishnan is seen as the representative of an imperial British culture and Sushila presents an ideal Indian woman, who is innocent, responsible and faithful to her duties as a daughter, mother and wife. Although both have been portrayed contrastingly, yet they cannot imagine a complete happy married life without each other.

Mr. Brown, another character in *The English Teacher*, the principal of the college where Krishnan works, with his "greenish eyes" (179) is so indifferent to the Indian culture, tradition and languages that he cannot speak even one local language of India. This white man always thinks that he is the best, and superior to the native, and that it is white man's institution and language that the locals have to adopt, accept and follow.

Narayan has mostly dealt with Indian life and has not focused much on the British characters in his novels. Mr. Brown, the principal of Albert College, in *The Bachelor of Arts* and in *The English Teacher*, Mathieson, the owner of Mathieson Estate in *Waiting for the Mahatma* and Marco in *The Guide* are a few of his British characters. Many critics have asserted that R.K. Narayan has failed to depict the political unrest in colonial India and that he "is remotely detached from the broader implications of unrest in India" (Singh, 120).

Though Narayan did not portray the political situation of colonial and postcolonial India, his subtle and direct portrayal of British influence on India in his novels *The English Teacher* and *The Bachelor of Arts,* is worth noticing. His portrayal of Mr. Brown, the usage of English and the English education in India in *The English Teacher* keep him above Mulk Raj Anand and Raja Rao, especially his resisting English language and his study of English education.

R.K. Narayan learnt English at his primary education, he mastered the language of the colonizers first, leaving out his mother tongue, Tamil, and Sanskrit, under the impact of colonial imperialism. With his creative verve and imagination, he started writing short-stories and then novels. He mastered both the form and language of the colonizers, unlike Caliban who says: "You taught me language, and my profit on't. Is I know how to curse. The red plague rid you, For learning me your language!" (*The Tempest* Act I (ii) 361-65).

Narayan does not rebuke the English man rather attempts to present reality. He tries to present the real picture of India and Indian culture to the West, which had a lot of prejudices and false knowledge of the Indians presented by the British writers like E.M. Forster and Kipling. M.M. Hota says that a handful of Indian novels have given the West more understanding of Indians as a people than a hundred years of Western writings could have done. Certainly, Narayan has presented life of people, which even his contemporary writers have failed to do.

Narayan is a postcolonial writer who learnt the language of the colonizers and chose fiction as genre, which originally belongs to the Western world. He wrote fourteen novels and many volumes of short-story collections. *The English Teacher* can be interpreted in three phases as found in *The Beginning Theory*:

> At another level the double or hybrid identity is precisely what the postcolonial situation brings into being. The shift in attitudes in the 1980s and 1990s was towards post-colonial writers seeing themselves as using primarily Asian or African forms supplemented with European-derived influences, rather than as working primarily within European genres like the novel and merely adding to them a degree of exotic Africanisation (Indianisation). (Barry, 196)

The postcolonial literatures are therefore bound to go through a period of transition in three phases, namely adopt, adapt and adept.

In the adopt phase, the writer's willingness or interest is to adopt the form of the West, as it stands, assuming that the form has a universal validity and acceptance. Though initially, Narayan finds it extremely difficult to reach a Western author for publication, the forward by Graham Greene to *The Bachelor of Arts* enables him to get the novel published. The form which E.M. Forster and Kipling had used for portraying an unreal and degraded India is used by Narayan to present a stark reality of Indian lifestyle, its culture, and religious beliefs. He is admired and appreciated for depicting the Indian consciousness. Graham Greene, who first recognized and appreciated in Narayan the potentials of a great writer and his universal appeal as a novelist, in the Foreword to *The Bachelor of Arts*, writes: "It was Mr. Narayan with his 'Swami and Friends' who first brought India, in the sense of the Indian population and the Indian way of life, alive to me. His novels increase our knowledge of the Indian character certainly, but I prefer to think of them, as contribution to English Literature, contribution of remarkable maturity" (iii). With their 'adopt form of fiction' of the West, Narayan has gained recognition and appreciation around the world. He was introduced to American readers in 1952, and was honoured with the Sahitya Academy Award for *The Guide* in 1961, and later, the Indian Government conferred on him Padma Bhushan in 1967.

The second stage is known as adapt phase where a writer aims to adapt the European form to Indian subject matter. The writer, therefore, assumes partial rights of intervention in the genre. In the adapt phase, Narayan looks at the Western world partially. He does not use much of modern literary techniques like, stream of consciousness; his novels are plain, direct subtle and optimistic in nature. He neither condemns the British Characters nor does he give them much importance. He presents them as they are and fits them into the context. He partially intrudes into the lives of the colonizers, but he is conscious of not crossing the boundaries for demeaning and dislocating the characters.

The third phase is known as adept phase where the writers become confident of their own creativity, a kind of declaration of cultural independence. The writer remakes the form according to his own interest and specifications, without referring to the European norms. He feels free from all restraints of the colonization and concentrates on his cultural, national, religious and political aspects.

Narayan deals with the subject matter that is purely Indian and that does not have the impact of colonization. Most of his novels are truly imbibed in Indianness, which deal with day-to-day life of the ordinary characters. *The English Teacher* depicts the story of an English Teacher, his personal loss and his contribution as a teacher to the growth of a practically advanced India, keeping aside the theoretical knowledge. Though Mr. Brown feels that the contribution of English education has been beneficial to the growth of local youth, Krishnan rejects his claim by quitting his job as a college teacher and accepting a job of a school teacher, where he feels more contented, teaching children with his own creative mind rather than teaching the young students, the literature of the colonizers which he is now least interested in. *The English Teacher* further opens the door for examining the impact of the colonizers' language, English, resistance to English education in India and cultural imperialism. One of the major impacts of colonialism in India was "the language of the colonizers", that is, English. Its impact was immense, both in terms of loss and gain. As a language of the colonizers, English gained momentum and spread rapidly overshadowing many regional and classical languages like Tamil and Sanskrit:

> The encounter between English and most so-called Third World languages did not occur under condition of independence and equality. English, French and Portuguese came to the Third World to announce the arrival of the Bible and the sword. They came clamouring for gold, black gold in Chains or gold that shines as sweat in factories and plantations. (Wa Thiong'o, 31)

The importance of English was mainly for business purpose and to teach the colonized the so-called 'civilized way of living'. The purpose of colonizers was to communicate with the natives in order to keep them in chains for longer time, to inflict pain and to rule them the way they wanted to. Narayan's resistance to the linguistic imperialism is seen in the very beginning of the novel. Krishnan and his other colleagues are summoned by Mr. Brown: "Could you imagine a worse shock for me? I came across a student of the English Honours who did not know till this day that 'honours' had to be spelt with a 'u'" (5-6). For Mr. Brown, it is shocking that in a colonial India, anyone could be so careless in learning the language of the ruler. He feels angry not because he has a social cause in teaching the inferior people his language; rather he is shocked that the language of the law-makers and rulers has not been paid attention to. He knew "the importance of the English language" and "the need for preserving its purity" (2). The colonizers have been extremely particular about their language and culture, religion, and literature and art. Through language, they also want to succeed in enforcing their literature, culture and heritage on the marginalized and the ruled. The ruler knows that the ruled does not have power and right to resist. The colonial power has been so dominant that the subject cannot resist through his activities. Forcing English as a language of communication, the colonizers suppressed the colonized more severely. Wa Thiong'o reflects the purposes of the colonizer in enforcing the language: "It was the gun which made possible the mining of the gold and which effected the political captivity of their owners, it was language which held captures their cultures, their values, hence their minds" (31). Introduction of the language, as he says, restricted not only the cultural and religious aspects of the colonized, but also restrained the colonizers to think and communicate in their own native tongues. Thiong'o says that the first reason to adopt the English language was "to suppress the languages of the captive nations" (31) and the second "made of captivation was that of elevating the language of the conqueror" (32).

Mr. Brown, the only White man representing the entire White race as colonizer, has been extremely indifferent not only to the local languages but also to local lifestyle, dress code, religious belief and practices. Krishnan, as a colonized and as a learner of the language of the colonizers, resists when he tells Gajapathy about Mr. Brown: "I felt irritated and said: "Mr. Gajapathy, there are blacker sins in this world than a dropping vowel.... Let us be fair. Ask Mr. Brown if he can say in any of the two hundred Indian languages. The cat chases the rat. He has spent thirty years in India" (6). Indeed, the dropping of a vowel in 'honour' is not a grave sin, and what Narayan attempts to say indirectly through Krishnan's reaction is that the White men have exploited the Indians in various ways, be it economic, political, social, individual or linguistic.

Their sins are more heinous than a native not learning the colonizer's language—the impact of slavery in Tea-Plantations in India, the ill-treatment to the soldiers and the youth, the exploitation of women, of natural resources and many more to count. Many critics have been of the notion that Narayan did not write on political upheavals in India, and that he kept himself away from the conflicts. Narayan is rather diplomatic in his expression and the critics have not completely understood him. He mentions sarcastically that there are much blacker sins committed by the colonizer in dealing with the colonized. The impact of colonialism has been so extreme that even today, spelling mistake in English is not tolerated; or rather be it, in any language, wrongly written words often get bad treatment from the teachers.

The politics of representation continues as Dr. Menon, Gajapathy and Krishnan go on debating over a mis-spelt word. There is a sense in Mr. Menon's statement as he says: "American spell honours without 'u'" (16). The consciousness and awareness of the colonized, like Mr. Gajapathy and Krishnan, is quite appreciable. They resist against the system in their own ways. While talking about the west, Gajapathy says:

> Politics need not butt in everywhere. There are times when I wish there were no politics in the world and no one knew who was ruling and how. This would keep a little clearer, freer thinking in all matters. The whole of the west is in muddle owing to its political consciousness, and what a pity that the east should also follow suit. It is like a need choking all the human faculties. (16)

In the history of Civilization, it is always the West that has taken credit for most of the things. As a few countries of Europe have ruled the two-third part of the world, they still dominate through political influence, economic superiority and religious authority, either directly or indirectly.

The introduction of English, as a means of communication in educational institutions as well as government offices and public places had dual impact of benefit and loss. Benefit in the sense, people could learn a lot from the West through a British, they spoke regional languages and their loss was that they could not communicate in their own languages to the colonizers:

> The colonizer's mother tongue, that which is sustained by his feelings emotions and dreams that in which his tenderness and wonder and expressed, thus that which holds the greatest emotional impact, is precisely the one, which is least valued. It has no stature in the country or in the concert of peoples. If he wants to obtain a job make a place for himself, exist in the community in the world, he must first bow to the language of his masters. In the linguistic conflict within the colonized his mother tongue is that which is crushed. (Memmi, 107)

The irony of learning English is that most of the natives/colonized did not even understand the meaning of sentences. Krishnan, as English teacher, scolds a student for not understanding English written in the texts. He tells Ramaswami: "You are very bad in English" (14). He personally takes initiatives to teach to the best of his ability. He does not succeed in his attempt, perhaps knowing fully well that the texts were only theory oriented. They did not have national or regional interest or connection at all. Krishnan's episodic description of his activities reveals that he does fulfill his duty without fail: "I spent the rest of the period giving a general analysis of the mistakes I had encountered in this batch of composition—rather, very, as such for hence, split infinitives, collective nouns, and all the rest of the traps that the English language set for foreigners" (15).

Krishnan's knowledge of English is used in helping the colonized students; he cares for them without revealing it. Mr. Brown, being the only White character in the novel, shows his superiority over the Indian race. His linguistic competence in English is of no use to the native speakers as he tries to bully everyone. The impact of English language, after the colonialism, has, in a way, helped the colonized people to know more about the West, which is not available in the regional languages. Emerson rightly observes:

> All the colonial people have been brought into the modern world under the age of an imperialism which superimposed a European language into the native tongue. The imperial language served three principle purposes which have an obvious learning on the effort to secure national cultural identity. It was the language of instruction at least for higher education, it was the instrument through which intercourse of all the varieties could be maintained with the advanced Europeans and European-descended people, and it was frequently the 'lingua franca' within each of the several nations between them, as witness the cultural role of English. (at the Sandung Asian-African conferences of 1955) (Emerson, 137)

English spread and acquired recognition wherever the British colonialism had set up its roots, endangering many native languages to near elimination. *The English Teacher* represents the English language as a legacy of the colonizers even after the colonial period of the native land. Mr. Brown is a mouthpiece of British imperial power while Krishnan and his collegues are the colonized subject, who, under the impact of colonialism, have to follow the instructions of colonizers.

The English Teacher also presents a kind of cultural imperialism through the introduction of the literature of the colonizer's country to the colonized state. British colonialism also established Western civilization and culture. This affected and influenced the native's education system. The impact of the introduction of English language at higher education level was great. It gave access to British culture, art, music, literature and religious beliefs to the people of colonial India. The immediate impact of English overshadowed the natives, the native cultures, languages and lifestyle. Narayan, in *The English Teacher,* presents Krishnan as a subject to British colonialism, whereas as a teacher of English, he has to learn and teach British literature. Krishnan discusses:

> I got up at eight everyday, read for the fiftieth time, Milton Carlyle and Shakespeare, looked through compositions, swallowed a meal, dressed and rushed out

> of the hostel...I returned to my room, my duty in the interval had been astonishing, cajoling and browbeating a few hundred boys of Albert Mission college, so that they might mug up, Shakespeare and Milton and secure high at marks and save me adverse remarks from my chiefs at the end of the year. (5)

Krishnan gets up at eight in the morning, which is often practiced by the natives, as in India, people wake up early in the morning before the daybreak. Krishnan's lifestyle shows how he has been influenced by the cultural practices of his superiors, the colonizers. His life becomes mechanical and boring where he enjoys neither his professional nor his personal life. Owing to the fear of failing in the exam, the students only mug up the lessons without understanding, which signifies that the British cultural imperialism in India was forcefully spreading. Krishnan's possession of an alarm clock marks how mechanical and controlled his life has become. Growing at the village set up, people did not need a watch to perform their duties and responsibilities. The clock controls Krishnan's life like Mr. Brown or any other colonizer: "I had an alarm clock on which I could sometimes depend for giving the alarm at the set time.... It had a reddening face, and had been oiled and repaired a score of times. It showed the correct time but was eccentric with regard to its alarm arrangement" (8). Narayan consciously sees the alarm clock as representative of the colonial rule, on which all the actions are set up. As Mr. Brown has "greenish eyes" (179) so the clock has "reddening face" (8). Both are two faces of the same coin, called colonialism. No one can control the clock and its time. In the same way, the natives cannot control or stop the growing imperialism in front of them. The clock produces a shattering amount of noise, sometimes goes off by itself and starts off by itself. The clock and the colonial rule perhaps go hand in hand. In colonialism, everything moves based on time. The colonized subjects are commanded into action by the strict rules of time. Everything in life moves according to time. Krishnan, unconsciously or habitually, becomes the slave of the clock which does not give him a complete assurance to assist in working him up. Clock is the invention of the West, and is introduced to the East or 'the inferior other' only to make their life more mechanical and controlled. A culture, depending on time, is followed by the West or the colonizers and influences the colonized by overpowering their native culture and cultural practices.

E.M Forster, in his *A Passage to India*, represents India and Indian culture from an outsider's point of view:

> How can the mind take hold of such a country? Generations of invaders have tried but they remain in exile. The important towns they built are only retreats their quarrels the malaise of men who cannot find their way home. India knows of their trouble.... She calls 'come' through her hundred mouths, through objects ridiculous and august. But come to what? She has never defined. She is not a promise only an appeal. (135)

Foster's perception and description of India, Indian consciousness and culture are not real. No nation would allow another nation to come and set up its authority through cultural transmission and economic influence. There is always resistance if the native land is influenced by the other nation. Krishnan detests such influences in his own ways, and indirectly, he resists English literature "as newly a man who has mugged earlier than the introduction and the notes in the verity edition of Lear. I did not do it out of love for them or for Shakespeare but only out of love for myself" (12). Krishnan does this mechanical profession only for one hundred rupees that he is paid. Educated in an English background and then making English as his own profession, Krishnan adopts English culture.

The English culture and teaching have influenced him so much that even his wife, Sushila, does not remain untouched by it. Sushila is a typical Indian woman, she respects her husband and does not go against his wish. Krishnan does not ask Sushila to read the Indian classics or Tamil books, rather he mentions only English books of his rulers: "You have neglected your books: Have finished Ivanhoe? She had been trying to get through Ivanhoe for years now, and Lamb's tales from Shakespeare" (42). Though Sushila is fond of books, she does not show particular interest in English books. Her interests lie in her culture and her country, not in her colonizer's culture and literature. According to Gayatri Chakrovarty Sprivak, a woman is doubly marginalized between the discourse of her native man and colonizer. The colonized man and, colonizer offer little hope for the Third World women to speak.

Sushila's character is presented as a typical Indian woman, as a daughter, wife and mother. She is an ideal householder, representing every other Indian woman. She knows how to run her household without violating or angering her husband. She performs her *puja* regularly and practices what she has learnt from her parents: "Srinivasa—'the greatest god'. You need not visit Thirupathi Hills to see him. If you visit him here—he grants all your boons and blesses all your efforts...". She held up a coconut, a packet of camphor, plantain and betel leaves" (63). Sushila is the only representation of a woman of the Third World country in the novel who is given more attention. She remains silent; however, at the same time, she does not want to be influenced by the Western way of life.

Krishnan struggles with himself till the end of the novel to choose between English and Tamil. He says: "I hadn't yet made up my mind as to which language was to be enriched by my contributions to its literature" (45). In the end, he chooses the language of the colonizers for his creative expression. His character goes through many changes. In the beginning of the novel, he is a colonial subject of the British rule, imperialism and British culture. He is not resilient but receptive to everything that is British. His profession makes him a follower of the British system. Sushila's arrival makes him understand his dilemma. She is an embodiment of Indianness and Indian culture who makes her husband feel Indian, think Indian and live Indian. Krishnan struggles between his colonizer's life-style and his own native culture. Finally, he rejects British education system and becomes a true Indian in a sense, dedicating his life for the creative and practical education of children.

Through English education and English as a medium of expression in higher education, the impact of English on the colonized is natural. Everything becomes English and English way of life. *The English Teacher* does not depict much of Indian classics and books, as much as the English literature books and authors are mentioned—Taine's *History of Literature*, Works of Milton, Carlyle and Shakespeare, Wordsworth, Shelley, Kant, Patter, Browning, Palgrave's *Golden Treasury*, *Pride and Prejudice*, *Ivanhoe*, Lamb's *Tales from Shakespeare* and Bradley. Narayan himself has been a subject to the colonial rules, interestingly he does not portray much of English culture except in *The English Teacher*, *The Bachelor of Arts*, *The Guide* and *Waiting for the Mahatma*.

The afore-mentioned works of English literature and the authors, if chronologically ordered, cover the entire period of British Literature till the publication of *The English Teacher* (1945). Narayan does not mention any other contemporary English writer of his time. Nevertheless, it is clear that Krishnan, as an Indian and as the colonized, has to know the literature of the colonizers and learn his culture in order to be more professional in his job to earn his livelihood. A large population of Indian subjects was illiterate and it was indeed difficult for the colonized to cope up the English education and English as a language. This has resulted in confusion over one's own language, culture and identity. And Loomba rightly mentions: "Colonialism, as we have seen, perhaps, often violently, physical territories, social terrains as well as human identities.... The colonial experience is a live experience in the consciousness of these people.... The experience is a continuing psychic experience that has to be dealt with long after actual colonial situation formally ends" (185).

As Loomba says that the impact of colonialism is difficult to end. It not only changed the lifestyle of the people but has also affected the psyche of the colonized. Krishnan and Sushila are the two forces of colonizer and colonized. Sushila dies only after coming in contact with dirty toilet of Western style. She feels disgusted, horrified and suffers from typhoid. Colonialism and its effects live in the mind of the people until there is a complete change in the 'once colonized', which does not happen realistically because the subject or the Orient cannot do away with the impact of hundred years of colonization. Said rightly opines: "The orient is not only adjacent to Europe, it is also the place of Europe's greatest and richest and oldest colonies, the source of its civilization and languages, its cultural contestants, and one of its deepest and most recurring images of the other" (1). The ruled cannot break away from its colonizers' civilization. Krishnan, however, resigns his job at the Albert Mission College, and will work at a school, yet he cannot part with the influence of colonial forces. He still is a part of the colonizers' culture, language and lifestyle: "The Orient is an integral part of European material civilization and culture. Orientalism expresses and represents that part culturally and even ideologically as a made of discourse supporting institutions, vocabulary, scholarships, imagery and doctrines and even colonial bureaucracies and colonial style" (2). Krishnan, as a subject, can only resist the colonial system but cannot reject it. It has been a part of social and professional life. Mr. Brown, as an Occident, though remains indifferent to Indian Languages, is still a part of his colonized land for more than thirty years.

The English Teacher depicts the idea of English education in India. Set up in the colonial India, the rulers of the land tried to enforce their education system on native people. Much like *Lord Jim* and *Heart of Darkness* by Joseph Conrad and Shakespeare's *The Tempest*, *The English Teacher* was also written much before postcolonial theory came into existence. Narayan does not portray the British as exploiter directly, but the novel fits into the postcolonial paradigm as it deals with British and Indian cultures and British and Indian education systems. Most parts of the novel focus on the British education system in India and its impact on the native learners: "A notable feature of the novel is the attitude to education it presents. Krishnan is very unhappy with the absurdities in the type of education given to the students" (Sharma, 52). The entire system of education appears faulty. It fails to impart to the students a sense of discipline from within, self-respect and self-reliability. The students feel uncomfortable at the theoretical knowledge of History. The literature has nothing to do with their own nation, culture and language. In fact, it is the literature of the colonizer that they are forced to read in the English education system, when they tell Krishnan: "Attendance takes most of our hours sir" (12). Krishnan reflects and feels sorry for his inability to create interest in the students: "These poor boys are now all attention, cowed by your superior force. They are ready to listen to you, and write down whatever you may say.... Some boys are already sitting up alert ready to note down the pearl droppings from my mouth" (13). Though he tries his best to teach the literature of the other nation, especially that of his colonizers, he himself does not feel at home: "Four periods of continuous work and I had not prepared even a single page of lecture" (11). He somehow feels that he is not doing his work efficiently and "was doing the wrong work" (5). He struggles between his emotions and moral responsibilities, his Western lifestyle of the colonizers and his own cultural practices and values. He detests everything, yet he has to go on. Pheng Cheah speaks about the colonial education and its impact on the native land and its people: "Colonial education is a sin because it stole the nation's future by corrupting the children of the indigenous elite. But the neocolonial state commits an even more heinous crime" (372). He feels that colonial education has destroyed the existing system of the natives. The natives are left without a choice with the enforcement of English education system to all the colonized states of the world. This does not solve the problem of the natives. Krishnan regards teaching only a way of earning money: he is far away from the touch of social service. The entire education system is cut off from the old noble traditions, where attendance does not matter; what matters is the quality of education and the sacred relationship between *guru* and *shishya* (teacher and disciple). Krishnan's disappointment as a teacher reflects his state of mind: "In sober moment perhaps I would reflect on the question of obedience. Born in different households perhaps, petted, pampered and bullied by parents, unless brothers, all persons known to them and responsible for their growth and welfare.

Who was I that they should obey my command? There between me and them?" (12). The British education system did not constructively succeed in colonial India. Krishnan, being an Indian, is an alien to his own native students, where he feels aghast in the world of colonizers. It also reflects Macaulay's attempts to bring about the British education:

> That the real aim of the minute of education was to construct an efficient interface between India and the British administration is apparent from Macaulay's text. He says, "we must at present do our best to form a class who may be interpreters between us and the millions who we govern; a class of persons, Indian in blood and color, but English in taste, in opinions, in morals and intellect." (193)

Macaulay, who is responsible for the introduction of English education in India, had an extremely rigid and imperial attitude. As a result, the colonized did not enjoy the system but slowly and gradually revolted against it. Krishnan, at the end of the novel resigns the job of a teacher of college, while his father-in-law, as Krishnan remembers, studies literature, completes the degree and does not look for job rather goes back to take care of his fields in the village: "He was B.A. of the olden days, brought on Patter and Carlyle and Scott and Browning, personally looked after by Dr. William Miller, Mark Hanter and other eminent professors of Madras College; he was fastidious and precise in handling the English language.... After passing B.A. he refused to enter the government service, as many of his generation did, but went back and settled in his village and looked after his land and property" (19). Krishnan's father-in-law would certainly get a respectable position. Had he joined a government job, he would have prospered. His decision was extremely courageous, perhaps he did not want to be treated mechanically by his colonizers, perhaps he realized that being 'self' is much better than being at the mercy of others for the livelihood of the family.

The inner struggle and psychological turmoil of Krishnan is quite natural as his beloved wife falls sick. The mental agony, that he undergoes, detaches him from the superficial colonial culture and its education. He remembers: "Once again all Milton and Shakespeare and Bradley jostled each other in struggle for existence. There were four library books on my table but I had not even opened once" (66). His taste for English books gradually undergoes a change. He is influenced by the headmaster whose school his daughter Leela attends. Admiring the headmaster, he comes to know that the school opens for children even on Sundays. This is perhaps for the first time that Krishnan's attitude changes. The headmaster lives a simple life, and contrary to Krishnan, dedicates his life to little children without much expectation. Simplicity, sincerity, honesty, and dedication of the headmaster teach a good lesson to Krishnan and make him aware of his own double standards. He is a teacher at college, where he is unable to enthuse the students and is dissatisfied with his profession. The headmaster, on the other hand, feels satisfied and expresses his willingness and dedication to work for the poor. He knows his school, the needs of the children and his moral responsibility. He has only a seat for the visitors and does not have a chair and table: "We are a poor country, and we can do without luxuries. Why do we want anything more than a shed and a few mats and open air? This is not *a cold country* for all the heavy furniture and elaborate buildings" (135). The headmaster is much contented with what he has for school. He does not believe in spending money for costly furniture and buildings and never expects any aid from the government. He ridicules the idea of depending upon the government for any financial aid. He feels the need for bringing changes and reformation in the existing education system and his purpose is crystal clear: "The main business of an educational institution is to shape the mind and the character and of course games have their own values" (135). The words of the headmaster open the eyes of Krishnan and he begins to seek the reality and joy of serving humanity with his own way education rather than depending upon colonizer's education system. The consciousness and knowledge of the headmaster regarding imperial rules is noteworthy. He even detests copying the white men. He urges to be original and authentic in one's own approach and way of life. He ridicules even British sports: "Why worship sports, the eleven stalwart idiots who bring in a shield or a cup? It is all a curse, copying, copying, and copying. We could have as well been born monkeys to justify our own power of imitation" (135). The headmaster's philosophy of life, his patriotic sport and social welfare cannot match Krishnan's personality. After the colonialism of British in India, there are two colonial legacies that Indians practise and have excelled. One is English and the other is Cricket. After Independence, India has practised and adopted these two legacies of colonizers. The English language has become *lingua franca* of the nation, limiting Hindi, Sanskrit and Tamil, and many other regional languages to count. Cricket has become a 'religion' in India, viewed passionately and played regularly. In other words, India has revolutionized the existence of cricket. It has replaced hockey, the national game of India, in its popularity and has become highly commercial.

Krishnan's visit to the headmaster is a turning point in his life. He changes his attitude towards British Education system and feels that "a national education of system must have three basic features; first, it must be national in extent, second it must be national in context, third it must be national in administration" (Prabhanandha, 118). He becomes conscious of the wrong work he has been doing without realizing it. He feels disturbed for what he has been doing so far. He hates his selfish interest. He feels that "a national system of Education cannot be different to the cultural heritage of the nation—the language and literature, art and philosophy, etc. of the people" (119). He wants to revive the old Indian tradition of open air schools seen by the saintly teachers in ancient India. Certainly as per the set up of the novel and the time it was written, there is a spirited attack on the modern system of education. Krishnan resists the whole idea of British education which was started with selfish interests. He "could no longer stuff Shakespeare and Elizabethan metre, and romantic poetry for the hundredth time into young minds and feed them on the dead mutton of literary analysis and theories and histories, while what they needed was the lesson in the fullest use of mind" (178). The Occident's attitude towards the Orient has always been one of exploitation and proven and dominance. Krishnan could no longer stand the Western system of education which has eliminated his own culture, language and issue of national interest; he feels agitated towards the system and says: "This education had reduced us to a nation of morons, and we were strangers to our own culture and camp follower of another culture, feeding on leavings and garbage" (178). He decides to restore his own culture which he missed for a long time. In the words of Swami Vivekananda, "To me (him), the very essence of education is concentration of mind, not collecting of facts" (Prabhananda, 42). Krishna, with his imaginative, innovative and creative ideas, perhaps succeeds in establishing an educational system which brings overall growth of a child's personality. The moral, spiritual, and intellectual growth, all could be enhanced through a practical way of teaching. As a poet, he regains his confidence, finds meaning in his life, accepts the offer of the headmaster and is keen to take up a job at a school, where subject-matter, talk, lectures—all would be of his own nation, culture and society. His eyes are opened; he ponders: "what about our own roots?"... I am up against the system, the whole method and approach of a system of education which makes us morons, cultural morons; but efficient clerks for all your business and administrative offices" (179).

Krishnan's character becomes complete and perfect. As mentioned earlier, he undergoes a transformation like that of Raju in *The Guide*. His awareness and his voice against the colonizer's system of English education and English language, as the medium of expression at the higher education level, lead him to resign his job and join a school where he could be of use and help to children and could constructively guide them and mould their future and personality.

To sum up, the postcolonial elements in the novel such as English as a language, cultural imperialism, resistance and British education system for the colonized prove Narayan as a postcolonial writer. Though he did not revolt against the colonization and British empire, Narayan's indirect attack on the British language and education system makes him committed writer of 'once colonized' India. *The English Teacher* is the novel close to his soul and he has only indirectly hinted the impact of colonialism without hurting the sentiments of the colonizers.

Works Cited

Barry, Peter. *Beginning Theory: An Introduction to Literary and Cultural Theory*. Manchester: Manchester University Press, 1995.

Cheah, Pheng. *Spectral Nationality: Passage of Freedom from Kant to Postcolonial Literature of Liberation*. New York: Columbia University Press, 2003.

Emerson, Rupert. *From Empire to Nation: The Rise of Self-assertion of Asian and African Peoples*. Calcutta: Scientific Book Agency, 1970.

Forster, E.M. *A Passage to India*. Harmondsworth: Penguine, 1979.

Loomba, Ania. *Colonialism/Postcolonialism*. London and New York: Routledge, 1998.

Memmi, Albert. *The Colonizer and the Colonized*. New York: Orion Press Inc., 1965.

Narayan, R.K. *The English Teacher*. Mysore: Indian Thought Publications, 1955.

Prabhananda, Swami. *In Search of Our National Roots for a Philosophy of Education*. Kolkata: The Ramakrishna Mission Institute of Culture, 2004.

Rajan, Balachandra. *Under Western Eyes: India from Milton to Macaulay*. New Delhi: Oxford University Press, 1999.

Said, Edward. *Orientalism: A Western Conception of the Orient*. New Delhi: Penguin Books, 1995.

Shakespeare, William. "The Tempest". *The Complete Works of Shakespeare*. Ed. London: Oxford University Press, 1972.

Sharma, K.K. *Four Great Indian Novelists: Some Point of View*. New Delhi: Sarup & Sons, 2002.

Singh, Krishna Kant. *Social Perspectives in R.K. Narayan's Novels*. Jaipur: Book Enclace, 2002.

Thiong'o, Ngugi wa. *Moving the Centre: The Struggle for Cultural Freedoms*. Oxford: James Currey Ltd., 1993.

3

What about Our Own Roots? Problematising Education and Philosophy in R.K. Narayan's *The English Teacher*

Arun Kumar Mukhopadhyay

The very concepts of alienation and 'rootlessness', the loss of one's own cultural moorings, can justifiably be claimed to be characteristic, more or less, of any realist fiction writer of a nation that inscribes an experience of colonization leading to a distinctive cultural marginalization. In the case of R.K. Narayan, who is essentially a writer of the 'individual', the idea of 'roots' is, interestingly, not confined to the search of his characters only. Instead, it is also seen to form a major part of his writerly self. It is pertinent to note that Narayan once said to Ved Mehta that having roots in family and religion are the essential qualities of being a good writer. Thus, the protagonist's search for roots in this novel, far from being an overt manifestation of a nativist attempt at constructing an Indian view of life in a society of bi-cultural hybridity, becomes technically a strategy of resistance, a strategy of postcolonial reverse-narrative.

Narayan's *The English Teacher* (1945) is the story of Krishnan, the protagonist, whose search for his cultural roots takes him along a process of evolution to forge independently a philosophy to assimilate his emotional, intellectual and spiritualities with his country or society. In fact, the writer's treatment of education and philosophy, in this novel, forms a derivative part of an abiding quest of the protagonist for the truth of his identity in his native cultural roots. In course of the novel, Krishnan, the English teacher at Albert Mission College in Malgudi, where he was once a student, finally resigns his post in favour of an option for teaching in a nursery school of an indigenous model. What is significant is that, such an evolution in him, being initiated primarily though by his ingrained antipathy for the system of English Education in colonized India, is necessitated in the ultimate reckoning by some sort of spiritual enrichment, gained after a strenuous meditation and psychic communion with the spirit of his dead wife. Maturity in Krishnan can be traced in terms of his tension between his conventional modes of existence and the ideal sort of a harmonious existence, sensed in his quest for the inexorable law of life, or truth. As the novel begins, Krishnan is shown as an established 'English Teacher', who is dissatisfied with the very system of teaching the youngsters for his own livelihood. Intellectually, Krishnan is quite aware of the discrepancy between his aspiration and achievement, and naturally, the resultant experience is a vague work-weariness in him that spills over the very opening pages of the novel: "The urge had been upon me for some days past to take myself at hand. What was wrong with me? I could not say, some sort of vague disaffection, a self-rebellion I might call it. The feeling... always leaving behind a sense of something missing" (5).

The very beginning of the novel sets the tempo of a search in Krishnan—a predicament faced by any sensitive individual who seeks to problematise the question of identity of the 'marginal' in a colonial society. The ironic recounting of his daily life, by Krishnan himself, highlights the need for some inspiration that his soul aspires for:

> I took stock of my daily life. I got up at eight every day, read for the fiftieth time Milton, Carlyle and Shakespeare, [...] so that they might mug up Shakespeare and Milton and secure high marks and save adverse remarks from my chiefs at the end of the year [...]. I was

> constantly nagged by the feeling that I was doing the wrong work. (5)

In the use of the very expression "to mug up Shakespeare and Milton",[1] Narayan perhaps attacks, through Krishnan, the very credo of colonialist education, which seeks to iconize the Western literature and history at the cost of marginalizing the entire gamut of literature and history of the colonized 'others'. "To mug up Shakespeare and Milton" and reproduce the same verbatim on the examination-script—have been set as criteria for a brilliant result. Narayan seems to be critical about the faulty evaluation system of the Western education that fails to take into account the intelligence and originality of the learners. The 'workweariness' in Krishnan, further aggravated by a 'perpetual self-criticism', as Krishnan himself admits, comes to the fore once again when the Principal summons all the English teachers to his room one day to convey to them his sense of shock after he has noticed a student spelling 'honours' without 'u'. He describes such an experience of his as a blot on the ennobling efforts of the colonizers to preserve the importance and purity of the English language. Krishnan can see a sense of pride and supremacy in the role of Brown as a self-appointed custodian to the Indians learning English: "Brown's thirty years in India had not been ill-spent if they had opened the eyes of the Indians to the need for speaking and writing correct English. The responsibility of the English department was indeed very great" (6). To Krishnan, all this seems to be a fiasco, projecting an attempt to catch and garner the chaff instead of the grains (which alone should be preserved with proper care). His indignation at the supposed gravity of the offence (i.e. dropping, 'u' from the word 'honours') bursts out in his interaction with Mr. Gajapathy, an Assistant Professor and Krishnan's senior in office. Gajapathy considers such a mistake as 'disgraceful' and Krishnan cannot help blurting out: "Mr. Gajapathy, there are blacker sins in this world than a dropped vowel". Krishnan's stand is, however, unequivocal: the Western colonisers have done a sacrilegious onslaught on the Indian culture and tradition; therefore any mistake on the part of the natives in learning a foreign language is not anything to be ashamed of. Moreover, Krishnan's approach to the problem is unbiased: acquisition of any language by any foreign learner entails some stumbling blocks to everyone, irrespective of the rank and status of the learner—coloniser or colonised. What happens to the poor fellow, who drops 'u' from 'Honours', may apply as well to Mr. Brown, who even after spending thirty years in India, will fail to translate into any one of the two hundred regional languages a simple expression like 'The cat chases the rat'" (6). In the character of Krishnan, readers notice Narayan's exposition of the postcolonial urge to ignore the exaltation of the West, a trend well set since the publication of Macaulay's historical 'Minute'.[2] Such an urge is characteristic of India's social condition of the Colonial period, when the introduction of English education led to the fragmentation of the traditional models of education. It is relevant to discuss here briefly the introduction of Western Education *vis-à-vis* the conventional modes of education in Colonised India. The incompatibility between the two ideals of education had a deep sociological repercussion insofar as it led to a distinctive cultural amnesia in the colonized people. The direct patronage of the Britishers began to establish, slowly and steadily, a new form of cultural elitism in Colonial India. Gauri Viswanathan, in *The Beginnings of English Literary Study in British India*, has asserted that the spread of English education led to Britain's ideological control over the people of India—"maintaining control of the natives under the guise of a liberal education" (*Oxford Literary Review*, 9, 1987, p. 17). In her *The Masks of Conquest* (1989), Viswanathan further observes that Britain's English Education Policy shrewdly furthered the Colonial interests through the controlling tactics of imperial textuality: "A discipline that was originally intended in India primarily to convey the mechanics of language was thus transformed into an instrument for ensuring industriousness, efficiency, trustworthiness, and compliance in native subjects" (93).

However, Krishnan's repudiation for the standardized, mechanical system of English teaching, once again, comes to the surface as he broods over the probable reaction of his students to his own poem on nature, composed on his new experience of getting up early for an outing. Reading a poem should be, ideally speaking, an experience in itself. But teaching poetry in the classroom often proves to be a debacle in the absence of an acceptable methodology. The annotator's desperate efforts to convey a meaning, the teacher's doubly desperate efforts to wrest a meaning from the annotator and the poet—all transform the poetry class into a gruesome experience that the students have to withstand with 'grim tolerance'. Through Krishnan's meticulous choice of words, Narayan throws into focus the failure of the Westernized system of education during the colonial period in igniting vision or creative imagination in the mind of learners, since the system could neither enable the learners to assimilate an appropriated culture nor make the Western culture compatible with the indigenous traditions. Krishnan's experience broadly corresponds to Narayan's critical attitude[3] to the existing system of Education. The spirit of search in Krishnan does not, however, die out after its initial outburst as discussed in the beginning of this chapter. One day, as he is making roll-calls, one of his students requests him to defer the roll-call to the last few minutes of the class, as the process of noting attendance takes most of the learning hours. The teacher refuses to do so with a showman's insolence and thus manages to silence the murmur with a threat to mark all of them absent. Later on, these thoughts, crossing over Krishnan's mind, goad him on to a remorseful self-analysis which has been suppressed by his overbearing consciousness of being an English teacher: "...who was I that they should obey my command? What tie was there between mine and them? Did I absorb their personalities as did the old masters and merge them in mine?" (12).

Krishnan has the clarity of outlook to take stock of his 'being' in the network of the colonial system of education in India: "I was merely a man who had mugged earlier than they, the Verity edition of Lear and guided them through the mazes of Elizabethan English. I did not do it out of love for them or for Shakespeare but only out of love for myself" (12). Such a clean confession shows Krishnan's disillusionment with the

Western model of education which obstructs conformity between earning and learning. Notwithstanding the lack of personal motivation for teaching in the existing set up, Krishnan bears his cross, but is baffled further by the discovery of an incompatibility between the craze for learning literature on one hand, and the lack of requisite accomplishments on the other. With a characteristic touch of irony, Narayan underscores this vain colonial mentality in the form of a conversation between Krishnan and one of his pupils, Ramaswamy. In spite of his inability to perceive the meaning of a poem, Ramaswamy writes two pages on it in his note-book.

> Krishnan: Does this poem make no sense as far as you are concerned?
>
> "No sir..."
>
> "Then why do you write so much about it?"
>
> "I do not know, Sir". (14)

Krishnan expresses his doubts also about the educationists' insistence on the subtleties and niceties of English grammar which, instead of encouraging, practically impedes the progress of the learners in the colonized society. He mentions his feelings in one of his classes on composition where he is set at correcting the grammatical errors made by his pupils: "I spent the rest of the period giving a general analysis of the mistakes I had encountered in this batch of composition…the traps that the English Language sets for foreigners" (15). But, in spite of a deep-seated unrest in his profession, Krishnan's happy family life, with his wife Susila and daughter Leela, is suddenly disrupted when his wife dies premature and, interestingly, the circumstances, in which Susila falls ill and dies of typhoid, have a striking resemblance to Narayan's personal experiences as recorded in his autobiography *My Days*.[4] However, such an unforeseen catastrophe in personal life hurls Krishnan into an abysmal depth of despair and gloom. Here, at this stage of Krishnan's life, as Ian Mackean observes, the "element of unpredictability" (that has begun encroaching upon Krishnan's life ever since he had moved out of his cloistered existence in the college hostel in order to live with his family in Malgudi) delivers its severest blow and life almost comes to a stand still for Krishnan. But true to the mettle of Narayan's heroes, Krishnan also shows the power of adapting himself to the changed circumstances. Right from his disastrous experiences in life, Krishnan is shown to have acquired a feeling of reality (or 'truth' in a broader sense) in his ordeals of life in the new set of experiences. Narayan records Krishnan's thoughts in the cremation ground with a superb rhetorical touch: "Flames appear over the wall.... It leaves a curiously dull pain at heart. There are no more surprises and shocks in life.... Nothing else will worry or interest me in life hereafter" (96). Now, the new responsibility thrust upon him—to keep himself going with an equal care for the little girl to the exclusion of any outside help—makes Krishnan now all set to play the role: "God has given me some novel situation in life. I shall live it alone, face the problems alone..." (97). Krishnan's maturity after Susila's death comes at an astonishing pace. Profound shocks and sorrows in his personal life serve to sublimate his being to the state of a detached stoicism: "Condolences, words of courage, lamentations, or assurances were all the same. I had become sort of professional receptacle of condolence and sympathy" (98). The phrase 'like a receptacle of sorrow and pain' reveals the significance of Krishnan's realization that has moorings in the rudimentary tenets of Hindu Philosophy. A perfectly stoic man, *Sthitapragya,*[5] remains unperturbed by any blow of sorrow or misfortune. According to *The Gita*, a balanced individual, indifferent to pain and pleasure, has the potentiality for an ideal existence. Krishnan's mental state, to some extent (at least a semblance to such an existence), corresponds to the therapeutic ethics of Hindu religion and philosophy. The rest of the story, so far as Krishnan's action is concerned, is with a fair measure of justice, an exemplification of *Karmayoga*[6] or the doctrine of 'activity in detachment' as propounded in *The Gita*. In this connection, Ian Mackean has described Krishnan's experience as an odyssey away from the 'academic world' to the 'Law of Life'.[7]

Death of his wife restores to Krishnan's life the 'reality' that has been so far perceived through the filters of academic perspectives offered by literature or rationalism in a cloistered life. The sterility of Krishnan's literary approach to life is reinforced a number of times in his confessions that he has been reading Milton, Carlyle and Shakespeare for 'the fiftieth time'. Later on, his effort in lucubration to record his impression of the angelic entity of his wife turns out to be mere a copy of a poem by Wordsworth. Again, his venture to read a book on Plato, too, is abandoned at the very first attempt. Krishnan's search for balance, in the matrix of the timetested Indian philosophical convictions, is otherwise the reaction to the futility of academic disciplines in countering the basic issues of life and death and thereby providing men with a wholly workable set of values. In one of his attacks on literature as a mere academic discipline in the Westernized world, Krishnan says, much later in the novel, to his pupils: "Don't worry so much about these things—they are trash, we are obliged to go through and pretend we like them, but all the time the problem of living and dying is crushing us" (149).

This self-adjustment, however complete in itself as the inner pattern, fails to match the outer order—Krishnan's vocation of teaching English in a colonized environment. If Indian tradition and spiritualism restore balance to Krishnan, the man, it is the lack of the same roots in his professional life that fails to motivate Krishnan, the teacher. The prevalent system of English education in India appears to be a fiasco and as artificial as a forcible imposition of one culture on another without a scope of osmosis between the two. The resultant reaction is one of lethargy and lack of interest. The aggravation of these tendencies cannot be fully subscribed to Krishnan's personal trauma; instead, right from the beginning of his career, the development of the teacher in Krishnan follows a uni-linear progression. One day, as Krishna is preparing to leave for home, he is saddled with an extra-class on language. He implores his senior, Mr. Gajapathy, to spare him that trouble on the ground of his lack of interest in language teaching. His feelings bear out a clean note of confession: "...as a student I had found language torture, and as a teacher I still found it a torture" (104).

In fact, any performance, when denied the supply of some natural and original sustenance, reverts to a drab and dull discharge of formalities. The same thing happens in Krishnan's case also: "...it seemed to me all the same whether they listened or made a noise or whether they understood what I said or felt baffled, or even whether they heard it at all or not. My business was to sit in that chair and keep my tongue active—that I did. My mind itself could only vaguely comprehend what was being read..." (104). Right at this juncture of life, where social identity no longer receives adequate spiritual support from within, Krishnan receives a catalytic connection—a letter from an expert in automatic writing, telling Krishnan of a possibility of communication with the spirit of his dead wife. Proximity with this man and regular sittings with him initiate Krishnan into the mystic peace of the world of the dead and, Krishnan's new knowledge serves as the passport for an entry into a new world of communication. Gradually, Krishnan learns, in a process of meditation, a power of spiritual perception so as to receive messages from his deceased wife. This spiritual communion enriches Krishnan's life and sensibility so as to make him discover and sift the abiding from the meretricious in personal as well as in professional life. Here, at this stage of life, Krishnan's experience of a different ideal of education is occasioned by none other than Leela, his daughter. Leela's growing interest in her new school incidentally brings the headmaster of her school in contact with Krishnan to whom this experience adds a new dimension to his search for identity as a teacher. Such an achievement (i.e. the expected dimension) seems to be realized (as Krishnan feels after meeting the headmaster and later visiting Leela's school) only after a departure from the mechanized and institutionalized world of adult education into some primeval, pure and simple experience that is not yet disrupted by any system of the adult society. The eccentric and visionary headmaster and the children, in general, of Leela's school bring a Midas touch to Krishnan's self as a teacher. A visit to Leela's school at the behest of the headmaster unravels to Krishnan an epitome of a created universe of pure, unmixed joy. Glittering alphabets on partitioning screens between classrooms, models and paintings of men, trees, animals, skies, rivers with every conceivable playthings made by the headmaster such as the see-saws, swings, sand-heaps and ladders—all like the circus party in Dickens's *Hard Times*,[8] stand for the phantasmagoria of such spontaneity and vitality that encourage life. However, the catalyst in the transformation of Krishnan's realization is none other than the crazy, visionary headmaster who points out: "these are the class rooms [...]. For us elders to learn" (124).

The headmaster, a champion of the ideal of childhood, has devoted his life to this nursery school since he received the prediction of death (which, however, proves false). This futility of prediction by a mystic in the headmaster's life bears an ironic closeness to Krishnan's journey from predictability to unpredictability in Krishnan's experience of Susila's death, which thwarted the doctor's assurance of recovery: "No complications. A perfect typhoid run". Ian Mackean stresses, thus, the role of unpredictability in Krishnan's life: "The scientifically-based prediction of life is thwarted by death and the mystical prediction of death is thwarted by in life" (*par* 14). To Krishnan, this headmaster acts as the curtain raiser to the law of unpredictability and the primeval simplicity, spontaneity and natural energy in the world of children which is untarnished by the deadening, stifling educational system with its dogmas and principles. The protective measure to save such 'angels', the 'real gods on earth', is, according to the headmaster, the "Leave-Alone System" as in practice at this school. Such a system, in his view, does justice not only to the children with versatile potentiality, but also to the elders, who can shake off the stigma of inhibition, the constrains of the adult world: "The Leave-Alone System,...will make them wholesome human beings, and also help us, those who work along them, to work off the curse of adulthood" (148).

The headmaster finds his roots, metaphorically speaking, in the children's world as ideal kind of living: "When I watch them, I get a glimpse of some purpose in existence and creation" (125). After an initial misgiving, Krishnan finally comes to believe in his ideals and views. Though Krishnan is finally seen to leave his college-job and resorts to a more genuine and authentic lifestyle as a teacher of Leela's primary school, such a radical decision to renounce the stifling, mechanized world of adult education is duly preceded by mental preparation coming in the wake of his growing perception of his own tradition and native culture. However, this is the turning point in Krishnan's life. The emerging reality is spelt out in an unequivocal manner as a revelation: "I had a feeling that I was about to make a profound contact in life" (125). Later, Leela and her friends in the school unravel to Krishnan a pure, sacrosanct world of spontaneity and naturalness. Their instinctive energy is not stifled, nor inhibited by the moribund educational system or canons of upstart morality of the world of the grown-ups. The headmaster of Leela's school, Krishnan's pathfinder, holds the view that "children have a simplicity to which all human conduct must be reduced" (140). The headmaster is against such a modern education that consigns 'angels' to a strangling system of data-consumption. He thinks that the glorious state of childhood has been tarnished by our educational systems and his feelings are expressed in unequivocal terms: "Most of us forget that grand period...a most balanced and joyous condition of life...for the future of mankind we should retain the original vision..." (147-48).

Krishnan's view of the children's world as a countermeasure against 'the curse of adulthood' finally matures after his wife's message, and this comes to be more intensified through the influence of the headmaster, who forsakes his quarrelsome wife and children to seek his new *janma* in his school. The headmaster's views regarding modern education in the colonial India emphasize the problematic of cultural usurpation by the British leading to a distinctive cultural amnesia in the colonized and the resultant moral bankruptcy: "Multiply your expenses and look to the government for support, and sell your soul to the government for grant. This is the history of our education movement.... The main business of an educational institution is to shape the mind and character..." (135).

This goal of education, as set by the imperialist policymakers, evokes bitter feelings in Krishnan. With a mounting distaste for the academic bias of modern education that is divorced from 'truth', Krishnan (rather his creator Narayan himself) pines for a cultural historiography instead of a mere historicisation of some inane chronicles and literary achievements of a foreign culture: "Why do they make so much of the history of literature? They have to make a history of every damned thing on earth—as if literature could not survive without some fool compiling a bogus history...I will tell the boys what is sense and what is non-sense...they are being fed on literary garbage and that we are all the paid servants of the garbage department" (150). The innate urge in Krishnan to re-establish and reformulate the native culture is enkindled at the offer of the headmaster: "I want you to take charge of my school and see that it does not go to ruin" (161). Krishnan's initial hesitation at the proposal makes the headmaster ask: "But do you think you are happy in your work"? It is noticeable that Krishnan's immediate reaction to this question of job-satisfaction is one of helpless cynicism: "But who cares for happiness in work? One works for the money..." (161). However, he gets over this form of cynicism regarding routine activities, and finally, we notice in Krishnan, an urge for self-development. The headmaster's destiny acts as a sort of revelation to Krishnan who, for all these months, had been pursuing self-development as a "perpetual excitement ever promising some new riches in the realm of experience and understanding even with an awareness in sensibilities" (168).

At this stage, a chance visit of Krishnan's mother has a salvaging effect on his sensibility which has been groping for an avenue for self-fulfilment: "It seemed to restore for a moment one's sense of security, the solid factors of life, and its warmth and interests" (172). After a couple of weeks, she leaves taking with her the grand-daughter, who by now blooms with the warmth of a mother's touch. One week-end, Krishnan pays a visit to his ancestral house and finds Leela in 'splendid health', perfectly accommodated to the delightful company of cousins and above all, the presiding affection of her grandparents. Krishnan comes back and remains preoccupied in his lonely house with the illuminating reflections on the inevitability of loneliness and separation as the 'law of life'. The last chapter of the novel projects the last phase of Krishnan's journey on his quest for roots (to the exclusion of everything else); for the set of values and way of life, sanctioned by native culture and spiritual tradition. The very opening lines set the tempo of a Titanic will to cut across all barriers to reach the fountain-head of inspiration: "My mind was made up. I was in search of a harmonious existence and everything that disturbed that harmony was to be rigorously excluded, even my college work" (178). Depressed with the dissemination of colonial education and culture, he resolves to resign from his college. His grudge against the cultural imperialism of the British educationists is evident in the following lines: "I could no longer stuff Shakespeare and Elizabethan meter and Romantic poetry for the hundredth time into the young minds and feed them on the dead mutton of literary analysis and theories and histories, while what they needed was education in the fullest use of the mind" (178).

Notably, the expression 'education in the fullest use of the mind' highlights one of the basic concepts of Indian thoughts and philosophy that all cognitive disciplines, including education, must be basically directed to the development of the mind. Viewed in this perspective, English education in pre-independence India only indulges in the appropriation of a cultural sycophancy by the natives: "This education has reduced us to a nation of morons; we were strangers to our own culture and camp followers of another culture, feeding on leavings and garbage" (178). Through Krishnan's agonized perception (of being 'strangers to our own culture and camp followers of another culture'), Narayan perhaps attacks a major sociological trend, a growing tendency for cultural sycophancy in the intelligentsia of India in the colonial period. The colonized middle class, with orientations in English, began to look upon the colonizer's language as a model of cultural elitism. This subsequently led to the development of the Babu class. The emergence of this Babu class had its repercussions and Meenakshi Mukherjee has shown in her book *The Perishable Empire*, how this new form of social elitism served to dismantle the regional language and gradually substantiated the rival claims of the English language. However, with an acute sense of incompatibility between his inner self and his social entity as a teacher, Krishnan feels depressed with dull methods of teaching. It seems that development of true literary sensibility is almost impossible in a borrowed language. Thus, even Shakespeare and Keats have been reduced to the level of mechanical examinations and critical notes: "What fool would be insensible to Shakespeare's sonnets or the 'Ode to the West Wind' or, 'A thing of beauty is a joy for ever'? [...]. But what about examinations and critical notes? Didn't these argely take the place of literature?" (178).

Krishnan's painful reflections remind one of the immortal lines written by Tagore on the character of education in the colonial period: "We rob the child of his earth to teach him geography; of language to teach him grammar...."[9] Ian Mackean's essay with a thoughtful title ("What about our own roots?") is justifiably summed up with a classification of roots that Krishnan's self quests for: "It could apply to all of us as adults alienated from our roots in childhood; to modern Indians alienated from their native cultural roots; and to humanity as a whole in that, we have become rational human beings alienated from our roots in the unknown" (*par* 32). With the unflinching zeal of a visionary or an idealist, Krishnan now hands over his resignation letter to Mr. Brown with a precise but straightforward confession: "Sir, what I am doing in the college hardly seems to me work. It does not please my innermost self [...]. I can afford to do what seems to me work, something which satisfies my innermost aspirations" (179-80).

Renunciation of a life, dominated by the Western cultural influence and withdrawal from the adult world in search of an inner peace, bring Krishnan into a realm of experience where this human mind becomes ultimately "clean and bare and a mere chamber of fragrance" (184). The novel comes to an end with an apocalyptic vision. The moments of ecstasy amalgamates past, present and future all in one and Krishnan imagines himself to be waking up to find Susila by his side; he has a sublime realization: "...where the boundaries of personality suddenly dissolve into a moment of immutable joy —a moment for which one feels grateful to Life and Death" (184). The surrealistic note with which the novel comes to an end does not appear artistically convincing to a critic like Srinivasa Iyenger. He wonders: "Is Krishna dreaming? Is it any more than an apocalyptic vision of Krishna's psychic ecstasy? Even so, isn't this a resurrection greater than life" (370)! In defence of Narayan, one can consider K. Chellappan's view of Indianness as 'a mode of perception'. He finds Narayan's vision and art embedded in the basic awareness of an Indian view of life in which illusion and reality, the mundane and the spiritual, the cosmic and the human, the tragic and the comic easily exchange places and what matters, is only 'a change in the mode of perception'. When the doors of perception are cleansed, life becomes immense and holy. In such a case, Narayan's factual narrative of a subdued life suddenly explodes into disorder which is the beginning of order and reveals depths of reality unknown and unexpected. So, in Narayan, there is an Indian rendition of "the ambivalence at the heart of reality in terms of a fusion/confusion of values, earthly and spiritual..." (Chellappan, 52).

In fact, Indian English fiction fits into that form of writing where the writer attempts for an ideal fictional historiography of a nation threatened by the cultural imperialism of colonial powers. Judged in this perspective, Narayan's *The English Teacher* is an attempt, in the person of the protagonist, to construct a kind of self-image through the discourse of drawing sustenance from indigenous roots that re-defines the intrinsic cultural, philosophical and social values. In this novel, Narayan transmutes, as Meena Sodhi has pointed out, life's experiences through the mode of aesthetic self-distancing in the persona of Krishnan. In conclusion, it might be said in this connection that Krishnan's quest is a metaphorical passage of an Indian whose sensibility drives him through the ordeals of the hybridisation of culture to the assurance of his native cultural roots and traditional values that explores the true import of education and philosophy. Such a culture, with its original network of values and convictions, strengthened by the 'timeless history' of India, offers materials for Krishnan's 'proper synthesis of life'. Krishnan's search for 'roots', realized in terms of his own tradition, practically endorses the opinion of Elleke Boehmer: "Tellingly, it is the same transition and cultural change of heart—a move from dependency to self-reliance and greater wholeness—that India as a nation will also make" (176).

Notes

1. Narayan writes in his essay "My Educational Outlook": "Educational theories have become progressively high-sounding, sophisticated and jargon-ridden (like many other subjects aspiring to the status of a science), but in practice the process of learning remains primitive. In the field of education, the educator and the educatee seemed to be arrayed in opposite camps, each planning how best to overwhelm the other" (106). Narayan is equally dismissive of the examination/evaluation system. In the same essay, he recollects his discussion with a teacher of political science, who had a progressive outlook on evaluation system. When he expressed surprise at the prevalent system of 'hiding the questions till the last moment' from the students, Narayan, with characteristic irony, explained: "We believe in mugging up; on an average 200 pages per subject, and fifteen subjects in a year. One who can demonstrate that he can recollect three thousand pages in the examination hall will be considered a first-class student in our country, although he need not understand a word of what he reads, or remember a syllable of what he has read after the examination. The whole aim of our education is to strain the faculty of our memory" (109). Emphasis added.
2. The following is an extract from Macaulay's Minute on Indian Education, 2 February 1835 that exalted English language with a comparative inferiorization of other native languages like Sanskrit and Arabic: All parties seem to be agreed on one point, that the dialects commonly spoken among the natives of this part of India, contain neither literary nor scientific information, and are, moreover, so poor and rude that, until they are enriched from some other quarter, it will not be easy to translate any valuable work into them. It seems to be

admitted on all sides, that the intellectual improvement of those classes of the people who have the means of pursuing higher studies can at present be effected only by means of some language not vernacular amongst them. What then shall that language be? One-half of the committee maintain that it should be the English. The other half strongly recommend the Arabic and Sanskrit. The whole question seems to me to be, which language is the best worth knowing? I have no knowledge of either Sanskrit or Arabic.—But I have done what I could to form a correct estimate of their value. I have read translations of the most celebrated Arabic and Sanskrit works. I have conversed both here and at home with men distinguished by their proficiency in the Eastern tongues. I am quite ready to take the Oriental learning at the valuation of the Orientalists themselves. I have never found one among them who could deny that a single shelf of a good European library was worth the whole native literature of India and Arabia. The intrinsic superiority of the Western literature is, indeed, fully admitted by those members of the committee who support the Oriental plan of education. *(par* 1-3). Emphasis added.

3. Narayan writes in "My Educational Outlook": "If a classification is called for I may be labelled 'anti-educational'. I am not averse to enlightenment, but I feel convinced that the entire organisation, system, outlook and aims of education are hopelessly wrong from beginning to end; from primary first year to Ph.D., it is just a continuation of an original mistake" (106).
4. In his autobiography *My Days*, Narayan writes: "*The English Teacher* is autobiographical in content, very little part of it being fiction. The English teacher of this novel, Krishan, is a fictional character in the fictional city of Malgudi; but he goes through the same experiences I had gone through and he calls his wife Susila, and the child is Leela instead of Hema" (134-35). The concept of *Sthitapragya* is explained in *The Gita* by Lord Krishna: Prajahati jada Kaman sarvan Partha manoggatan Atmanyebatmna tushta sthItaprajnostadochyate (Oh Partha! when Jiva forgoes desires arising out of illusions and the mind thus purified, receives satiety in the soul itself, it can be called sthitapragya.) *Bhagavad Gita*, II-55.
6. *The Gita*, explains the concept of '*Niskama karma*': *Tasmadsakta satatang karjang karma samachara Asakta hacharan karma paramapnoti purusha* (He who works always

without any attachment, deserves the attainment of the Supreme Knowledge.) *Bhagavadgita*, XI -19.

7. Ian Mackean, in his article on Krishnan's journey in *The English Teacher,* describes the change in Krishnan's perception (that has a close parallel to Narayan's) after the failure of predictions regarding the recovery of Susila: Now he is discovering how ordinary people encounter the big issues of life and death, not as seen through the perspective of literature or philosophy, and not in a way that would imply that some profound universal conclusions could be drawn, but as they actually experience it in everyday life. And Narayan himself, insofar as we can identify him with the character of Krishnan, is writing at the level of those ordinary people. He does not adopt the position of a novelist presenting the reader with fictitious characters which he has created, and which are under his control, as for example Charles Dickens does, but in the guise of Krishnan he places himself firmly among the ordinary people, and breaks down the boundaries between real life outside his novel and the life within the novel. Just as Krishnan faces life without illusions, so Narayan seems to create his novel without the usual illusions of the novelist such as pre-planned plot and fictitious characters (*par* 16-17).
8. See, The Norton Critical Edition of Dickens's *Hard Times.* Dickens's treatment of Sleary's circus party in the novel stands for the world of fancy, of pristine joy that encourages life. In the novel, the circus party technically parodies the fetters of fact that the theories of Adam Mill and Bentham delivered on English life/education in the Victorian Age.
9. In the essay entitled "A Poet's School," Tagore has emphasized the necessity of an 'empathetic sense of interconnectedness with the surrounding world'. The following extract seeks to validate the poet's idea: We have come to this world to accept it, not merely to know it. We may become powerful by knowledge, but we attain fullness by sympathy. The highest education is that which does not merely give us information but makes our life in harmony with all existence. But we find that this education of sympathy is not only systematically ignored in schools, but it is severely repressed. From our very childhood habits are formed and knowledge is imparted in such a manner that our life is weaned away from nature and our mind and the world are set in opposition from the beginning of our days. Thus, the greatest of educations for

which we came prepared is neglected, and we are made to lose our world to find a bagful of information instead. We rob the child of his earth to teach him geography, of language to teach him grammar. His hunger is for the Epic, but he is supplied with chronicles of facts and dates...Child-nature protests against such calamity with all its power of suffering, subdued at last into silence by punishment (116-17). From Personality, 1917. Emphasis added.

Works Cited

Boehmer, Elleke. *Colonial and Postcolonial Literature*. New York: OUP, 1995.

Chellappan, K. "Indianness as a Mode of Perception". *Anthology of Recent Criticism on R.K. Narayan*. New Delhi: Penchraft, 2000.

Dickens, Charles. *Hard Times*: Norton Critical Edition. Ed. Ford, George and Sylvere Manod. New York: Norton and Company, 1990.

Halsall, Paul. Thomas Babington Macaulay on "On Indian Education", July 1998. 17 Oct. 2007. <http://www.fordham.edu/halsall/ mod/1833macaulay-india.html>.

Iyenger, Srinivas. *Indian Writing in English*. New York: Asian Publishing House, 1973. 358-85.

Mackean, Ian. "What about our own roots? Krishnan's journey in R.K. Narayan's *The English Teacher*". 13.10. 2007. <http://www.literature-studyonline.com/essays/narayan.html>.

Mehta, Ved. "Profiles: The Train Had Just Arrived at Malgudi Station". *The New Yorker*, September 15, 1962.

Mukherjee, Meenakshi. *The Perishable Empire: Essays on Indian Writing in English*. New Delhi: OUP Paperback, 2002.

Narayan, R.K. "English in India: The Process of Transmutation". *Aspects of Indian Writing in English*. Ed. M.K. Naik. New Delhi: Macmillan India Limited, 1979. 19-23.

———. *My Days*: A Memoir. Mysore: Indian Thought Publications, Indian Reprint, 1995.

———. "My Educational Outlook". *A WRITER'S NIGHTMARE: Selected Essays* (1958-1988), Penguin Books, 1988.

———. *The English Teacher*. 1945. Mysore: Indian Thought Publications, 1989.

O'Connell, Kathleen M. "Rabindranath Tagore on education". 17 Oct. 2007. http://www.infed.org /thinkers/tagore.htm .

Sodhi, Meena. "R.K. Narayan: His Life into Art". *R.K. Narayan: An Anthology of Recent Criticism*. Ed. C.N. Srinath. Delhi: Pencraft, 2000.

Srimad Bhagvadgita: Eds. Jagadishwarananda, Swami and Swami Jagadananda. Kolkata: Udbodhan Karjalaya, 2007.

Viswanathan, Gauri. *Masks of Conquest: Literary Study and British Rule in India*. New York: Columbia University Press, 1989.

4

Revisiting R.K. Narayan Through Eco-criticism

Kishwar Zafir

To his credit, R.K. Narayan has fourteen novels and a good number of short-stories—renditions which are light yet sensitive. The factor binding his novels and the stories, at the most basic level, is that all his novels and most of his short-stories are set in Malgudi. Malgudi, a small south Indian town is, therefore, the microcosm, which, in all capacity, represents the society at large. It is a localization, yet it can be viewed as being anywhere in India. However, though Malgudi does represent Indian sensibilities to a great extent, it remains a creation of the mind—a vision, a dream town. In it, one can find ample number of characters, both round and flat. In fact, the town itself can be called a character, continuously developing and evolving.

The city, however, seems to be largely unaffected by political and historical conditions, and sometimes even by natural causes. Even through a drought, as in *The Guide*, people's sensibilities do not take a beating, which is perhaps why V.S. Naipaul says: "The Indian of Narayan's novel is not the India that the visitor sees. He tells the Indian truth. Too much that is overwhelming has been left out: too much has been taken for granted" (225). Of course, it should always be kept in mind that Narayan's world is imaginary, purely fictional.

When one has read all the novels and the short-stories, one can safely say where what is; as if one talks of a town or city one has come to dwell in over the years. The names and details of the streets, stores, public amenities, and even the people living in various streets, appear in one novel after the other, and the community is essentially close knit with just a few intruders. This, then, is the prowess of the man who says he likes, in Mukherji's words, "peopled places" (87), and is most comfortable when discussing them against their backdrop. This is why, on the part of the reader, one can explore "those loved and shabby streets and see with excitement and a certainty of pleasure a stranger approaching past the bank, the cinema, the haircutting saloon, a stranger who will greet us, we know, with some unexpected and revealing pleasure that will open a door to yet another 'human existence" (Greene, vi).

Amidst all this milieu of human characters and townscape detailing, we find that due attention has not been paid to the landscape, or the nature, or the ecology of the area in and out of Malgudi. In this regard, William Walsh observes: "The physical geography of Malgudi is never dealt with as a set piece but allowed to reveal itself beneath and between the events" (123). A town, peopled and charactered to its hilt, is yet missing out on one of the most important aspects of any given place—nature. This brings us to the subject of my paper—discussing Narayan's work through an eco-critical perspective.

The word 'eco' has its roots in science, but has been used in the English scenario for quite some time now. One of the most basic definitions of ecocriticism has been given by Glotfelty, who puts forth that "ecocriticism is the study of the relationship between literature and the physical environment" (xviii). There is, however, no single fixed definition for eco-criticism and many ecocritics do away with restrictive definitions and assess literature from a 'green' point of view. Mazel suggests that whichever way we put it, "eco-criticism seems less a singular approach or method than a constellation of approaches, having little more in common than a shared concern with the environment" (2). Basic definitions and concepts apart, there have been various phases of eco-criticism over the last few decades, in which the paradigm has shifted from the first wave to the second wave. There have come up several ecological philosophies and the application of any of these can be used to analyse a text of literature.

Deep ecology is based upon an eight point platform, put forward by Arne Naess in 1972. The upshot of this is that deep ecologists demand a return to, what Gerard calls, "monistic, primal identification of humans and the ecosphere" (21). Social and Marxist Ecology views capitalism, globalization and competition as threats to the environment and suggests a renunciation of these oeuvres. Ecofeminism views the women as closer to nature and rejects the concept of feminization of landscapes by man. It argues that women are more compatible to save the earth from further destruction.

The ecocritical examination of a text is not only about the author's interest in the non-human natural environs, but about how the approach of the entire text is, which, in other words, means to look at how nature is treated upon as a whole in the setting of the text, as well as by the characters peopling the text. Most of nature, consistently over the past, has been looked upon as opposite to culture, and therefore, nature is treated as an exclusion. The creation of a master identity, in this case, humans in general, is the reason for the creation of "the inferior other" (Plumwood, 42). It is for this reason that most people, including writers, treat the non-human natural words as soulless and spiritless, mere presences for the utility of man.

In Narayan's fiction, there is so often, so much stress on human characters that nature begins to lose its identity in the scheme of things. It begins to become 'the other'.

The Mempi Forest near Malgudi, and the River Sarayu are two such natural presences. They are so much a symbol of permanence that they are taken for granted. The forest serves its purpose as a source of timber, and that is all that the Malgudians are bothered about. The Sarayu too serves its own purpose. Though a number of mundane activities take place on its banks, it is usually referred to passively by the people, and never assumes an important place in their psyche. The lotus pond, outside the town, too, is a prominent feature and appears in many novels. It is beyond the Sarayu, towards the north, in a garden. In *The English Teacher* and *The Financial Expert*, we find the garden discussed as a wilderness; beautiful yet fore-boding in its ugliness, with its overgrown trees, and plants having gone wild. Margayya, the financial wiz, can only look at it as a land gone to waste because of neglect, otherwise it could definitely have yielded a thousand or more rupees.

The garden is where the lotus pond is located. It is the place where the red lotus, required for pooja purposes, is found. We can sense the depletion of natural resources, such as water bodies, from Malgudi, when the priest tells Margayya: "There were perhaps ten spots in a town where you could pick up a lotus in former days, but now our world is going to pieces because we have no more lotus about" (51). The priest's belief is that the loss of the ponds, and the world going to pieces are the outcomes of non-availability of lotus for religious purposes, not because of man's role in destroying nature. It highlights the ignorance the Malgudian harbours towards nature.

Giving due importance or no importance to nature is always looked upon by Narayan's characters through the lens of religion, and ultimately, it is decided that nature is for the benefit of man and not vice-versa. Vasu, the taxidermist, in *The Man Eater of Malgudi,* kills an eagle flying in the sky, and offers to stuff eagles for pooja purposes. Promptly enough, he is frowned upon by the Malgudians and is referred to as a "rakshasa" (231). He earns this contempt because he has dared to kill the messenger of Vishnu; not because he has done a cruel act towards a living creature. Later on, in the same novel, Nartraj cannot stand the idea of Vasu killing the elephant, Kumar, because it is an unholy act; not because it is a cruel act towards nature: "Elephants? Who could kill an elephant" (249)?

A Tiger for Malgudi discusses the life of an animal from the point of view of a tiger, Raja. The feelings, the lion harbours upon the loss of its mother, and in captivity, or as "Supreme Lord of the Jungle" (13), are akin to human thoughts and emotions. In the end, the tiger adopts *sanyas* while living with a hermit. All this is fine, but the question here is as to why has the writer made his animal character depict exactly the same emotions as that of human beings; and why has he not treated it from the animistic point of view?

In *The Bachelor of Arts*, when Chandran leaves his house, he leaves behind a disturbed father who gives up tending his garden. It should, however, be noted that no other task is left untended except the gardening.

Looking at Narayan's works of non-fiction, we find glimpses of such instances where nature has been talked of as 'the other'.

In the essay "Gardening without Tears", which appears in the collection *Next Sunday*, the writer says: "There is something in gardening which affects what may be called the norms of human temperament" (*A Writer's Nightmare,* 51). The gardener, according to Narayan, is a cantankerous person, ever scared of trampling feet and unwanted chickens. In all the mention of the garden, the two prime purposes that come up are—gardening for the purpose of procuring flowers for pooja and gardening for utility purposes. The garden that affords "merely visual pleasure" is not even given description (51). Also, in the end, the writer refers to plants as being man's best friend, not because they are a pleasure to have around, but because they are "silent, unobtrusive and (more or less) responsive" (51).

In the essay "The Winged Ants", from the collection *Reluctant Guru*, we come across the writer asking the use of the creation of the winged arts. The only reason that he doles out a line of praise for any non-human living organism (in this case, the white ant or termite) is that it helps in getting rid of paper waste. In the essay, "Elephant in the Pit", of the same collection, the writer neither shows apathy, nor sympathy for the cruelty meted out to the elephant, which is merely being captured for the purpose of human entertainment.

An essay that is written in the positive note, however, is 'Monkeys' in the collection *Later Essays*, but is it because they are the 'descendants of the great god Hanuman' (195).

To say that Narayan's views regarding nature are completely unostentatious would be wrong, for among all this projection of nature as a utility tool only, we find instances where there is a compassionate undertone also.

Natraj, in *The Man Eater of Malgudi*, comes from a house where one of his many grand uncles gave him a coin to buy sugar for the ants. His uncle even told him not to scare away the crows and sparrows who came to partake of their food as "they have as much right as we to the corn that grows in the fields" (67). However, instances, such as this, make very rare appearances in Naryan's work. The concern, usually, is how to eke out the best possible benefit from nature.

Though Narayan is able to capture the "spirit of the place" (Naik, 14) with his writing, in detail, of human characters, he would have been able to perfect his presentation of the true spirit of a place by giving due attention to nature as one of the important forces in the being of his characterisation.

Works Cited

Gerard, Greg. *Ecocriticism*. London and New York: Routledge, 2004.

Glotfelty, Cheryll. "Introduction: Literary Studies in an Age of Environmental Crisis". *The Ecocriticism Reader: Landmarks in Literary Ecology*, Ed. Cheryll Glotfelty and Harold Fromm. Athens and London: University of Georgia Press, 1996.

Greene, Graham. "Introduction". *The Financial Expert*. Mysore: Indian Though Publications, 1984.

Mazel, David. *A Century of Early Ecocriticism*. Athens and London: University of Georgia Press, 2001.

Mukherji, Nirmal. "Some Aspects of the Literary Development of R.K. Narayan". *Banasthali Patirika*. Vol. 13, 1969.

Naik, M.K. "The Spirit of the Place". *Literary Endeavour*. Vol. III, Jan-June 1982.

Naipaul, V.S. *An Area of Darkness*. London: Andre Deutsch, 1964.

Narayan, R.K. *A Tiger for Malgudi*. Mysore: Indian Thought Publications, 1983.

Narayan, R.K. "A Writer's Nightmare". *Selected Essays*. 1958-1988, New Delhi.

———. *The Financial Expert*. Chennai: Indian Thought Publications, 2008.

———. *The Man Eater of Malgudi*. Delhi: Hind Pocket Books, 1979.

Plumwood, Val. *Feminism and the Mastery of Nature*. London and New York: Routledge, 1993.

Walsh, William. "Sweet Mangoes and Malt Vinegar". *The Novels of R.K. Narayan, Indo-English Literature*. Ed. K.K. Sharma. Ghaziabad: Vimal, 1977.

5

Renunciation: An Indian Way: V.S. Naipaul's Interpretation of R.K. Narayan's Novel *Mr. Sampath*

Javaid Ahmad Lone

One cannot truly and critically know a system unless one is not outside the system. One needs either to detach from the system, which one belongs to, or seek some other's help in order to gain the full knowledge of it. Detachment is one of the primary keys to gain an objective view of a thing. This kind of detachment can be both emotional and physical, or it can be one of the two. Detachment is a vast term to deal with. I will try to return to the concept later on in this paper, but presently, I intend to use this term in a sense, for example, to get the help of another person to help me in knowing myself better. It is in the same way as one needs a mirror to know one's facial features. A question may arise in this context—which I think is an important question—and that is, can a completely detached person know a field of knowledge without a risk to misunderstand it? It will be as risky as an alien is asked to conduct a research, say for example, on human knowledge systems. The conclusion, in short, is that we need a detached 'insider' to help us know the fault-lines in our knowledge of ourselves.

V.S. Naipaul, the writer of Indian origin and a grandson of an expatriate Indian Brahman, I think, will be always welcome to point his critical finger towards the fault-lines of changing Indian ways of life. India is not his home, but he himself says that he cannot reject India altogether or be totally indifferent to her (Naipaul, Foreword, x). He is a detached 'insider' (to call him attached outsider will be too gross a thing for him).

In his second book on India, titled *India: A Wounded Civilization*, he ventures to know India on two different levels: physical and literary. To know India physically, he travels throughout the country and for knowing her on literary level, he chooses a small number of writers. The writer who catches his attention the most is none other than R.K. Narayan. Narayan, the first generation Indian English novelist, has been diversely evaluated by critics. His art is different from his two contemporaries, Mulk Raj Anand and Raja Rao. Narayan is the "novelist of individual man," while Anand and Rao are respectively the novelists of social and metaphysical men (Naik, 1). Some critics see his style "as an old, rickety, wooden spinning wheel squeaking and rattling noisily" producing the thread with "no sign of fineness" (Shrivastava, 203), while some others believe him to be one of the world's three great modern writers. They equate him with William Faulkner and Hemingway (Raizada, 4). The speciality of Narayan is in the Indianness of his fiction. To know Narayan is to know India—with her past and her present. It was only during his 1975 visit to India that V.S. Naipaul could claim to have understood the real essence of Narayan's works. He had till then read him—as most of the critics do—as a writer with ironical skill and comic flavour.

> To get down to Narayan's world, to perceive the order and continuity he saw in the dereliction and smallness of India, to enter into the ironic acceptance and relish his comedy, was to ignore too much of what could be seen, to shed too much of myself: my sense of history, and even the simplest of ideas of human possibility. I did not lose my admiration for Narayan; but I felt that his comedy and irony were not quite what they had appeared to be, were part of a Hindu response to the world, a response I could no longer share. And it has since become clear to me—especially on this last visit, during a slow reading of Naratyan's 1949 novel

> *Mr Sampath*—that, for all their delight in human oddity, Narayan's novels are less the purely social comedies I had once taken them to be than religious books, at times religious fables, and intensely Hindu. (Naipaul, 11-12)

R.K. Narayan is one of those rare literary personalities in Indian literary history "who have realized life as they have lived it" (French xiii). It is the theme of withdrawal and renunciation on different levels which repeats itself in Narayan and which strikes Naipaul the most. *Mr. Sampath* is one of the less known novels of this versatile genius. The main character of the novel *Mr. Sampath* is not Sampath himself, but another character, named Srinivas, whom Naipaul calls a 'contemplative idler' (Naipaul, 12). His contemplative inaction is not that of prince Hamlet, nor has he set any great goals for himself. He has tried many jobs but has got no satisfaction. Being a Brahman, he starts reading Upanishads. After reading, he can do nothing but to write. He comes to Malgudi from his ancestral place, called Talapur, to edit his own paper. Being a family man, he never informs his wife or other family members about his new address. It is only through his paper itself that they come to know about his whereabouts. He finds his "domestic duties an extra burden" (Narayan, 36). But to escape from the guilt of negligence, he takes the responsibilities of his family: "Am I guilty of the charges of neglect?" he asks himself. "Family duties come before any other duty. What if I don't accept the position? I am sure, if I stick to my deeper conviction, other things like this will adjust themselves" (Narayan, 33).

When he starts his paper named *The Banner*, he declares that his paper has nothing to do with politics or any war. What he is concerned with is "the war that is always going on—between man's inside and outside" (Narayan, 6). Narayan's heroes possess a unique sensibility. They "[...] are aware of the social and the political changes, but they do not take sides, nor do they commit themselves to any ideology. Narayan imbues with reality in the social relationship and the sense of responsibility only to the extent it helps him to bring out their human qualities" (Singh, 57). While brooding over the functioning of the whole world, he sees a great balancing phenomenon. Nothing seems to him wrong, nothing right; everything works according to a set plan in the vastness of life. He thinks himself no more important than a leaf in a torrent. The vision of the Indian primitive past engulfs him completely. The rhythmical sounds of the cymbals and the rattle-drum of the *sadhu* and his assistants, who have been summoned to cure Ravi's madness, work upon Srinivas's psyche. He sees Lord Rama on his way to Lanka, walking through Malgudi when it was only a jungle. He sees the Buddha coming the same way, "preaching his gospel of compassion, centuries later," when Malgudi was a mere village (Narayan, 207). He sees philosopher Shankaracharaya treading the same path "during the next millennium...preaching his gospel of *Vedanta*" (207). One after the other, he sees the Christian missionary with his *Bible*, the European merchant and the soldier paving way for modern India: "Dynasties rose and fell. Palaces and mansions appeared and disappeared" (207). Srinivas is reconciled with the acceptance of *Karma*. Everything he sees is just and balanced (Naipaul, 15). H.C. Harrex calls Narayan's novels "the comedies of karma" (qtd. in Singh, 32). "To weave the present and the historical past together very skillfully" is the favorite province of Narayan's art (Kalinnikova, 20). The three great theories of *maya, tyag,* and *karma* are the essence of indian Hindu philosophy. According to Will Durant:

> The Hindus were deeper than the thinkers of Europe, because their interpretation of the world was internal and intuitive, not external and intellectual; the intellect divides everything; intuition unites everything; the Hindus saw that the "I" is a delusion; that the individual is a phenomenal, and what the only reality is the Infinite One—That art Thou. (Durant, 442)

V.S. Naipaul also tries to fit the concept of *karma* within the idea of Gandhian non-violence, a contemporary phenomenon in Narayan's time. When the exorcising magician brutally canes Ravi, Srinivas abandons his idea of stopping him:

> The vision had given him a view in which it seemed to him all the same whether they thwacked Ravi with a cane or whether they left him alone, whether he was mad or sane—all that seemed unimportant and not worth bothering about. The whole of eternity stretched ahead of one; there was plenty of time to shake off all follies. Madness or sanity, suffering of happiness all the same.... It didn't make the slightest difference in the long run—in the rush of eternity nothing mattered. (Narayan, 208)

Naipaul equates Srinivas's quietism with the concept of *karma* and Gandhian non-violence. It is nothing but "surrender". To quote Naipaul: "It is a religious response to worldly defeat" (Naipaul, 15).

To a common reader of Narayan, like me, Srinivas seems to be responsible for Ravi's madness. Because he neither stops him to pursue Shanti—the heroine of their film, who turns out to be Ravi's old dream girl—nor does he help him to do so. He only advises Ravi to open his third eye to burn *kama*—the instinct of love/lust—as Shiva does in their film *The Burning of Kama*. Srinivas knew that Ravi can never restrain himself. He also knew the fact that even as a painter, Ravi was not able to paint any image other than Shanti's, as she was his only muse. Mr. Sampath, Ravi's rival in love, has yet another ideology. Sampath gets swept by Shanti's charm and beauty, though we know that he is already a family-man. He always tries to remain with her and even wishes to have her as his second wife. His principle in life is that "[...] a man must shut eyes tight if it proves useless to look any longer" (Narayan, 58). It is an irony that Sampath, who believes in keeping his eyes shut, comes forward to play the role of Shiva, the god with a third eye, against Shanti, who acts as Parvathi in the film. It is intolerable for Ravi, who has been asked to be a true Shiva and open his third eye; when he sees his dream girl with Sampath, he plunges into the film studio in a fit of frenzy and destroys the whole effort of the film crew. Being too weak, Ravi is not able to obey Srinivas's mythical advice. Thus, he loses his senses. As a believer of the *karma* and eternal equilibrium,

Srinivas thinks himself to be no one to stop any forthcoming event in his or in the lives of his near ones. H.M. Williams has a point to make. He observes that "Ravi may go mad for love of a twentieth century film-actress semi-nude before the cameras and lights of Mr. Sampath's studio, but his cure is undertaken not by psychiatrists but by Indian magicians usning the immemorable spells of their ancient craft" (3).

Srinavas is a detached observer of the great universal equilibrium, a *sanyasi*, though not in a literal sense. His *sanyas* or renunciation is not physical but psychological. He has his faith in an overall structure of Indian mythology and historical sense. Although Srinivas is not a fake *sanyasi* like Raju (*The Guide)*, Jagan (*The Vender of Sweets)* or like his old landlord, yet at the same time, he is one of them who believe in keeping in touch with the outer world while finding some solution to the eternal question of existence. Narayan's *sanyasis* never lose touch with the world of reality. Jagan takes to *sanyas* but he does not forget to carry his cheque-book with him. Raju renounces only after a sense of defeat and is always reluctant to move forward in his renunciation. S.R. Ramteke rightly opines that "[...] the heroes of Narayan depend upon chance or luck for their happiness or unhappiness; if things go contrary, they run away and sometimes even become sanyasi" (xvi).

The characters of Narayan's novels may appear rebellious at times but we see them returning and behaving according to the norms of their society. They never continue their revolt. They feel disillusioned and thus abandon their rebellious attitude in order to get their lost social recognition once again. Rosie (in *The Guide*) returns to Marco and Shanti (in *Mr. Sampath*) leaves Sampath after an amorous escape from their social norms, ready to live a life of a typical Indian widow as she is one. In the same way

> Chandran (*The Bachelor of Arts*) renounces the earthly world out of sheer reluctance to its irrational and ridiculous nature of social customs, but finally returns to his family, marries in the same old traditional way and settles down in life. Savitri's high caste (*The Dark*

> *Room*) creates a deeply psychological barrier between herself and Mari and Ponni of the lower caste, who rescue her from drowning. She too in her attempt to assert her individuality leaves her husband, though in the end she has no other alternative left yet to accept defeat in life. She returns home to her unrepentant husband. (Ramtake, xvii)

To return to their original position is equivalent to their *sanyas*. They renounce their individual rebellious attitude in order to return to the collective realm where they have to obey the "universal" norms because they, as Ramtake observes, "cannot stand the collective force of the society as a whole" (xvii).

In conclusion, we can sum up that the renunciation in Narayan is double-sided. Some of his characters renounce the world to mix with the Universal Soul in order to gain their peace of mind, while others renounce their individuality to gain social accreditation. We know that Narayan lived in an age of "metaphoric change" (Biswas, 5). The semi-urban Malgudi evolves with his every new fictional work. A railway station, new shopping malls, printing presses, cinemas, and film studios change Malgudi from a village to a town and finally into a city. Narayan may parody the forms and patterns under the Western influence but his themes remain as firmly associated with the archetypal myths of Indian scriptures as his ever changing Malgudi keeps to be a microcosm of 'Hindu India'.

Works Cited

Biswas, Saravani. *A Study of R.K. Narayan's Novels: A Celebration of the Carnival*. New Delhi: Atlantic, 2010.

Durant, Will. *The Story of Philosophy: The Lives and Opinions of the Greater Philosophers*, New York: Pocket Books, 2006. French, Waren. Preface. *Perspectives on R.K. Narayan*. Ed. Atma Ram. Ghaziabad: Vimal, 1981. xvii-xxxii.

Kalinnikova, E.J. "Indian Myths and Legends in R.K. Narayan's Interpretation." *Perspectives on R.K. Narayan*. Ed. Atma Ram. Ghaziabad: Vimal, 1981. 17-37.

Naik, M.K. *The Ironic Vision*, Delhi: Sterling, 1983.

Naipaul, V.S. "Foreword". *India: A wounded Civilization*. London: Picador, 2001. ix-xii.

———. *A Wounded Civilization*. London: Picador, 1977.

Narayan, R.K. *Mr. Sampath*. Mysore: Indian Thought Publishers, 1971.

Raizada, Harish. *R.K. Narayan: A Criticzal Study of His Works*. New Delhi: Young Asia Publications, 1969.

Ramteke, S.R. "Preface". *R.K. Narayan and His Social Perspective*. New Delhi: Atlantic, 2008. v-vi.

Shrivastava, Ramesh. "What is so Great in R.K. Narayan?" *Perspectives on R.K. Narayan*. Ed. Atma Ram. Ghaziabad: Vimal, 1981. 199-210.

Singh, Krishnakant. *Social Perspectives in R.K. Narayan's Novels* Jaipur: Book Enclave, 2002.

Singh, R.S. *Indian Novel in English*. New Delhi: Arnold Heinemann, 1977.

Williams, H.M. "Precarius Innocence: Patterns in the novels of R.K. Narayan." *Perspectives on R.K. Narayan*. Ed. Atma Ram. Ghaziabad: Vimal, 1981. 1-16.

6

Decentering the Centre: A Post-structuralist Study of R.K. Narayan's *The Dark Room, The English Teacher* and *The Guide*

Kavitha Gopalakrishnan

> One can describe the world of today to the people of today only if one describes it as capable of alteration.
>
> —Bertolt Brecht

R.K. Narayan's novels have been read and analyzed by his readers time and again. But one unique characteristic of his works is that it offers itself to be read in innumerable perspectives. They have something for every reader and critic, and hence disappoint none. Post-structuralist study has opened new avenues for re-reading Narayan's works. Derrida's deconstruction theories make it evident that we can never fully understand or know anything, as the interpretation of words differ from one individual to another. The article in *e-notes* further clarifies this:

> There are no texts which are meant in the same way by readers because readers occupy different subjective positions of articulation. The rhetorical claims of the text are integrated or transformed through the parallel rhetorics of common sense and the everyday against which they are read. Post-structuralism has provided a necessary shift from a critical focus on text alone to the

> dynamics ot culture and consumption reflected in the reader. (n.pag.)

This paper aims at a post-structuralist reading of R.K. Narayan's *The Dark Room, The English Teacher* and *The Guide*. Debunking or decentering the massive structures is the key function of post-structuralist study. The most significant aspect of Derrida's deconstructionist thought surrounds the notion of decentering. In his article "Structure, Sign and Play", included in the text *Writing and Difference* (1978), Derrida observes:

> ...the structurality of structure...has always been neutralized or reduced...by a process of giving it a center or of referring it to a point of presence, a fixed origin. The function of this center was not only to orient, balance, and organize the structure...but above all to make sure that the organizing principle of the structure would limit what we might call the play of the structure. By orienting and organizing the coherence of the system, the center of a structure permits the play of its elements inside the total form. (278)

Derrida views that the concept of centre does work, but it is not essential and hence always changes. Center is needed to form a structure but immediately it escapes from the so-called centrality. Derrida conveys that the idea of center is illusory and constructed. He also brings forth the notion of rupture or decentering, wherein he states that the center is at the center of totality, and yet, since the center does not belong to the totality, the totality has its center elsewhere. He dismisses the binaries of structuralism which are in hierarchical order, in which the first term has privilege over the other. The binaries are not true representations of external reality, rather they are simply constructions. The 'signifieds' are not fixed. When it seeks meaning, it becomes a 'signifier'. So, there is a chain of signifiers. It means that there is no centre, no totality. Derrida further says that center and margins are equally important as one depends on the other; and hence, there is no center and no margin. Thus, the center is no longer the center. Hence, meaning is not determined in the text. The prime objective of deconstruction is not to destroy the meaning of the text, but to show how the text deconstructs itself. The theory brings forth the idea that meaning is infinite. We, hence, need not be satisfied with a meaning; we can go further in search of meaning.

Re-reading the works of R.K. Narayan, in the light of post-stucturalist theories, like deconstruction, lends an added depth and an extra dimension to these works. On reading Narayan's novels in this light, we see how his novels disrupt the structure of family, of society, societal or moral standards and provide an in-depth study of the society or the changing traditions of the society. His works, thus, critique the long standing structures in society and inadvertently make an attempt to shake the foundations of these structures.

The Dark Room displays the puncturing of male patriarchal structure. It recreates a middle-class family structure, showcases its functioning, unravels the power play in it, and displays the moral value structure and the changing nature of it. The opening paragraph of the novel introduces the three major characters—Ramani, Savitri and Babu. But beyond that, it showcases the structure of the typical middle-class Indian family and how this structure really works. When Savitri says Babu has fever, Ramani states: "No, he hasn't. Go and do any work you like in the kitchen, but leave the training of a grown-up boy to me. It is none of a woman's business" (1). The nature of this interaction between Ramani and Savitri sets the tone of the novel. Ramani's dominance and Savitri's subordination is clear. This is ratified again in the succeeding paragraph: "I don't know when I shall have a little decent food to eat. I slave all day in the office for this mouthful. No lack of expanses, money for this and money for that. If the cook can't cook properly, do the work yourself. What have you to do better than that?" (2).

Savitri endures the rage with the conventional submission of an Indian woman. As a result, peace prevails in the house. This seeming order or structure shakes when Shanta Bai is taken as the woman probationer at Engladia Insurance Company. Previously, Ramani had a routine life. He performed everything in a structured manner and the people around him performed accordingly: "At eight-thirty Savitri's ears, as ever, were the first to pick up the hoarse hooting of the Chevrolet horn.... Ramani as a rule sounded his horn at about a furlong from his gate, two long hoots which were meant to tell the house hold, 'Ranga keep the shed door open when I reach there, if you value your life' (9). But with the entry of Shanta Bai, the routine structure, the family structure and even the power structure is shaken: "At two o'clock he went home. He drove the car into the garage with as little noise as possible, opening the gate and the garage door himself" (65).

The matters worsen when Gangu, who happens to see Ramani at the cinema hall with another person (Shanta Bai), shares the information with Savitri. Savitri, as a result of it, is totally shattered, and walks out of her home at midnight and attempts suicide by drowning herself in river Sarayu, only to be rescued by Mari. Walking out of the house at midnight by itself is indicative of debunking the patriarchal structure and the power structure. She herself wonders:

> Am I the same old Savitri or am I someone else? Perhaps this is just a dream. And I must be someone else posing as Savitri because I couldn't have had the courage to talk back to my husband. I have never done it in my life. I couldn't have had the courage to walk through the streets at midnight. I am afraid to go even a hundred yards from the house unescorted; yes, afraid, afraid of every thing. (90-91)

It is only at this critical juncture that she sees through the structure of patriarchal society and her folly in not asserting herself earlier:

> What can I do by myself? Unfit to earn a handful of rice except by begging. If I had gone to college and studied, I might have become a teacher or something. It was very foolish of me not to have gone with my education. Sumati and Kamala must study up to B.A and not depend for their salvation on marriage. What is the difference between a prostitute and a married woman?—the prostitute changes her men, but married woman

> doesn't; that's, but both earn their food and shelter in the same manner. (93)

She stays at Ponni's and Mari's hut for a while, but memories of her home and her children force her to return. She realizes her dependency on her home and family. She returns but cannot truly be her old self. When Ramani cracks a joke in order to bring in a semblance of normality, she attempts to laugh but fails. She reflects thus: "A part of me is dead" (160).

Savitri's return to home confirms the cyclic reversal of situation. Narayan takes dig at most middle-class families, where the husband and wife put on a facade and stay together because of their kids and for convenience. The women in these families may show streaks of individuality and may sometimes voice against male domination, but do not assert as they cannot exist outside the family structure. Nevertheless, Narayan makes an attempt to decentre the centrality of male domination and puncture the structure of patriarchy. He has given woman sensibility due respect with the detailed portrayal of Savitri.

The English Teacher, one of Narayan's best novels, can also be seen as the exemplum of post-stuctural study. The novel delineates the ramification of Western culture that revolutionizes the entire outlook of Indian intellectuals. The new age Indian educational system, modeled on the Western ideology, is questioned and debunked. In the novel, Krishnan, an English teacher at the Albert Mission College, represents one who is deeply influenced by the Western culture in India. He is representative of all educated Indians who have lost ties with the country and its tradition. Kapil Kapoor, in a National Seminar, says thus:

> I am reminded of Ananda Coomaraswamy who uses the expression "educated Indians" and then gives a footnote—"That is how victims of Indian education are described". One of the effects of mainstream education is to marginalize inherited learning which though much restricted is very much alive.... The main stream education has certainly had one very clear effect and that

> is—it has uprooted us in the sense that there is complete disjunction with our tradition of thinking. (n. pag.)

Narayan too debunks the existing educational system which produces Indians with English spirit and English habits. He also questions the so called 'rational/analytical' perception. He also delineates the 'physicial and metapsysicial'. Krishna's conversation with his dead wife cannot be digested by rational brain. Such metaphysical experiences shake the foundations of world reasoned out by Man. In *The English Teacher*, Narayan decenters reason and rational thinking of man which does not accept anything that cannot be proved or substantiated.

In *The Guide*, Raju and Rosie decenter the moral value system and build a new one based on utilitarianism. In doing so, they debunk the structure of society and societal norms. Rosie, encouraged by Raju, decides to follow her dreams and walks out of her marital life with Marco. They start living together and Raju's mother leaves them as she does not like their relationship. Eventually, Raju becomes Rosie's stage manager and moulds her career in an impressive manner. He, however, gets involved in a case of forgery and gets a two year sentence. Rosie still has the photograph of Marco which is indicative of the fact that however far an Indian woman moves away from the structure, the centre always exerts a gravitational pull on their lives.

When we analyze the three novels, we realize that change happens, not as a result of any grand plan, but as a result of a person's reaction to a series of challenging situations, which arise once we begin to break the structure and move away from the centre. Savitri realizes herself when she moves away from her safe structure of family; change in Krishna happens when he begins to take steps away from the protective environment of the school; and Raju comes in terms with himself when he moves away from the materialistic, worldly world. In all the three novels, a disrupting factor jolts them into reality. It is only when they are threatened of being sidelined by this factor, do they realize that the centre, to which they had clung all their life, is not really worth and that the things, they had sidelined, are actually worth taking the centre stage. Savitri realizes that her own self is as important as her husband's; Krishnan realizes that selflessness is what gives ultimate happiness; Shanta Bai is the catalyst in deconstructing the safe structure of marriage and family; Susila and the Headmaster disrupt this safe cocoon of predictable life Krishnan was leading; and Raju's meeting with Rosie and the subsequent term in jail pulls Raju out of the materialistic structure he was tangled in. Narayan seems to be pondering over the question—whether a structure rears or sears individuality? The three novels implicitly suggest that structures are cloistered and one must break away from it to assert individuality. Savitri walks out from her home and realizes that her individuality lies in the house, Krishnan leaves the college to come to terms with his true self and origins and Raju leaves the worldly life and materialistic pursuits to attain at least a moment of spiritual bliss.

In these novels, objects attain prominence as they occupy an important place in the lives of respective owners. The bench in *The Dark Room* and its missing are very prominent. It had an important place in Savitri's life—it occupied a centre stage. This is decentered when the bench is taken to the office by Ramani for furnishing Shanta Bai's room. This is symbolic of the fact how Savitri, who occupied the centre, is now sidelined and of the fact that Ramani is being more and more estranged from the house. In *The English Teacher*, the clock had an important place in Krishnan's life. When Susila, his wife, sells off the old clock, he takes time to come into terms with the fact. Susila is the person who acts as an impetus to break from his cloistered structure of Western Education and brings charm and unpredictability to his life. The selling of the clock astounds him and it hints of the events to come—Susila's death despite assurance from the doctor and Headmaster living in spite of the prediction of the astrologer. The decentering of the clock is symbolic of the fact that things happen unaware and one must accept what ever life offers in its course.

The conventional family structure is also demolished in all the three novels. The notions of bonds, attachments and relations are redrawn. In *The Dark Room*, the husband-wife relation is on a boss-subordinate level and the children are literally scared of their father. In *The English Teacher*, Krishnan-Susila relation is simply inexplicable. Susila guides Krishnan even after she leaves the material world. In *The Guide*, Marco-Rosie relationship breaks as Rosie builds and maintains relationship with Raju.

A final post-structuralist reading of these books highlights the fact that "culture", as a system, is also debunked. The cross cultural influences that go deep into the psyche of its characters also lend to a new dimension of study. In *The English Teacher*, we see that Narayan depicts his protagonist attaining spiritual harmony by communicating with his wife (part of Indian beliefs) which contradicts his Western values. In the death of Susila and the life of the headmaster, Narayan critiques the modern Western science and ancient Indian mysticism. In *The Dark Room,* the Engladia Insurance Company and Shanta Bai can be seen as Western influences, Ponni and Mari can be seen as standing for rustic Indians. In *The Guide*, the coming of railways, the commercialization and materialistic pursuits can be attributed to the East-West cultural encounter. The cross-cultural influences break the existing cultural structure that the characters had based themselves on. These influences thus force them to set new "centers" to cling on to.

Thus, we may say that Narayan questions the established structures and tries to subvert or even demolish some of them. It is on account of these factors that Narayan's stories fascinate even the readers of our age. He thus succeeds in describing today's world, as Brecht says, in an interesting manner; as he describes it as capable of alteration.

Works Cited

"Decentering the text". *e Notes*. 14 July 2011. n.pag.Web.

Derrida, Jacques. "Stucture, Sign and Play in the Discourse of the Human Science."

Kapoor, Kapil. "Decolonizing the Indian Mind." Patan: Dept. of English, North Gujarat University, 2001. n. pag. Web. 8 Feb. 2011.

Narayan, R.K. *The Dark Room*. Chennai: Indian Thought, 1956.

———. *The English Teacher*. Chennai: Indian Thought, 1955.

———. *The Guide*. Mysore: Indian Thought, 1958.

Writing and Difference. Trans. Alan Bass. London: Routledge, 1978. pp. 278-294.

7

Quest for Self in the Novels of R.K. Narayan

Bina Biswas

My main concern is with human character—a central human character from whose point of view the world is seen, and who tries to get over a difficult situation or succumbs to it or fights it in his own setting (RK Narayan to William Walsh in a *B.B.C interview* in 1968).

In fact, the handling of an individual character, in the context of his/her growth and maturity, forms the core of Narayan's awareness as an author. In the 1940s, when R.K. Narayan undertook the editorship of the quarterly journal *Indian Thought*, he had the following literary ambition in his mind, as he reminisces in his autobiography: "I packed into the manifesto all my ambition: to phrase our culture properly; to utilize the English language as a medium for presenting our cultural heritage—Indian classics and philosophy from Sanskrit and a score of other regional languages...and to encourage original English writing of the highest quality" (*My Days*, 153).

It is noteworthy that protagonists in Narayan's fiction and his short stories, in an explicit/implied way, show an urge to live their culture and remain alive to this. This fulfils their creator's editorial ambition too. Incidentally, Narayan's works turn out to be unique culture-texts where the hunt for identity, by principal characters, projects a journey through certain types of experiences characterized by a conflict and tension between the iron grip of tradition and the collision of modernity. The critical focus of this paper is specifically on major novels of R.K. Narayan where the quest for identity by the characters emerges to be the most important and crucial in their cultural awakening of the 'self'.

The expression 'own setting' (quoted above) refers to the Indian context, a cultural self symbolised by Malgudi, which not only reflects the huge, ageless gamut of Indian life and its traditional values, but also reserves the potential for regeneration and growth. The idea of discovery of 'roots' in Narayan's works is in turn set in Narayan's 'weltanschauung' and this can be explained by N. Ram in the article "Malgudi's Creator": "The idea of being rooted in a society and civilization—in one's own culture, traditions, values, changing local milieu, modernity and family—is important to Narayan's development as a writer and also to his assessment of other writers".

Narayan's 'hoi polloi', who crowd Malgudi, embody the indigenous and pristine cultures in India and her 'vox populi'. Perhaps every chief character in his fiction and some in his short-stories are engaged in a quest for native roots and uniqueness, and in this voyage, he/she discovers a distinct space in the social milieu of Malgudi which reminds one of the Bakhtinian 'chronotope'.[1] Though 'identity' dovetails into many connotations in postcolonial literary criticism, in R.K. Narayan's fiction, it refers to a bona fide space of a cultural re-settlement and rehabilitation of the 'self' through one's primordial rootages of native culture and its ethics. Almost every central character in Narayan's novels seeks to lodge him/her and tries to parley the problematics of roots and identity in terms of his/her own subject position. It necessitates a process of critical choice leading to an ideological evolution and development. The present paper establishes, though synoptically, the role of 'roots' or ethics in four major novels of R.K. Narayan and some of his short stories from *Malgudi Days* (1982).

In *The Bachelor of Arts* (1937), protagonist Chandran's trials and tribulations can be problematised in the background of an adolescent's quest for identity in the world of adults. His sudden repudiation, an outgrowth of his obsession for an individual self-hood in protest against the totalitarianism of the adult world (symbolised by his parents for not allowing him to marry a girl of his own choice), is but an act of deviation from the existing patterns of behaviour which assumes return of a straying personality to the familial/societal folds and confines, sooner or later. Only after recognizing the worth and meaning of 'family' and the re-location of 'self' in society, he aspires for a life of freedom 'from distracting illusions and hysterics'. He proceeds towards his goal by re-adjusting himself to a life that commingles familial sensibility as well as social affiliations. This novel conforms to Narayan's treatment of 'family' as an institution of Indian society. 'Family', in Narayan's fiction, externalises the unitary form of life that establishes the pattern of life in the community and the society. The layout of relationships among the members of the family, the set of rules for behaviour that have been sanctioned by tradition, the anxiety and tension of living in the joint-family supply the individual with the immediate space where his/her susceptibility operates. In the following extract from Narayan's essay, "English in India: A Process of Transmutation", one can easily spot the writer's urge for social re-orientation, an indigenisation of the form and content of the English novel:

> The eternal triangle, such a stand-by for a Western writer, is worthless as a theme for an Indian, our social circumstances not providing adequate facilities for the eternal triangle. We, however, seek excitement in our system of living known as the 'Joint Family'. The strains and stresses of this kind of living on the individual, the general structure of a society emerging from it, and the complexities of the Caste system, are inexhaustible subjects for us. (21-22)

In this context, Meenakshi Mukherjee talks about the role of [joint] family in Indian English Fiction. Taking a cue from Narayan's disapproval of the 'eternal triangle' as a theme, Mukherjee, in her book *The Twice Born Fiction* (2001), writes: "The joint family is a formidable force even when the love interest is absent [...]. It represents the voice of authority and tradition and serves as a microcosm of a hierarchical society which the individual has to rebel against in order to attain his personal identity."

In the whole fictional world of R.K. Narayan, 'family' is treated as a space, an infinite that doles out individuals with explicit roles with 'complexities, demands and muddle of kinship' and at the same time, locates them in a larger gamut of time and place. The 'family' emerges as units with cultural and sociological sameness; the characters are moulded into an intricate awareness of values and norms that validates an allegiance to traditional 'ways of life'. It, at the same time, reserves the potentiality for negotiating and accommodating the influences of change/modernity too. This sort of cultural flexibility in the role of 'family' is evident in the growth of one of Narayan's protagonists like Chandran in the novel *The Bachelor of Arts*. This novel is also important in reflecting the 'horoscope motif', another conventional practice deep-rooted in the Indian psyche even today. The heated exchange between Chandran and his mother, regarding the former's individualistic attitude toward marriage and a unyielding, stand of a purist in the other:

> Chandran: 'I shall marry this girl and no one else'.
>
> Mother: 'But how are you sure they are prepared to give their daughter to you?
>
> In reply Chandran says: 'They will have to'.
>
> Mother: 'Extraordinary! Do you think marriage is a child's game?' (193-94)

The mother's declaration stresses the traditional approach to marriage as a thoroughly 'negotiable and socially, and also religiously, approved family-contract'. Customarily, marriage is seen as a part of a providential design that has to be reckoned with along with the 'horoscope matching' before a social marriage is finalized. The author has pledged to this time-tested practice of securing astrological reassurance by tradition-ridden families before the agreement of a social 'arranged' marriage:

> In an English novel, for instance, the theme of romance is based on a totally different conception of man-woman relationship from ours [...]. We believe that marriages are made in heaven and a bride and groom meet, not by accident or design, but by the decree of fate, the fitness for a match not to be gauged by letting them go through a period of courtship but by a study of their horoscopes; boy and girl meet and love develops after marriage rather than before.

In another major pre-independence novel of Narayan, *The English Teacher* (1945), Krishnan's disappointment proceeds from the academic iconoclasm of the West in the colonised education. Krishnan's bitterness against the cultural imperialism of the British educationists is manifest in the following lines towards the end of the novel:

> I was going to explain why I could no longer stuff Shakespeare and Elizabethan metre and Romantic poetry for the hundredth time into the young minds and feed them on the dead mutton of literary analysis and theories and histories, while what they needed was lessons in the fullest use of the mind.

The expression 'education in the fullest use of the mind' talks of one of the "basic concepts of traditional Indian thoughts and philosophy that all cognitive disciplines, including education, must be basically directed to the development of the mind". English Education in pre-Independence India only treats in the requisition of a cultural obsequiousness by the natives: "This education has reduced us to a nation of morons; we were strangers to our own culture and camp followers of another culture, feeding on leavings and garbage".

As a young student, at a missionary school in Chennai, R.K. Narayan's first encounter with the English language is a story of bewilderment. "Born in 1906, Narayan was five years old at the time, part of a middle-class Brahmin family of second-generation immigrants from rural South India. The family was new to the city, and still close to ancestral ways at home. An almost religious solemnity had attended Narayan's formal introduction to Tamil and Sanskrit, when, presented with a tray of corn, he was asked to shape the first two letters of the alphabet in both languages." But Tamil and Sanskrit carried badges of inferiority and occasions for jokes at school, along with everything else that belonged to the old Hindu world broken into by British colonialism. Narayan, the only Brahmin boy in the class, faced mockery by the Christian teachers. "The 'first' language at school was English, taught from a textbook that was imported all the way from England and looked much more sturdy and glossy than the textbooks produced in India. Its glamour also came from the mysteries it contained." The child's license to daydream made Narayan naturally attracted to the world of freedom, to the freelance writer's life. He too had to struggle to establish himself as a writer and convince his family and publishers too.

To Krishnan, his daughter's school appears as an archetype of a created universe of wholesome, pure joy based on the conventional system of education where the construction of environment makes learning an automatic activity instead of a pedagogic routine. Dazzling alphabets on screens between "classrooms, models and paintings of men, trees, animals, skies, rivers with every conceivable playthings made by the headmaster, such as, the see-saws, swings, sand-heaps and ladders—all stand for the primeval simplicity, a phantasmagoria of such spontaneity and vitality that encourage life". Krishnan's self-pity ('I was doing the wrong work') at the beginning of the narrative, directs him to a seek for a free identity (an essentially Western phenomenon) and "he finally finds his moorings through a peculiar change in circumstances involving the death of his wife and his psychic communication with her in telepathic messages under the auspices of a spirit-medium". This change in him, aided by the idea of the weird and idealist Headmaster of his daughter's school, shows Krishnan a revelation of the ideal system of education. It re-shapes his identity by making him recognise the existing aspects of his own tradition and culture that can stand firm against the cultural invasion of the West. Krishnan's resignation from his college and his decision to teach in an indigenous school indicate and establish a cultural conversion of heart. Krishnan is finally able to re-locate himself in terms of the indigenous culture and principles of education that helps him to rediscover the abiding 'Law of life'. While offering a plea for conventional, value-based education, the novel also upholds another philosophical aspect bordering on occultism, of Hindu culture—the practice of communicating with the dead or that of automatic writing by a spirit-medium.

In his autobiography *My Days* (1999), R.K. Narayan has categorically told that the circumstances in which Krishnan's wife died and the consequent psychic communion between the husband and the spirit of his dead wife correspond to the writer's real life experiences. In the context of Indian philosophy and mysticism, the transmigration of human souls through generations, the supreme pre-occupation of spiritualism concentrating on the elimination of self which restricts one's view of personality, it is relevant to quote Narayan's realisation in *My Days*:

> The full view of a personality would extend from the infant curled up in the womb and before it, and beyond it, and ahead of it, into infinity. Our normal view is limited to a physical perception in a condition restricted in time, like the flashing of a torchlight on a spot, the rest of the area being in darkness. If one could have a total view of oneself and others, one could see all in their full stature, through all the stages of evolution and growth, ranging form childhood to old age, in this life, the next one, and the previous ones [...]. Somehow, for the working out of some destiny, birth in the physical world seems to be important; all sexual impulses and the apparatus of sexual functions seem relevant only as a means to an end—all the dynamism, power, and the beauty of sex, have a meaning only in relation to its purpose.

When the entire fictional opus of Narayan is taken into account, one notices that the pursuit of exploration in the characters is not only restricted to a strict social concept of roots and identity but a quest of universalism.

Recent literary studies on Narayan establish certain disturbing spaces of socio-familial problematics in some of Narayan's post-independence novels. It is noticed that the search in the character[s] here offers a 'sub-text' for a parallel quest for beingness and transcendental truth. This transmutable twist in the search involves a prominent postcolonial strategy to evolve a flexible identity-formation or to subvert, between imperial systems and native subversion. An astonishing satire on imagining nations, maps, and Europe figures in R.K. Narayan's *Swami and Friends*, Swami is trying to draw a map of Europe. Several issues and questions crop up in the boy's mind: "It puzzled him how people managed to live in such a crooked country as Europe...How did the map-makers find out what the shape of a country was? How did they find out that Europe was like a camel's head?"

Most of the Third World countries emerged from under the colonial rule after a prolonged anti-colonial struggle. After the independence, there was a homecoming, bonhomie in Africa and Asia. The literature of the 1950s and 1960s marked the celebration of freedom through nationalism and the euphoria of decolonization. The most preferred mode was 'realism' (Ben Okri's Magic Realism). Brenda Cooper defines magic realism as striving to 'capture the paradox of the unity of the opposites', contesting polarities such as history and magic, the pre-colonial and the pre-industrial present, life and death. We find biculturalism, nationalism, humanism and the postcolonial identity of the new born nations in the writings of Chinua Achebe, Wole Soyinka, and these were the earliest themes of Raja Rao, R.K. Narayan, George Lamming, Patrick White, Derek Walcott and others. The discovery of the self, assertion of cultural identity, respecting one's own cultural roots, rituals, icons and belief systems became visible in the postcolonial literature. Numerous authors explored the post-colonial nations' disenchantment and disillusion.

Postcolonialism matters a lot in the academic echelons of India today as a phenomenal discourse that is closely connected to the nation building process, although trying to think of the major Indian voices, who have added substantially to this discourse, one is left primarily only with four or five names, those of Mahatma Gandhi, Gayathri Chakraborti Spivak, Homi K. Bhabha, Harish Trivedi, Ranajit Guha and more recently, the more popular Ramachandra Guha in the realm of history. Edward Said's *Orientalism*, the book *The Empire Writes Back* and further work done by Bell Hooks as well as the formidable Fanon seem to sum up the giant contributions of postcolonialism as a loosely held together counter or alternative discourse to the power of the USA, Europe and the "developed" world that shows itself even now in policies that sweep across cultural, economic, national, ethnic, class, racial, gender, and sociological or political divides. It would be wrong to assume that resistance and anti-colonial encounter—Narayan and Anand in India—had explored in considerable depth the ill-effects of colonial rule, racism, and exploitation even before political independence from their colonial masters. In Narayan's ever-popular *Swami and Friends*, the scripture teacher, Ebenezar, described by Narayan as a 'fanatic', rejects Hinduism and rants and raves against Hindu idolatry: 'Oh, wretched idiots!' the teacher said,... "Why do you worship, dirty, wooden idols and stone images? ...What did your Gods do when Mohammed of Gazni smashed them to pieces?" Narayan, here, shows how colonial rule and English education rejected native belief systems as a preliminary moment to install Christianity as the only true faith.

The sense of search in the principal characters of Narayan's two post-Independence novels *The Guide* and *The Vendor of Sweets*, concludes in a different sphere of reality, a space which conforms neither to an unqualified form of tradition nor to the codes of a mechanised society, but to a process of an evolving possibility, a plane of transcendence from the designated subject-position. This transcendence finally provides an authentic realisation of the truth of existence that is exclusively Indian. In *The Guide* (1958), Railway Raju's guiding skill, his adoption of the role of an impressario with 'a water-diviner's instinct' to promote the dancing talent in Rosie, his progress towards the position of a con-man in the postcolonial Indian society, is a typical phenomenon of the West that, in his case, leads to self-deception insofar as Raju consciously dissociates himself from his native cultural roots in his consequent moral degradation brought about by his penchant for appearance rather than reality. On the other hand, Raju's mother represents traditional values. She sings hymns to God in her evening prayer, lights a lamp in the God's niche with the faith that, as S. Girija has pointed out, the Gyan-Jyoti will remove ignorance and enlighten the mind. She "believes that if there was one goodman it would rain for his sake and all the world would bennefit..." (Girija, 29). Though the novel traces Raju's steady progress into self-delusion upto a considerable extent, in the last part of the novel, one finds the conviction of Raju's mother coming true as there is a teleological progression in the character of Raju in terms of the values of his spiritual tradition. Raju's end unmistakably substantiates a denial of self "for the first time he was doing a thing in which he was not personally interested" (237-38) with an urge to merge with an ultimate spiritual reality. In Raju's end, we find a new beginning, the emergence of a transcendent reality characteristic of Indian culture where the illusion merges with reality, the vesture becomes the essence, thereby justifying the Indian spiritual goal of *Advaitya* or non-duality in existence. The theme of transcendence in Raju's role of a saint, no doubt, evokes an impression of a spiritual, mystic phenomenon, but from the sociological point of view, this element is also a major part of that part of Indian culture which continues to exist, according to Ramesh Sree, in the "collective unconscious mind of the Indian psyche" (211). Again, observance of fasting as a ritual for invocation of rain is not a rarity in Indian tradition and interestingly enough, Narayan, in his autobiography *My Days*, mentions a similar fast that was intended successfully to bring rain to a drought-stricken place and he admits that this experience acted as the starting point of his novel *The Guide*:

> A recent situation in Mysore offered the setting for such a story. A severe drought had dried up all the rivers and tanks; [...] as a desperate measure, the municipal council

> organized a prayer for rains. A group of Brahmins stood knee-deep in water (procured at great cost) on the dry bed of Kaveri, fasted, prayed, and chanted certain mantras continuously for eleven days. On the twelfth day, it rained and brought enormous relief to the countryside.

In *The Vendor of Sweets*, Jagan's experiences show an arduous progress of realisation through the mazes of cultural conflict between tradition and modernity. Jagan's Gandhism serves to posit his character within the stronghold of tradition/ideology whereas Mali, his son, is an instance of extreme individualism which is a pronounced Western trait. Mali's ways of life have only a shattering effect on Jagan who, notwithstanding his lack of critical and intellectual self-awareness of the Gandhian ideology, has lived so long with an unswerving commitment to tradition. The Mali-Grace episode, with their practice of living-together, seems to be a sacrilegious intrusion into Jagan's household (that entails a 'sanctity of usage' over generations) and his personal life that has been a happy continuity with the past. Jagan's retirement to Nallappa's grove, which Afzal Khan thinks to be symbolic of India's mythical and mystical retreat, parallels India's tradition of the *Vanaprastha* stage of *Ashramadharma* that recommends withdrawal from worldly/familial obligations as preparatory to *Sannyas* at an advanced stage of life. The quest for 'truth', that has so long remained unrealised to a superficial Gandhian like Jagan, now seems to appear in its real form to the awakened soul, the rejuvenated *sattva* of Jagan who has now found out an ideal space to authenticate his existence. Apart from the abiding theme of India's traditional *Barnashrama* system, the novel also highlights a few other minor aspects of Indian tradition, viz. *Namavishekam* (a ceremony in which a new born baby is given a name through some religious rites) and the *Tonsure pratha* or the sacrifice of hair (symbolic of one's ego) to God for the fruition of an honest desire. It is a practice still in vogue in holy places like Prayag in Allahabad and Tirupati temple. Another aspect of Indian tradition treated in the novel is the offering of *manat* or holy promise to God so that barren women like Jagan's wife, Ambika, can be blessed with children. One more traditional value in the novel is that of reading scriptures as a means of self-purification. Initially, the readers find that while Jagan apparently reads the sacred lines of *The Gita*, his mind is alert to the noise of sizzling and frying in the kitchen of his shop or to the blue airmail letters from Mali in America. But constant tuition, coupled with real-life experiences; bring the belated synthesis of the teachings of *The Gita* in his life leading, to an acquisition of the *Sthitapragya* state of existence which displays a stoical attitude to pain and pleasure.

In the over all analysis, the predicaments of Raju and Jagan ideologically present an initiative on the part of the characters to authenticate a space for belonging, the 'truth' in one's identity in 'one's own setting', through the roots of India's spiritual tradition and culture. Such an identity testifies to the 'inner strength' of Indian life, as Narayan has explained in his essay "India and America": "It is through subtle, inexplicable influences, through religion, family ties and human relationships in general let us call them—psychological 'inputs', to use a modern term—which cumulatively sustain and lend variety and richness to existence".

The limitations in Narayan's characters are the limitations of the still-raw and shapeless society in which they have their being—limitations that are not overcome, but merely avoided, by leaps into fantasy and myth that such ready-made forms as magic realism facilitate. Narayan, as the first writer of his kind, was always far from attaining an intellectual overview of his circumstances. Early realist writers, like him, usually stay within, and share the prejudices of, the particular historical moment they find themselves in; sometimes offering, as Narayan does in his later novels, quasi-religious explanations of chaotic nature of their world.

The protagonists' hunt for a genuine self, instead of being an ill exercise of nativism on Narayan's part, subscribes to the mode of postcolonial reverse-narrative in which, the writer celebrates *ad via negative*, the inner reserves of Indian life, the manumission aspect of Indian culture. Noemia De Sousa, in her 'If You Want to Know Me', describes herself thus: "This is what I am empty sockets despairing of possessing of life...."

Note

1. Krishna Sen cites Bakhtin's definitions of 'chronotope' in her study of Malgudi as a chronotope on the basis of a living intersection of regional and universal/human traits: "...Malgudi is more than a physical location—it also has a mythic dimension, which enables Narayan to invest his realistic stories with moral and metaphysical significance" (*Critical Essays on R.K. Narayan's The Guide*).

Works Cited

Afzal-Khan, Fawzia. "R.K. Narayan: A Realm of Mythic Realism". *Cultural Imperialism and the Indo-English Novel.* Pennsylvania: The Pennsylvania State University Press, 1993. 27-57.

Boehmer, Elleke. *Colonial and Postcolonial Literature*. New York: OUP, 1995.

Girija, S. "Indian Customs and Conventions Depicted in the Writings of R.K. Narayan". *Studies in Indian Writings in English*. Ed. Mittapalli, Rajeswar and P.P. Piciucco. Vol. 1. New Delhi: Atlantic, 2000, 26-33.

"India and America". *A Writer's Nightmare Selected Essays 1958-1988*. New Delhi: Penguin, 1988, 233-40.

Karnani, C.K. "R.K. Narayan: The Novelist without Depth". *Glimpses of Indo-English Fiction*. Ed. O.P. Saxena. Vol. 2. New Delhi: Jainsons, 1985.

Mukherjee, Meenakshi. *The Twice Born Fiction: Themes and Techniques of the Indian Novel in English*. Delhi: Pencraft, 2001.

Naik, M.K. *The Ironic Vision: A Study of the Fiction of R.K. Narayan*. New Delhi: Sterling Publishers, 1983.

Narayan, R.K. "English in India: The Process of Transmutation". *Aspects of Indian Writing in English*. Ed. M.K. Naik. New Delhi: Macmillan, 1999, 19-23.

Narayan, R.K. *Malgudi Days*. Mysore: Indian Thoughts Publications, 1999.

Nayar, Pramod K. *Postcolonial Literature: An Introduction*. Pearson, 2011.

8

R.K. Narayan's *The Bachelor of Arts*: Regional Ambience, Universal Appeal

C.L. Khatri

If, historically, Bankim Chandra is regarded as the father of India English novel, practically, R.K. Narayan can be called its pioneer in the sense that he is the first novelist who ushered in a new age and created a long chain of followers. In this way, he gave rise to a tradition of Indian English novel. Special about Narayan is that he is an indigenous novelist, a product of 'Malgudi' who lived by writing fiction, a rare feat to achieve in those days. His world is limited as the world of Jane Austen, but he lived in it and lived its life. That's why he could portray the locale naturally and authentically with ease and grace and could create characters, who became an archetype through a succession of novels. Schoolboy, Swami in his first novel, *Swami and Friends*, becomes the college guy, a graduate in *The Bachelor of Arts* and the graduate evolves into a teacher in *The English Teacher*. It is not only the character that grows up, matures and assumes new roles, but also the place 'Malgudi' that grows and develops with the passage of time so much so that C.D. Narasimhaiah views 'Malgudi' as a character.

R.K. Narayan is intensely regional like Thomas Hardy and Phanishwarnath Renu, and it is being intensely regional in ambience that he makes a universal case in theme, character and effect. Hardy's description of his major fictions as 'novels of character and environment' equally applies to the novels of

R.K. Narayan. A regional novel deals with the physical features of the region, people, locality, life, customs, habits, traditions, superstitions, etc. The novelist brings to light uncommon features of the common people of the region. It may be a geographical place or a mental place, but it is created and peopled in such a way as to represent any other place. So, it becomes a microcosm of the country and of the world at large. 'London' of Eliot's *The Waste Land* can be New York, Paris, Tokyo, Berlin or Bombay. Likewise, Malgudi need not be identified with a particular geographical location. It would be an act of limiting its implications. It is a small town of south India; it has a railway station, a college, a cinema hall and other amenities available in a small town. And like most of the Indian towns, it is situated on the bank of river Sarayu. At an immediate level, it represents south Indian semi-urban life, people and culture. He has deliberately created a town for the locale of his all novels, partly because a semi-urban locale has the qualities of both, urban and rural India, and partly because R.K. Narayan does not belong to the rural culture. He is essentially a writer of semi-urban sensibilities. He was born and brought up in Madras and then shifted to Mysore. C.D. Narasimhaiah comments: "Himself a product of the Hindu middle class, sharing the beliefs, superstitions and perhaps the prejudices of his class in a small town and viewing its going on with sympathy but also with a keen eye for the comic in the life around him, he had qualified himself to be a writer of his own class and the provincial town. Actually the odd men or rather, the oddities in men, in the ordinary men, seemed to evoke his interest most but they are invariably common men with a marked potential for the uncommon, trying to win attention to themselves: how do such men struggle towards maturity, such maturity as they can achieve within the accepted religious and social framework?" (103). So, naturally, he created in his novels and short stories, the life he lived and saw intimately. Iyengar rightly says: "Malgudi is Narayan's Casterbridge but the inhabitants of Malgudi, although they may have their recognizable local traits, are essentially human and hence have their kinship with all humanity. In this sense, Malgudi is everywhere" (360).

Malgudi forms the setting of all the novels of Narayan. It is a symbol of India. It is the 'Wessex' of Hardy; it is the 'West Champaran' of Phanishwarnath Renu. He gives a vivid and realistic picture of 'Malgudi' with its past, present and a growing Malgudi so much so that it becomes a part of the living tradition and not mere an island of his imagination. What happens in Malgudi, happens all over India. But there is a difference between Hardy's 'Wessex', Renu's 'West Champaran' and Narayan's 'Malgudi'. Hardy, in fact, resurrected the old name of the locality, 'Wessex', or land of the West Saxons which comprises Dorset, Wiltshire, Hampshire, parts of Berkshire and Somerset; Renu's *Maila Anchal* is an attributive denominator of a place in Bihar that is 'West Champaran'; but 'Malgudi' is not an actual geographical place in the map—it is a 'country of the mind' created as a sample of the middle-class life in a semi-urban India. Even after a gap of around seventy years, his *The Bachelor of Arts* is read with a homely feeling. It touches the chord of our hearts and takes us back to our own past as a student in the college and a sort of empathy is created with the struggle of Chandran, the protagonist of the novel, for maturity, survival and for psychological and economic independence.

It is an interesting point to remember that R.K. Narayan's India, opposed to Raja Rao's metaphysical India, is folk India —social and traditional India, living with its own age old system, almost detached from the socio-political India of Mulk Raj Anand. Perhaps this is the reason why Graham Greene finds in his novels 'a second home' (introduction to *The Bachelor of Arts*). Shiv K. Kumar rightly opines:

> Graham Greene, in his introduction to Narayan's first novel *The Bachelor of Arts* expresses the eagerness of Western readers to read about Real India (with a capital R) and not the India which has been a mere literary region of mystery, of strange spiritual quests, of superstitions, of jungle adventures—a Kim here or Fielding there, an anglicized Sri Ganesh in Maugham's novel, *The Razor's Edge*, or John Masters' latest literary effusion *Bhawani Junction*. Such fiction only evokes in

> the minds of Western readers vague scene of "an historical woman in a cave, adultery at Simla, greased cartridges, heroic Gurkhas advancing to the drums of the Fore and Aft, mutinies on barrack squares.... But Indian writers have now done a great deal in lifting the veil off this mysterious India. (116)

So, it was the regional ambience, quite new to the English readers of Indian novels, that created a global interest at that time. And it will ever remain relevant even if all towns are turned into cities and those days are gone forever. We will have to turn to the fictional world of R.K. Narayan if ever we wish to look back to our past, feel the life and live for a moment in that Indian ambience.

Regional ambience is not so much revealed in terms of topography and the description of nature, as we find to a greater extent in Hardy's description of Wessex or in Renu's *Maila Anchal*. Regional ambience in Narayan's is more in terms of customs, manners, traits of human behaviour and inter-personal relationship in a rather homogenous society where people are familiar with one another. Through this web of life, the regional ambience unfolds itself and is transmuted into Indian ambience with tints of popular culture. The novel begins in a direct manner:

> CHANDRAN was just climbing the steps of the College Union when Natesan, the secretary, sprang on him and said, "You are just the person I was looking for. You remember your old promise?"
>
> "No," said Chandran promptly, to be on the safe side. "You promised that I could count on you for a debate. (1)

It is clear that topographical details are not prominent. They are there as much as they are required to give the effect of a place. But in the centre of his concern is the character, the individual, and all the actions revolve round the hero, whose attributes determine the action and the story moves through a set of events. Even the novelist has said in an interview: "My main concern...is with human character—a central character from whose point of view the world is seen and who tries to get over a difficult situation or succumbs to it or fights it in his own setting" (qtd. in Lakshmi Holmstorm, 124).

Chandran, though unwillingly, accepts the offer to be the prime mover of the debate on the subject—"Historians should be slaughtered first"—he speaks eloquently despite being a student of History and emerges victorious. This episode throws light on some 'archetypal failings' of Chandran. So through Chandran, Narayan tells us about the failings, incongruities, hopes and aspirations of the youth who are standing at the crossroad. He is a good orator but he is chosen for the wrong subject. In the debate, he seems the right man in the wrong box. The success only adds to his self-deception and ego. We see, for example, how he feels bored once he finishes off his speech: "Now that he had delivered his speech he felt that the speeches of the others in the hall were both unnecessary and inferior" (5). We feel that we, too, suffer form this cold indifference to others and self-centeredness in our everyday life. It is further reflected in Chandran when he desperately seeks complement form the secretary: "...how did you like my speech today?" (8). The secretary lavishly praises him. Now a few words of flattery calm the agitated soul down and make him change his opinion about the Principal, Prof. Brown. In the beginning, he frowns at Natesan, the secretary, when he calls his speech humorous. He even calls him a scoundrel. But a few words of flattery change his tune: "Another thing," said Chandran, "Don't for a moment think that I dislike Brown. I agree with you entirely when you say he is a man with a pleasant manner. He has a first-rate sense of humour. He is a great scholar. It is really a treat to be taught Drama by him. I was only trying to suggest that people saw humour even where he was serious. So please don't mistake me" (9).

Self-confidence turns into complacency and adds fuel to the spirit of independence and lofty idea about himself. In this juvenile zeal, he cuts his parents and teachers to size. When he returns to his house late, a habitual impulse of diffidence comes to his mind; but he shakes it off with the consciousness of his matured age: "He realized that what he usually did was a piece of evasive cowardice worthy of an adolescent. He was not eighteen but twenty-one. At twenty-one to be afraid of one's parents and adopt sneaky ways! He would be a graduate very soon and he was already a remarkable orator!" (11). He deliberately makes a noisy entry rather than sneaking into the house. And then, he goes to the Cinema Hall with his friend, Ramu. He frankly informs his father of his plan to go to cinema: "Father, Ramu will be here in a moment, please ask him to wait...we are going to cinema to night..." (12). In a traditional Indian family, a son is expected to seek permission form his father for going anywhere. Similarly, he thinks about Prof. Raghavachar: "As he came near the Professor's room, Chandran felt very nervous. He adjusted his coat and buttoned it up. He hesitated for a moment before the door. He suddenly pulled himself up. Why this cowardice? Why should he be afraid of Ragavachar or anybody? Human being to human being. Remove those spectacles, the turban, and the long coat, and let Ragavachar appear only in a loin-cloth, and Mr. Ragavachar would lose three-quarters of his appearance. Where was the sense in feeling nervous before a pair of spectacles, a turban, and a black long coat" (26).

C.D. Narasimhaiah calls it 'healthy disrespect for others' and believes that it makes survival possible for Narayan's heroes. However, Chandran's remark on Prof. Gajapathi is not simply adolescent prank but eccentric immodesty, born of an illusion about himself. He not only makes a sketch of an elephant for him but also refuses to show him his notebook: "Honestly, I have not taken down anything, sir. If you will excuse me I must go now. I have to see Prof. Ragavachar" (26). It is this trait in him that develops into romantic infatuation for a girl named Malathi and conflict with the traditional power structure. He reacts against too much interference of the family and relatives in matters relating to his personal life. His father wants to send him to Madras to study Law. And then there is suggestion of his marriage. Some want him to be fixed in the Railway. He himself wants to go to London: "Within six months of becoming a graduate Chandran began to receive suggestions from relatives and elderly friends of the family as to what he should do with himself. Till this time it had never occurred to him that he ought to be doing anything at all. But now, wherever he went, he was pestered with the question, "Now what do you propose to do?" (52). This is the way of the close-knit world in which people around us show their involvement, and concern for us. With the endless suggestions and repeated questions pouring in, he feels persecuted: "I am sorry, Father, that I ever passed the B.A... Why should everybody talk about my career? Why can't they mind their business?" (53). His father trains him to take them positively. Chandran wants to go to London to do doctorate, but his sudden love with an unknown girl about fifteen years old, whom he finds at the bank of Sarayu, changes his mind: "he would not have room for anything else in his mind" (54). He is lost in a whirlpool of conflicting thoughts. The conflicts are at two levels: First how far he should be conformist and how far non-conformist? How far he should succumb to the power structure of the society and family? And he resolves it by his decision that he would not let others decide his own course of action in life, in matters of marriage and career. He is not in open revolt mainly because he has got a considerate father. The second conflict is between his own choices—love, marriage and career:

> He went on his usual walk down to Nallappa's Grove, crossed the river, went up the opposite bank, and away into the fields there; but he caught himself more than once thinking of the girl. How old was she? Probably fourteen. Might be even fifteen or sixteen. If she was more than fourteen she must be married. There was a touch of despair in this thought. What was the use of thinking of a married girl? It would be very improper. He tried to force his mind to think of other things. He tried to engage it in his favourite subject—his trip to England in the coming year. If he was going to England how was he to dress himself? He had better get used to tie and shoes and coat and hat and knife and fork. He would get a first-class degree in England and come back and marry. What was the use of thinking of a married girl? Probably she was not married. Her parents were

> very likely rational and modern, people who abhorred the custom of rushing a young child into marriage. (55)

He is seen torn between the two poles—Malathi and his career. But ultimately, he surrenders before the image of Malathi. One day he follows her to her house and procures the necessary information about her and her parents with the help of his friend, Mohan, who, too, lives in Mill Street. He feels excited to learn that she is unmarried and that she belongs to a respectable Iyer family of his own caste. In this episode, it becomes evident that Narayan wants to show the transition taking place in the society but it is within the ambit of the system. Chandran, however modern and independent in outlook, has a sense of respect for the society, or rather an inherent fear of the staring eyes of the society. He does not muster guts to express his love for her. He cannot even stare in her eyes; he only looks at her from a distance with the fringe of his eyes. Even when he decides to talk to his father for the marriage, he fails to speak to him in his two attempts. It represents the consciousness of an age; and his intense desire for love and marriage indicates the advent of an age. This conflict is not the case of Chandran alone, but a clash between two generations at moderate scale. So, it presents the youth in transition asserting his individuality and fighting with his own diffidence created by the traditional moorings:

> Chandran prayed to God to give him courage, and went to his father to talk to him about his marriage. His courage failed him at the last moment, and he went away after discussing some fatuous subject. The next day he again went to his father with the same resolution and again lapsed into fatuity. He went back to his room and regretted his cowardice. He would be unworthy of Malathi if he was going to be such a spineless worm. Afraid of a father! He was not a baby asking for a toy, but a full-grown adult out on serious business, very serious business. It was very doubtful if a squirming coward would be any good to Malathi as a husband. (67-68)

On his third attempt, he succeeds in telling his mind: "Father, please don't mistake me. I want to marry D.W. Krishna lyer's daughter" (68). Though his parents are not interested in the proposition, they, after a little dilly-dallying, come to compromise. But then they have to keep in mind the social superiority assigned to bridegroom's parents, the amount of dowry the bride's parent can afford and, above all, the horoscope must match. It has been a practice that proposal for marriage should come from the side of bride's parent. It does not apply to the whole of India but to a large section of the Hindu society: "The fear of society was very imminent. Anything done contrary to this would make them the laughing stock of the community" (70). He is so much pained that he hates his parents and thinks that they love only money and not him. He finds his feelings expressed in a verse composed by Mohan and he passes that piece to his father.

> The parents love you, you thought.
> No, no, not you, my dear.
> They've loved nothing less for its own sake.
> They fed you and petted you and pampered you
> Because some day they hope, you'll earn a
> Bride who'll bring much money, so much and
> More and still more.... (72)

It offends the feelings of his father and mother who, ultimately, send Ganapathi Sastrigal, a matchmaker, to the Iyer family to invite proposal from that side. Both the families feel happy with the prospect of marriage, but it falls flat and Chandran's elated hopes are shattered once for all, when it is found that their horoscopes do not match. Chandran's father does not believe in it but Iyer is conservative and he politely refuses to marry his daughter with Chandran. Later on, Malathi is married to some one else. Chandran's cynical reaction against his father, his exuberance, impatience and then his frustration are quite understandable and are momentary impulses that make the novel all the more natural and authentic. Chandran, in this part of the novel, presents a romantic view of time and events that stand in contrast with his mother's 'awareness of an idealized order of events' prescribed in time honoured formulas. She is a conformist character who believes in the sanctity of custom and in fate—"you can only marry the girl you are destined to marry at the appointed time." So the episode presents the clash between individual choice; and, the social choice and the latter prevails over the social choice; and, the contrast is also between the early romantic Chandran and the latter anti-romantic Chandran. The emotional dilemma of the youth, his assertion of individuality and the accommodation of individuality, within the ambit of traditional family system, is a rare feat in those days and it gives the novel a universal appeal because it has been enacted in every society and in every age. The old generation will keep clashing with the new in ideology and they will learn to come to terms with each other. Chandran's father shows an example of honouring one's individuality. He never comes in the way of his son.

Chandran decides to go to Madras to his uncle for a change. But he prefers to go to a hotel where he falls in the company of a reckless man, Kailash. Chandran is led by him; but when it comes to drinking, he is rescued by his mother: "Excuse me. I made a vow never to touch alcohol in my life, before my mother." It emotionally appeals to Kailash, who says: "Then don't. Mother is a sacred object. It is a commodity whose value we don't realize as long as it is with us. One must lose it to know what a precious possession it is. If I had my mother I should have studied in a college and become a respectable person. You wouldn't find me here. After this, where do you think I am going?" (98-99). It throws light on our cultural moorings and strong bond of mother. She is a humanizing factor in Indian culture. Chandran soon gives up his company and leaves for Mylapore. There he dons a saffron robe and becomes a sanyasi. He writes a letter to his father telling him that he is on a tour and that they should not be worried if they don't hear from him for a long time. Thus, he sets on his journey mostly on foot, occasionally by bus, begging food and sleeping where the day's journey ends. There is nothing spiritual or religious about his journey. As the narrator describes:

> He was different from the usual *sanyasi*. Others may renounce with a spiritual motive or purpose. Renunciation may be to them a means to attain peace or may be peace itself. They are perhaps dead in time, but they do live in eternity. But Chandran's renunciation was not of that kind. It was an alternative to suicide. Suicide he would have committed but for its social stigma. Perhaps he lacked the barest physical courage that was necessary for it. He was a *sanyasi* because it pleased him to mortify his flesh. His renunciation was a revenge on society, circumstances, and perhaps, too, on destiny. (108)

In the course of his wanderings, he sits under a banyan tree and the news is spread that a holy man, under vow of silence for ten years, is sitting under the banyan tree in intense meditation. People throng there in great number with offerings and they seek his blessings. He reminds us of Raju, the guide in his later novel *The Guide*, who, too, becomes a *sanyasi* but not to return. Chandran is still fresh with noble impulses and doesn't like parasitic life and thus makes a retreat. C.D. Narasimhaiah makes a brilliant comparison: "The situation is very similar to what makes the Railway Guide a Swami in Narayan's later novel, *The Guide*. But whereas the Guide, a hardened scoundrel, could hold on and become a swami in spite of himself, the inexperienced Chandran, with the idealism of a youth fresh form the university, retrieves himself from the undeserved role of the ascetic foisted on him by others and goes away with remorse for 'humbugging' through life". Chandran's self realization and self-introspection result into a guilt consciousness in which he feels sorry for the pain he has given to his parents, sorry for cashing in upon the innocence of the people and also for what he has made of himself. Narayan narrates: "Sitting in the dark, he subjected his soul to a remorseless vivisection. From the moment he had donned the ochre cloth to the present, he had been living on charity, charity given in mistake, given on the face value of a counterfeit. He had been humbugging through life. He told himself that if he were such an ascetic he ought to do without food or perish of starvation. He ought not to feed his miserable stomach with food which he had neither earned nor, by virtue of spiritual worth, deserved" (111). He finds an answer to his 'degradation' in "Malathi" and "Love" and shakes off his self-deception and romantic illusion. He comes back to his home. But in reality, there is little change in his cynicism. At least his observation on friendship and love seems so. He observes: "Friendship was another illusion like Love, though it did not reach the same mad heights. People pretended that they were friends, when the fact was they were brought together by force of circumstances.... When the circumstances changed the relations, too, snapped.... Friendship-what meaningless expressions had come into use!" (118).

But there can be another point of view. When he returns to his place, after a gap of eight months, he naturally turns nostalgic and misses his friends and his college days. Whatever he says is his reaction in disappointment. Most of his rumblings are impulsive responses to a moment. And hence, I consider them in that perspective and do not attach any philosophic importance to them. His view on the transience of college friendship is a matter of fact observation prompted by the situation. But he soon overcomes his 'distracting illusions and hysterics.' He gives up the idea of going to England and secures the agency of *Daily Messenger* with the help of his uncle. He shows "a fleeting awareness of the larger irony of life" (Naik, 15), when he comments on the managers of the newspaper: "My life is in these fellows hands! Absolute strangers. Decision of my fate in their hands, absolutely! Why is this so?" (138). More than this, what touches me the most is the natural, simple and colloquial way of portraying the characters and the life they lead in that region. It has the grace, ease and naturalness without any linguistic embellishment and complex architectonic of narrative. To me, he is closer to Premchand in the portrayal of life and characters than to Hardy or Austen. Take, for example, a scene of husband-wife nagging:

> After Chandran had gone to his room, his mother said: "Why are you tormenting the boy?" Father did not

> vouchsafe an answer but merely rustled his paper. She repeated the question, and he said: "Why don't you leave it to me?"
>
> "If the boy wishes to stay here, why won't you let him stay? What is the use of sending him to England? Waste of a lot of money. What do our boys, who go to England, specially achieve? They only learn to smoke cigarettes, drink wine, and dance with white girls."
>
> "It is my hope that our boy will do something more than that."
>
> "If there is as much money in the paper as he says, why shouldn't he do that work?"
>
> "If there is; that is what I must know before I let him do it. I can't very well give him a cheque for 2,000 rupees and ask him to invest it, without knowing something about the persons that are running the paper, how long it will last, and other things. There is hardly any sense in letting him in for work which may last even a year! I have written to my bother. Let me see what he writes."
>
> "You have to write to your brother about everything," she said, rising to go in. "Only I don't want you to drive the boy to desperation." (128-29)

Eventually, Chandran starts the agency with all sincerity and devotion. He is married to Susila. He is shown working as an afflicted man once again in romantic illusion, natural for a newly married couple. K.R. Srinivasa Iyengar's observation is worth quoting:

> The story of their wedded life is a prose lyric on which Narayan has lavished his best gifts as a writer. Spring is no hard material substance: it is a presence, it is an unfolding, it is ineffable becoming that strains after Being. A thousand little occurrences, leaps of light, bubbles of sound, a thousand smiles revealing their rainbow magnificence through the film of tearful happiness or fulfilment, a thousand murmurs of ecstasy, meaningless worries, tremendous trifles, a thousand stabs of pain that are somehow transcended, a thousand

> shared anxieties, excitements and adorations; it is out of these that the texture of wedded happiness is wrought, and Narayan is an adept at giving form and meaning to this glory of holy wedded love. (367)

What surprises me is that the boy himself, along with his mother, goes to see his prospective bride even in that period of time when girls were not even shown to the boy's parents. It is certainly the effect of the change. But the change is on other side, too. Though Chandran does not like all these formalities, he resigns to fate. Does it not point to the way it accommodates both Sastrigal and Chandran and the way it overpowers Chandran's resistance and juvenile deviations? It is like the river Sarayu, symbol of the continuity and flexibility of our culture. I like this novel for its regional ambience in a wider sense. The region chosen is, of course, south Indian, but it becomes pan-Indian in its representativeness and even global when it comes to the grammar of love and juvenile sensibility. The simplicity of the language and style reflects the simplicity of the man and the age. All said and done, it is more a novel for the readers than a novel for critical aerobics.

Works Cited

Holmstorm, Lakshami. *The Novels of R.K. Narayan*. Calcutta: Writer Workshop, 1973.

Iyengar, K.R. Srinivasa. *Indian Writing in English*. New Delhi, 1987.

Naik, M.K. *The Ironic Vision*. New Delhi: Sterling, 1983.

Narasimhaiah, C.D. *Makers of Indian English Literature*. Delhi: Pencraft, 2003.

Narayan, R.K. *The Bachelor of Arts*. Mysore: Indian Thought Publications, 1991.

Page, Normon. *Thomas Hardy*. London: Routledge & Kegan Paul, 1997.

Tilak, Raghukul. *The Bachelor of Arts: Critical Study*. Barelly Prakash.

9

Reflection of the Third Space in the Novels of R.K. Narayan

Dhananjay Tripathi

It is almost a century since the literary firmament has been dominated by formalism or its off-shoots. Since Russian Formalism, which was initiated during 1920s, formalism has occupied the very centre of literary study and has not only inflated its orbit, by pushing all other approaches to the periphery, but has also come to the governing core. The cornerstone of the movement was an emphasis on the text and rejection of all the external references. To substantiate, we can quote Derrida, when he says "there is nothing outside the text". Derrida was already anticipated by J.C. Ransom—the first law of criticism is to recognize the autonomy of the work—and the Russian Formalists' emphasis on the devices creating literariness, which, as the tacit marginalization of the author, can be read in the same context. The approach surfaced with Eliot's statement that "honest criticism and sensitive appreciation is directed not upon the poet but upon poetry" (297). I.A. Richard's recommendation of close reading, without any smell of the author's personality, Paul De Man's author as 'grammatical pronoun' and Barthes' murder of the author and declaration of text as 'a tissue of quotations drawn from innumerable centers of culture' are nothing but tacit emphasis or the same current of thoughts.

Several knee-jerk consequents of the trend can be categorized as following: (a) they raised the value of the text; (b) they rejected the subjectivity or the authorial intent which leads to the shifting of focus from author to readers and sows the seeds of writerly text, rejecting the readerly text, which finally resulted in the concept of 'ecriture writings'; (c) they raised the importance of language as stressed by Russian Formalism, New Criticism, Structuralism, Deconstruction, stylistics, Discourse analysis and Bakhtin's theory of Dialogism; (d) the last and the most important consequence was the imposition of theoretical perspective in understanding the text.

As Srawani Biswas aptly opines: "Although the theories were there since Aristotle and they were supportive and narrating the meaning of the text. After the 1960s, the relation between text and theories underwent a radical change and slowly the prerogative of text, as the source of fixed meaning, came adrift and theories strengthened the hold on that" (01).

This long hegemony was first time challenged or apposed tacitly by Barthes himself in his essay titled "From the Work to the Text" wherein he writes: "It is not that the author cannot 'come back' into the text; however he can only do so as a 'guest,' so to speak. If the author is a novelist, he inscribes himself in the text as one of his characters...." (qtd. in Rajnath, 48). The claim that the author can 'come back' was further reiterated by the Geneva critics, who even went to the extent of saying that the text is the reflection of the author's 'cogito' and 'lebenswelt' (lived world). In fact, the Geneva Critics 'glimpse' the personality and unity of 'creative mind' in the writings. This shift of attitude from form to content, intrinsic to extrinsic value, universal to particular, writerly to readerly text and text to author is strengthened and substantiated with the features of postcolonial criticism which covers politics, culture, identity and race. This postcolonial debate finally results in the consideration of issues like 'double identity' (colonizer and colonized) and as Barry says, "at another level, the double or hybrid identity is precisely what the postcolonial situation brings into being" (196). This concept of duality or plurality of identity, culture, race and language is the most celebrated and, therefore, variously interpreted. But the credit of the significance, which the concept bears today, goes to

Bhabha, who explicated the horizons of the concept in his *The Location of Culture* (1994). In Bhabha's cultural discourse, 'hybridity' is actually an anti-chamber which leads to many other new areas of critical thoughts, which are not only new, significant and identical, but largely depend, for their meaning, on their similarities and differences with each other.

The word "'hybridity' is commonly used to refer to the creation of trans-cultural form; in fact the term refers to the cross-breeding of two species by grafting or cross-pollination to form a third 'hybrid' species" (Ashcroft, 118). It is worth mentioning here that hybridization could take place in many areas: language, culture, politics and race. Mikhail Bakhtin's concept of Dialogism is an example of hybridity happening in linguistic domain. Bhabha explicated the notion to describe the unique 'culture' and 'identity'. For him, "hybridity is the process by which the colonial governing authority undertakes to translate the identity of the colonised (the other) within a single universal framework, but then fails, producing something familiar but new" (Meredith, 02). Bhabha claims that new identity, culture, and position, etc. are given birth when the interaction of the colonizer and the colonized takes place and, this very space, which engenders something new, is referred to by him as 'the Third Space', which is the chief concern of this paper. However, in the process, it would perhaps be desirable to explicate the notions of In-betweenness, Mimicry and Ambivalent.

Bhabha's hybridity is basically the 'in-between space.' "In-betweenness", as Hoogvelt says, "is the straddling of two cultures and consequent ability to negotiate the difference" (qtd. in Meredith, 02). Thus, it can be concluded that the coming together or interaction of two cultures with all these notions and original features is called 'in-betweenness of cultures'. According to Nayar: "Bhabha sees borders as thresholds, in-between spaces where identities can be recast... the need to think beyond narratives of originary and initial subjectivity and to focus on those moments or processes that are produced in the articulation of cultural-differences. These 'in-between' spaces provide the terrain for elaborating strategies of selfhood—singular or communal—that initiate new signs of identities, and innovative sides of collaboration and contestation, in the act of defining the idea of society itself" (171). Thus, this process of 'in-betweenness', with the cultural ambiguity and ambivalence, results in hybridity of cultures which passes through mimicry and finally results in the 'third space'. Bhabha defines mimicry and says that it takes place "when colonial discourse encourages the colonized subject to 'mimic' the colonizer; by adopting the colonisers' cultural habit, assumptions, institutions and values, the result is never a simple reproduction of those traits. Rather, the result is a 'blurred copy' of the coloniser that can be quite threatening" (qtd. in Ashcroft, 139).

However, this paper aims at explicating the idea of 'third space' which is 'a space of relation between colonizer and colonized' and, Nayar puts it as "a site where:

> Colonial identity and native identity meet and often contest.
>
> Colonial discourse is both—at once asserted and subverted.
>
> There is deference and difference.
>
> There is split and a negotiation within colonial discourse.
>
> Mimicry and mockery occur." (171)

The idea of 'negotiation' is already stressed by Bhabha while explaining 'third space'. He opines: "It is the indeterminate spaces, the in-between subject-position that is lauded as the locale of the disruption and displacement of hegemony, colonial narratives of cultural structure and practices. Bhabha posits hybridity as such a form of luminal or in-between space, where the 'cutting edge of translation and negotiation occurs' and which he terms the third space" (qtd. in Meredith, 02). Articulating Bhabha's ideas of third space, Paul Meredith writes: "The third space is a mode of articulation, a way of describing a productive, and not merely reflective space that engenders new possibility. It is an 'interruptive, interrogative, and enunciative' space of new forms of cultural meaning and production, blurring the limitation of existing boundaries and calling in to question established category of culture and identity. According to Bhabha, this hybrid third space is an ambivalent site where cultural meaning and representation have no "primordial unity or fixity" (qtd. in Meredith, 03).

Thus, it can be argued that in-between the cultural discourse, the third space is the space where cultures, identities, understandings meet, contest, negotiate and after undergoing the process of mimicry and hybridity, there engender new culture, identity or understanding. Thus, the third space could be designated as a 'productive space' in cultural discourse, as Bhabha describes: "At the point at which the coloniser presents a normalizing hegemony practice, the hybrid strategy opens up a third space of/for rearticulating of negotiation and meaning" (qtd. in Meredith, 03). The same idea echoes in the writings of Elizabeth Birrmoje, as she says: "In third space, then what seem to be oppositional categories can actually work together to generate new knowledge, new discourse and new forms of literacy" (42). The idea can be finally substantiated by a quotation from Bhabha's own writing in his *Location of Culture* where he writes: "Third space...constitutes the discursive condition...that insures that...even the same signs can be appropriated, translated, rehistoricized and read anew" (qtd. in Moje, 43).

To apply the 'third space' to Narayan's writings, or rather to say that to read him in this context, is not an easy task because most of his writings precede even the emergence of the notion of the third space. However, I shall try to quote certain grey areas from his select novels, which show his conscious or unconscious anticipation or contrivance of the 'the third space'.

In his very first novel, *Swami and Friends* (1935), the episode of Swami's teacher, Mr. Ebenezar, who criticizes and denigrates the Indian culture of idol-worship and insults the Hindu God and praises Christianity in the class room—"'Oh, wretched idiots!' clenching his fist, Why do you worship dirty, lifeless wooden idols and stone images! Can they talk! No"

(04), and Swami's reaction, which is full of subtle humour and irony, wherein he asks and criticizes Christianity in the same manner of questioning: "If he did not, why was he crucified".... "If he was a God, why did he eat flesh and fish and drink wine?" (As a Brahmin boy it was inconceivable to him that a God should be a non-vegetarian) (04) is an example where two cultures can be seen at negotiation, confrontation and clash. And Swami's abandoning of the school with the remark: "I don't care for your dirty school" (107) is clearly a projection of cultural clash. The author's preference for the one that is marginalized is an example of 'the third space'.

Another example of cultural interaction and clash is the ambivalent response of Swaminathan towards the civil disobedience movement. At one point of time, he was not sure about his stand; but after listening to the lectures, he makes his stand clear and decides to reject the foreign clothes which symbolise occidental culture: "Swaminathan was going to mete it out by wearing only khaddar, the rough homespun" (96). If Swaminathan's stance is an example of cultural dissonance, Mani's reply is the example of apparent clash and denial of occidental culture: Mani says "of course", in Swami's reply to what he will wear: "Khaddar. Do you think that I will pay a paisa to those Lancashire devils? No they would not get it out of me" (96). These cultural negotiations are the examples of 'In-betweenness" of cultural discourse which open up the new possibilities of 'the third space' or a 'new culture' influenced by both the occidental and oriental culture, also hybrid in nature.

The reflection of the third space with all its nuances can also be seen in Narayan's second novel, *The Bachelor of Arts*. Narayan has the unique ability to satirize and suggest the solutions to some of the dominant problems through projection of the psychology of his characters. Chandran's reaction to the restriction imposed on the Indians to enter the English club in India is one example: "Chandran says, "all Europeans are like this. They will take their thousand or more a month, but would not do the slightest service to Indians with a sincere heart.... If ever I get into power I shall see that English men attend clubs along with Indians and are not so exclusive" (05). Chandran's speech can be taken as an example of cultural negotiation where he is comparing or rejecting outrightly the occidental and coming up with the third culture wherein he will admit and give importance to the occidental and will never allow it to become 'exclusive' or 'essential'. This interaction and negotiation of culture, which is rejecting essentialism and engendering a new trend, can be the anticipation of plurality of culture or multi-culturalism, which has resulted in the third space.

The cultural clash can be witnessed in some other incidents of the novel too; for instance, the proposal of Chandran's father to study in England is an example where a complete transformation of culture can be discerned. In the beginning, Chandran was happy with the idea of going to England: "What do you propose to do in England?" asks his father. He answers "I want to get a doctorate or something and come back, and then some quiet lectureship in some college will suit me wonderfully. Plenty of independence and leisure" (53). Chandran's conversation with Mohan, a poet, friend and ardent believer of Indian culture, made the idea ambiguous for him: "What have we to learn from English? I don't know when this craze for going to England will stop. It is a drain on the country's resources. What have we to learn from the English?" (61). After this conversation, Chandran's mind, which was enticed by English culture, fuses with cultural ambivalence and, after a cultural tug-of-war, he rather rejects the idea of going to England, as he says to his father: "Will you be disappointed if I don't go to England? ...I feel that going to England will only mean a lot of expense" (127). The whole episode can be seen in terms of cultural transformation.

In *The Vendor of Sweets* (1967), under the veil of conflict between tradition and modernity, Jagan is the representative of tradition and his son, Mali, that of modernity. However, after Mali's return from America, both change their roles to become the representatives of oriental and occidental cultures, respectively. Mali's personality is completely changed. He starts 'beef eating' in America and returns with a hybrid identity. Jagan's satirical question—"did Valmiki go to America or Germany in order to learn to write his Ramayana?" (51)—can be read in the same context. In fact, the conflict between Jagan and his American educated son can be interpreted at various levels, like "the division of east and west" (Walsh, 152). The portrayal of Mali, after his visit to America as 'inhuman', can be taken as an implicit rejection of the Western culture he had imbibed.

The theme of ambivalent relationship between two cultures and groups of society has been presented in Narayan's other novels as well. These novels present this ambivalent relationship in terms of the negotiations between the marginalized and the preferred. In *The Dark Room* (1938) and *The Painter of Signs* (1977), Narayan is concerned with the marginalization of women as 'other' and the impact of women movements and the changing status of women in Indian society. In *The Dark Room*, Savitri's suffering at the hands of her husband, Ramani, shows the treatment of women as marginalized and 'the other' in society. Savitri's speech, wherein she says—"I am a human being. You men will never grand that. For you we are plaything when you feel like hugging and slaves at other times. Don't think that you can fondle us when you like and kick us when you choose?" (75)—is an example of a clash of two genders where one is marginalized as the 'other'. The marginalization of women is also suggested by Ramani's reference of Savitri as his "possession" (50). Savitri further utters: "What possession can a woman call her own except her body? Everything else she has is her father's, her husband's or her son's" (75). These speeches of Savitri and her husband's careless attitude towards her clearly project the ambivalent relationship in terms of gender. Savitri has shown the half-backed individuality of woman by leaving her house, however, her returning symbolizes that that was a time when assertion of women's rights and their development had been only recently initiated.

The next novel of our concern is *The Painter of Signs* which shows the fully developed and matured impact of women liberation Movements, as Daisy is more assertive, educated, self-dependent, self-proclaimed and more individual. The novel has been read as "the power of women in Narayan's novels" (Olinder, 96-104). In fact, Savitri and Daisy are a contrast to each other in many ways. Daisy is more assertive and not compromising, unlike Savitri. She does not return and surrender after taking the decision to pursue her own path as she replies to Raman's pleadings that she should not leave him. She says: "Married life is not for me. I have thought it over. It frightens me, I am not cut out for the life you imagined, I cannot live except alone. It won't work.... I cannot afford to have a personal life" (179). In the same chapter, she is described as being very emotional but she controls herself and sticks to her aim. Narayan writes: "She looked up and said, 'calm yourself you will be happy married to someone very different. Seek a proper partner for yourself...you can, any girl will accept you—no, adore you. You are everything a girl dreams of'. For the first time she was sounding so emotional and personal" (180). However, soon after this conflict, she replies strongly that she cannot abandon her future ambition 'because [she has] a different life chalked out.' Thus, she stands in contrast to Savitri. While Savitri is the product of the 1930s, Daisy is living in the 1980s; and, so by their attitude, both justify the milieu they belong to. Narayan has presented two shades of ambivalent relationship between man and woman in these two novels. He has shown how a woman is marginalized and, even after her repeated attempts of assertion, she fails and surrenders to patriarchy in the first novel; but when he comes back to the same theme of ambivalent relationship after almost four decades, he returns with change and mature vision and portrays Daisy—the symbol of a modern woman. This shows that though the theme of ambivalent relationship recurs in his writings, his vision and understanding never remain stable. He is not an author with rigid vision or a utopian mindset, but rather an author of real life which he portrays with all its changing shades.

Now let us focus on an award-winning and one of Narayan's best pensive comedies, *The Guide*. Raju's step to change his look after Rosie's arrival, by discarding his old-fashioned *Khaki* bush-coat and *Dhoti* and wearing the silk *jibba* and lace *dhoti*, and his speech—"In my *khaki* bush-coat I would not have dared to take a seat beside him (Marco) or talk to him"—is the beautiful example of tacit mimicry. Marco's disliking of 'dance' which 'always stung him' made Rosie, who used to study the ancient works of art and culture such as *Natyashastra* of Bharatmuni, disappointed. She requested Marco, who was obsessed with local rock-carvings, in a very polite manner: "I think I will be very happy if I could do that. I have so many ideas. I would like to try just as you are trying to" (147) and Marco's reaction: "Oh, you want to rival me, is that it? This is a branch of learning no street-acrobatics" (147)—is clear undermining of Rosie's interest and tacit rejection after a harsh clash between two cultures by Marco, the latent representative of Western culture. This is an appropriate example of cultural imprisonment which gets freedom in the form of the third space with Rosie's association with Raju.

This ambivalent relation is also reflected through the rejection of colonial mechanism of the education system. As Thieme writes: "On one level this opposition functions as a device for criticizing the colonial education system despite Narayan's allegedly apolitical stance and his own English education, his early trilogy offers an implicit indictment of colonial education and in *The English Teacher* the criticism is more overt than Swami or *The Bachelor of Art*" (61). In *Swami and Friends*, the sad and reluctant attitude of the protagonist and his subsequent expulsion from two schools of Malgudi clearly suggest the rejection of the colonial education system. Throughout the novel, Swami is never happy or satisfied with the colonial school of Malgudi. In these two schools, he came to realize only the inferiority of Indians and their culture. He is happy only when he is away from his school whether with his friends, granny or alone in the town moving here and there; it seems that Narayan suggests that he favours only the 'live alone' system of ancient India. The idea can be supported by his own words in *My Days* where he describes: "My outlook on education never fitted in with the accepted code at home. Since revolt was unpractical. I went through it all without conviction, enthusiasm or any sort of distinction" (56). Swami's rejection of his school when he says: "I do not care for your dirty school" (107)—may be taken as Narayan's rejection of that schooling system which is celebrated in many schoolboy British fictions. Thieme is very appropriate in his conclusion when he says: "Despite his lightness of touch Narayan renders the school a site of struggle and subtly suggests the codes of English school-boy fiction, while ostensibly operating within its conventions" (29). This rejection of the British way of schooling becomes stronger in the next novels, *The Bachelor of Arts* and *The English Teacher*. Chandran's satirical approach to Mr. Gajapathy, the lecturer of English, and his subsequent rejection of his father's proposal to go to England are a clear suggestion of rejection of the colonial education system. The rejection of the colonial education system becomes more overt and prominent with his latest novels. Krishna's remarks and statements typify the clear-cut rejection of the education pattern inaugurated by the British. Being a teacher of English, he says: "What about our own roots?" I thought over it deeply and felt very puzzled. I added: "I am up against the system, the whole method and approach of a system of education which makes us moron, cultural morons, but efficient clerk for all your business and administrative offices" (178-79). He further criticizes Macaulay's method of teaching: "I replied, Sir, what I am doing in the college hardly seems to me work. I mug up and repeat and they mug up and repeat in the exam...this hardly seems to me work Mr. Brown" (97). The headmaster's philosophy, described in the last chapters of the novel, may be taken as the clear-cut alternative of the British system of education and the protagonist's resignation from the college and joining the headmaster's school is the symbolic rejection of the British schooling system which has also been criticized, though implicitly, in the next novel, *The Financial Expert*, where Maragyya is very much concerned about the schooling of his son, Balu. He would "send him to *Albert Mission College* and provide him separate room" (111) in new extension but Balu's failure in the high school exams, and later his moral corruption under the influence of Dr. Pal, is an example of overt rejection of the colonial schooling system.

After this brief discussion on the third space and Narayan's writings, it is abundantly clear that there is tremendous scope for further research in this hitherto untrodden area. One can at least conclude that though Narayan precedes the theory of the third space, nevertheless he has unconsciously anticipated it, and the theory of the third space, with all its mechanism and components such as mimicry, hybridity of culture and in-betweenness suggests that we are living in a cultural world which is open to new domains wherein no culture is perfect in itself.

Works Cited

Ashcroft, Bill, Gareth Griffiths and Helen Tiffin. *Post-Colonial Studies*. London: Routledge, 2000.

Barry, Peter. *Beginning Theory—An Introduction to Literary and Cultural Theory*. Manchester University Press, 2008.

Biswas, Sravani. *A Study of R.K. Narayan's Novels: A Cerebration of the Carnival*. New Delhi: Atlantic, 2010.

Eliot, T.S. "Tradition and Individual Talent", *English Critical Texts*. ed. D.J. Enright and Ernst D. Chickera. London: OUP, 1972.

Meredith, Poul Hybidity in the The Third Space.

http//www.iianz.waikato.ac.nz/PAPAERS/Paul/hybridity.pdf (retrieved on 13.01.2011)

Moje, Birr Elizabeth. "Working Toward the Third Space in Content Area Literacy", *Reading Research Quarterly*. Vol. 39 (1).

Narayan, R.K. *Swami and Friends*. Chennai: Indian Thought Publications, 1935.

———. *The Bachelor of Art*. Chennai: Indian Thought Publications, 1937.

———. *The Guide*. Chennai: Indian Thought Publications, 1958.

———. *My Days*. Chennai: Indian Thought Publications, 2006.

Nayar, P.K. *Contemporary Literary and Cultural Theory*. Pearson Longman, 2010.

Olinder, Britta. "The Power of Women in RK Narayan's Novels", *R.K. Narayan: Critical Perspective*. Ed. A.L. McLeod. New Delhi: Sterling, 1994.

Rajnath. *Critical Speculations*, Delhi: Doaba House, 1996.

Thieme, John. *R.K. Narayan*. New Delhi: Viva Books, 2010.

10

Old Wine in New Bottles: Traditionalism in R.K. Narayan's Novels

Shyam Bihari Tiwary

Unlike M.R. Anand, R.K. Narayan upholds the old traditional values of life prescribed by the ancient Indian culture and embodied in Indian epics, 'Shastras', 'Puranas', myths and mythologies. Naturally, he gives the philosophy of traditionalism which permeates all of his novels. It is the fountain-head from which his other philosophical concepts such as orthodoxy, superstiton and the role of fate in life flow as its inseparable channels. He presents his concept of traditionalism through the middle-class life of Malgudi. His novels show that success and happiness in life lie in resignation to and acceptance of the Shastra-approved traditional values. Human life is suggested as a journey in quest of self-identity or emancipation from the miseries of life. But influenced by man's modernism, ego and *karma*, and governed by fate and chance, human life moves in a zig-zag way and at last, comes to the same state which it started from, but with man's self-realization of his puny stature and the truths of life in the tradition-bound social set-up. In the novels of Narayan, "there is generally a flight," observes Iyengar, "an uprooting a disturbance of order—followed by a return, a renewal, a restoration of normalcy" (107). Any deviation from traditional norms results in disruption of regular, normal life. Chandran in *The Bachelor of Arts*, Savitri in *The Dark Room* and Mali in

The Vendor of Sweets run away in protest against their family traditions, suffer from a lot of troubles and later on come back, or are brought back, willingly or unwillingly, for a life better or worse.

The traditional world of Malgudi does not sanction romantic love, as it has its own custom of arranged marriage which is settled by parents after negotiation and horoscope-matching. Chandran falls in love with Malathi at first sight and is determined to marry her. But their parents stop marriage negotiation when the horoscopes of Chandran and Malathi do not match. Later on, Chandran has to marry Susila, a girl of his parents' choice. Sriram, in the novel *Waiting for the Mahatma*, loves Bharati and wants to marry her but the latter gives her consent for this only after obtaining approval from Gandhiji, who is her Godfather, Guru and guardian. Bharati acts as an ideal for modern girls by following Indian values and traditions. The marriages between Chandran and Susila and between Sriram and Bharati are supposed to give happiness in life. Unlike Chandran's parents, Margayya (*The Financial Expert*) regards horoscope matching only as a formality in the settlement of the marriage of Balu with Brinda, the only daughter of a rich man. He says to the astrologer: "Well probably I shall be able to add a couple of rupees to your usual charges...and if alliance concludes successfully, well, of course a lace dhoti and all honours for the pundit" (107). At last, the horoscopes are anyhow matched. Though Balu and Brinda are married, the consequent events show that their married life is not so happy as it was expected. Brinda has to suffer much on account of Balu's indecent way of life.

Malgudi has its own set sexual ethics, according to which, sex-aberration or perversion with any motive is bound to end in frustration and misery. Man and woman, living together as husband and wife, without getting married, are regarded as sinners. Hence, it is sacrilegious to violate the sanctity of sex. In *The Dark Room*, Ramani, a Branch Manager of Englandia Insurance Company, falls in love with Shanta Bai, the probationary insurance assistant, who has deserted her husband. His immoral relation with her terribly upsets his normal family life. Shanta Bai, who tries to thrive on her love with the crazy Ramani, fails to fulfil insurance business. She is at last forced to leave Malgudi in frustration. Ravi and Sampath, in *Mr. Sampath*, establish immoral relation with Shanti Devi, the actress. Ravi goes mad in frustration and is sent to the police lock-up. Shanti leaves Sampath for good. Also Sampath is forced to leave Malgudi in order to escape the notice of his creditors, Somu and others. When Marco, the husband of Rosie, in *The Guide*, comes to know about Rosie's immoral illicit relation with Raju, he grows angry and leaves her saying: "You are a woman who will go to bed with anyone who flatters your antics.... I don't want you here" (134). After separation from her husband, she lives with Raju as his wife under the assumed name, Nalini, without marrying him. Raju's mother, who is an orthodox woman, is dead against her son's way of life with Rosie. She tells Raju about Rosie: "Why can't she go to her husband and fall at his feet? You know living with a husband is no joke as these modern girls imagine" (137). She does not want Rosie to stay in her house. But Raju has no regard for his mother's sentiments. Hence, she leaves the house forever. In course of time, Raju's romantic love for Rosie (Nalini) changes into love for money that he gets through her dancing. He exploits her in a variety of ways. Not only this, he possesses Rosie's box of jewellery by forging her signature for which he is arrested and jailed. Rosie (Nalini) severs her relation with Raju at last. Thus, romantic love between Rosie and Raju not only causes miseries to them but also ruins their families. Mali, the only son of Jagan in *The Vendor of Sweets*, lives with Grace, his half-Korean, half-American girlfriend, without marrying her. This is against the wishes of his father as also against the social and ethical tradition. His son's living in sin terribly offends his moral sense. But their romantic love does not continue for long. Mali is arrested and jailed on the charge of prohibition and thereafter Grace plans to go back to her country. Disillusioned with his life and in desperation against his son's conduct and character, Jagan leaves his home forever. Raman, the painter of signboards, in *The Painter of Signs*, is in romantic love with Daisy, an officer of a Family Planning Centre. They do enjoy privacy like husband and wife. Raman intends to marry her, but his orthodox aunt questions: "What is her caste, what is her history? She ran away from home! Don't you know all that?" (154). Thus, she opposes Raman's marriage with Daisy because the latter's identity is quite unknown. When she finds Raman adamant, she leaves her house like Raju's mother and goes on a pilgrimage. Daisy first accepts the marriage proposal, though on some unconventional conditions, yet later on, she changes her mood and leaves Raman saying: "Married life is not for me...I can't live except alone" (178-79). She goes away from Malgudi in order to do social work. Both Raman and Daisy, thus, remain unmarried throughout their lives. Raman has no one in his family to look after him.

It is thus obvious that the people of Malgudi have their roots in traditional family systems and moral codes of conduct, against which they cannot revolt for freedom. Their revolts are bound to bring about despair and frustration which amount to their ultimate defeat. In Narayan's novels, traditionalism dominates and overpowers modernity whenever there is a clash between them. "Narayan seems to point out, overtly and obliquely," says Shantha Krishnaswamy, "the value of a hertiage, of a past. What the Shastras have prescribed is good for everybody" (96) for a peaceful, harmonious and happy life.

Most of Narayan's woman characters, excepting only a few, are typically Indian housewives. They are meek, docile, submissive and orthodox having traditional views of virtue and family life. They seem to think that their virtues lie in their perfection in the roles allotted to them in their male-dominated families. As they are fully aware of the fact that the happiness in life depends on the mutual understanding of husband and wife, they merge their individualities in their husbands'. They avoid quarrelling with them just to preserve the peace of the family life. They appear to be resigned to their fate, but they are the depositories of social and family traditions. Chandran's mother, Susila, Janamma, Ambika and Meenakshi, to name a few, are to all appearances happy. Janamma, though a minor character in *The Dark Room,* gives a clue to the happy married life in a traditional family. She tells Savitri: "As for me, I have never opposed my husband or argued with him at any time in my life. I might have occasionally suggested an alternative, but nothing more. What he does is right. It's wife's duty to feel so" (59). It appears that she is fully aware of and complacent with her duties and status in her male-dominated family. This is why she has adjusted herself to her family customs so as to lead a normal peaceful life. Though Savitri leaves her family as a token of revolt against the brutality and immoral conduct of her tyrannical husband, Ramani, she comes back (or is forced to come back) realizing that she can't remain happy in seclusion of her own home and family. The unconventional manner of resistance to her husband's conduct and character causes her so much suffering that she feels: "I am like a bamboo pole which cannot stand without a wall to support it" (189).

Indian epics, 'Puranas' and 'Shastras' are the depositories of ancient values of life and moral codes of conduct. Indian myths and mythologies were enunciated by Indian sages, seers and saints who were divinely inspired and blessed. They are commonly accepted, and acceptable even today, for a peaceful, happy and prosperous worldly life. These epics and Puranas have been sources of moral teachings to common man and of inspiration to the creative writers. Raja Rao, in *The Cat and Shakespeare*, refers to the Shiva Purana to show how God is, by His very nature, and without any cause, extremely compassionate and superemely benevolent to all. Savitri, in *The Serpent and the Rope*, symbolizes Savitri of the Mahabharata. She saves the spiritual life of Ramaswamy by reminding him of his pursuit of self-realization and illumination. In *Comrade Kirillov*, Raja Rao shows Kirillov's great reverence for Sankaracharya and his Nirvana Astaka. Allusion to the Ramayana is found in Anand's *Gouri*, though with a very different motive. Narayan shows that the values of life preached in our scriptures are still relevant to human life in the present context. Traditionalism becomes more pronounced in Narayan's frequent allusions to myths, mythologies, Puranas and epics in his novels, in order to show the content and continuous conflict between good and evil, right from the ancient times, in which the evil forces, however, powerful they may be, are ultimately destroyed by themselves or by some invisible power. Vasu, the taxidermist in *The Man-Eater of Malgudi*, is the symbol of evil. He is, indeed, an embodiment of the 'Asura', as described in the Sixteenth Chapter of *The Bhagvad Gita*. He is ugly, ferocious in appearance, amoral by nature and devoid of the sense of gratitude and sympathy. He possesses super human strength and takes cruel pleasure in inflicting pain to others. The novelist has presented him as a man-eater. He says: The man-eater is a man, not a tiger, a modern *rakshasa* (Miscellany, 5). He has an insatiable appetite for killing both dangerous and domestic creatures. This is against the ancient Indian philosophy of 'Ahimsa Parmo dharmah'. Not only this, he exploits the people of Malgudi in general and Nataraj, the printer, in particular. He silences all with threats. Nataraj, the symbol of God, is too weak and timid to do anything against Vasu. Even then, there is a smouldering conflict between the two, though Nataraj is always on the defensive. He fails to understand how to face Vasu and get rid of him. But Sastri, the Sanskrit scholar, refers to the epics and Puranas to show his faith in inevitable downfall of the evil. He says that Ravana, in *The Ramayana*, had enormous yogic and physical power and a boon from the Gods that he could never be vanquished...still he came to a sad end (96). In the Markandeya Purana, Mahishasura had acquired a boon of immortality and invincibility but was killed by Goddess Durga at last: "Then there was Bhasmasura who acquired a special boon that everything he touched should be scorched.... He made humanity suffer. God Vishnu was incarnated as a dancer of great beauty, named Mohini with whom the asura became infatuated. She promised to yield to him only if he imitated all the gestures and movements of her own dancing. At one point in the dance Mohini placed her palms on her head, and the demon followed this gesture in complete forgetfulness and was reduced to ashes that very second" (96-97).

God incarnates Himself from time to time for the redemption of pious souls, for diffusing the light of religion, for the suppression of Evil through the destruction of Evildoers and for infusing love and piety among the people through manifestation of His divine sports on the earth. Vasu plans to kill Kumar, the temple elephant, but he is found dead, the next morning, from concussion in a mysterious way. Vasu's mistress, Rangi, solves the mystery of his death. According to her, Vasu himself was responsible for his death. While trying to kill a mosquito settled on his forehead, he slapped it with all his might and killed himself. Sastri's remark is that Vasu's fist was meant to batter thick panels of teak and iron. He never hit anyone, in spite of any provocation, because "he had to conserve all that might for his own destruction" (242). Vasu is the modern counter-part of demon Bhasmasura. Both of them are killed at last by the strange powers of their own hands for their unethical, immoral and anti-traditional conduct and character. The novelist seems to show here that even in the modern age, there are Bhasmasuras like Vasu heading towards self-destruction for their evil deeds. Sastri says philosophically: "Every demon carries within him, unknown to himself, a tiny seed of self-destruction, that goes up in thin air at the most unexpected moment. Otherwise what is to happen to humanity?" (242).

Allusion to the ancient Ganga-Santhanu myth mentioned in the Mahabharata, is found in the novel, *The Painter of Signs* to present a similar context but with a slight difference in the ways and motives of characters. Raman, the painter of signs, proposes to marry Daisy, an officer of the Family Planning Centre, but Daisy accepts his marriage proposal on two conditions (as against one lay down by Ganga in the epic): "One that they should have no children, and two, if by mischance one was born, she would give the child away and keept herself free to pursue her social work.... If you want to marry me, you must leave me to my own plans even when I am a wife. On any day you question why or how, I will leave you" (158-59). Raman, like King Santhanu, promises neither to interfere with her duties nor to question her activities. In addition to other concepts, the novelist intends to place the selfless duty to humanity above worldly pleasures. Thus, it is found that through the allusions to the epics and puranas, the novelist juxtaposes antiquity and contemporaneity to show, in M.K. Naik's terms, "how the basic imperatives of the human conditions remain the same, in spite of differences in time, place, milieu and even the plane of existence" (88). Though it amounts to the conservatism of people's thought, it undoubtedly shows their devotion to the ancient Indian culture and tradition.

Religion is deep-rooted in Indian life. Indian writers view it from different angles according to their tastes and temperaments. Anand, the Marxist, does not believe in traditional religion and the concepts associated with it such as orthodoxy, superstition and fatalism which, in his opinion, are the hindrances in the way of human progress. Even then, the peasant community has deep-seated faith in the age-old philosophy of *Karma*. Krishna's mother in *Seven Summers* shows her faith in all religions. She yields to all kinds of superstitious beliefs. There are numerous examples to show that his minor characters have faith in religion, orthodoxy and fate. Though the novelist makes them objects of ridicule, he seems to admit that religion, orthodoxy and fatalism are the integral parts of Indian life. R.K. Narayan and Raja Rao, who believe in Indian religion, scriptures and culture and old values of life show in their novels that religion and its constituent parts can't be separated from life. Even though they cause conservatism of thought and some kind of inertness, they give a sort of systematic, normal life in Indian social set-up. Chandran's mother is conservative and orthodox in all matters. She performs 'puja' every morning with full faith in the protective power of God as also the people of Kanthapura in Raja Rao have faith in their goddess Kenchamma. There are plenty of examples in Narayan's novels to show the religiosity of characters. Superstition, orthodoxy, fatalism, belief in the theory of 'Karma' and life after death are implied in Indian religion. Swaminathan, though a child, has inherent superstitious belief in the benevolence of God and in His power to turn the impossible into possible. Also, Margayya, in *The Financial Expert*, worships goddess Luxmi for becoming rich overnight and for this he undergoes a penance for forty days. When Savitri, in *The Dark Room*, steps down the river, her conscience pricks because she has talked back to her husband and disobeyed him for which she may be punished by Yama in the Other World. She thinks: "In Yama's world the cauldron must be ready for me for the sin of talking back to a husband and disobeying him" (121). Malthi's father, D.W. Krishan Iyer (*The Bachelor of Arts*) says that the marriage between Malathi and Chandran is not possible because their horoscopes do not tally. In his letter to Chandran's father, he writes: "...I have known from experience that the marriage of couples ill-matched in the stars often leads to misfortune and even tragedy" (86). Valan and other villagers (*The Guide*) are of the view that a Saint is capable of curing a man of any disease as he has supernatural power for this. They also believe that Raju the saint (or pseudo saint) can do miraculous deed for saving the village from draught and famine. Ravi's mother in *Mr. Sampath* is highly superstitious. When Ravi goes mad because of his failure and frustration in love for Shanti, she thinks that he is possessed by some ghost. She believes that exorcising can surely restore him to his normal state. The adherence of the people of Malgudi to the commonly accepted theological or religious doctrines shows their orthodoxy on one hand and their traditionalism on the other. When Srinivas picks up his toothbrush and unscrews the toothpaste top, the old man (his house owner) remarks: "What is the world coming to? Everybody has taken a fancy to their toothbrushes; they are made of pig's tail. Why should we orthodox, pure Aryans go in these things? Have you ever tried Margosa or banyan twigs? They are the best and they were not fools who wrote about them in the Shashtras" (51). As mentioned earlier, Raju's mother and Raman's aunt are highly orthodox in their ways of life. Like them, Jagan is against his son's immoral life with Grace. He is haunted by the thought that his pious ancestral house has become polluted. This is why he makes desperate attempts to save himself from moral pollution by locking the connecting door to the room of Mali and Grace. Moreover, he is very dogmatic. He uses shoes made out of the hides of animals that have died natural death.

According to Indian religion and philosophy, *Karma* and fate play important roles in human life. Though these concepts appear to be inter-dependent, it is an established belief that in this *Karmabhumi*, fate is determined by *Karma*. As you sow, so shall you reap—is a universally accepted proverb. The exponents of the theory of *Karma* hold the view that the present existence of an individual is the effect of the past and its future would be the effect of its present existence. After wandering for eight months, Chandran comes home and marries Susila, the girl of his parents' choice, instead of Malathi. Chandran's mother says: "You can marry only the person whom you are destined to marry and at the appointed time. When the time comes let her be the ugliest girl, she will look all right to the destined eye" (158). She means to say that the marriage and its time are already settled in heaven. It is only performed on the earth. Nobody can go against what is allotted by destiny. Raju attempts several possible explanations for the movements of events in his life. What he says with a painful self-awareness shows his faith in pre-ordained fate: "It is written on the brow of some that they shall not be left alone. I am such one..." (49).

Savitri and Rosie also believe in *Karmic* laws, according to which, everyone has to bear the consequence of his/her deeds. They think that they have led a religious life and they have not deliberately committed any sin, so they will not be punished in the other world. This shows their staunch faith in the theory of 'Karma'. When Raju in *The Guide* is arrested on charge of forgery, Rosie (Nalini) tells him: "I felt all along, you were not doing right things. This is 'Karma' what can we do?" (193).

Joys and sorrows, rewards and punishments are the results of one's deeds done in the past. The 'Karmas' of human beings influence, control and condition their lives. Every action, good or bad, has its reaction. This is shown also by the narrator in Raja Rao's novel, *The Chess Master and His Moves*.

R.K. Narayan stands contrasted against M.R. Anand in his view of life and death. Anand, the anti-traditionalist, is of the view that there is only one vast universe with man, woman and other living beings. There are no two worlds, heaven above and the earth below. There is no spiritual world separate from the material world. The soul is the body and the body is the soul. But Narayan, who believes in ancient religion and philosophy, has an altogether different view of life and death. He says: "Perhaps death may not be the end of everything as it seems, personality may have other structures and other planes of existence, and the decay of the physical body through disease and senility may mean nothing more than a change of vehicle" (*My Days,* 146-47). This clearly shows his faith in the immortality of the soul as well as in life after death. This concept is found in *The Geeta*, in which Lord Krishna says that as after rejecting worn out clothes, a man takes up new ones, likewise after rejecting worn out bodies, the embodied one (soul) unites with a new one. Narayan's faith in life after death is quite obvious in his novel *The English Teacher*, in which Krishna succeeds in establishing spiritual contact with the sprit of his dead wife through occultism. Though she does not present herself physically, he feels her presence and talks to her. He comes to know from her the nature and meaning of life and death. In answer to one of his questions, she replies: "ours is also a life of aspiration, striving and joy. A considerable portion of our state is taken up in meditation and our greatest ecstasy is feeling the Divine Light flooding us" (158). Her spirit gives a detailed description of the spiritual world and shows how it differs from the material world. Krishna is fully convinced of the existence of life after death in some form or the other. It appears that Narayan also has a unique communication with the spirit of his dead wife. Though it seems to be very surprising, it has helped him very much. Narayan himself says: "His outlook may be unscientific, but it has helped me survive the death of my wife" (*My Days,* 135).

In addition to this, Savitri's fear of torture in the Other World and other philosophical musings of other characters on life, in Narayan's novels, confirm their belief in life after death. The comments of Srinivas on the derangement of Ravi's mind show his faith in a series of births. When the tiger (Raja), in *A Tiger for Malgudi*, describes the sufferings of his imprisoned life in the cage of circus, the Master comments: "You probably in a previous life enjoyed putting your fellow beings behind bars. One has to face the reaction of every act, if not in the same life, at least in another life or series of lives. There can be no escape from it" (42). This shows the Master's faith not only in present and previous lives but also in the 'Karma' which affects, and shapes life in general. There are numerous examples in Narayan's novels to show that the people of Malgudi have firm faith in religion, orthodoxy, superstition, life after death and *Karmic* laws which they have inherited also from their ancestors. In fact, almost all of his novels present, in Graham Greene's words, "a strong framework of social convention with which the author sympathises but which he does not share.... But the life of Malgudi...proceeds in exactly the same way as it has done for centuries" (vii). "The institution of sanyasa or the renunciation of worldly goods and attachment," says Luxmi Holmstrom, "is an ideal that remains constant in Narayan's novels" (72). According to the Hindu religion, there are four stages or 'Ashrams' of life—Brahmcharya, Garhasthya, Vanaprastha and Sanyasa (asceticism). It is only after passing through the first three stages that one can enter into 'Sanyasa' successfully.

Sanyasa, as an ideal of ancient Indian life, is very difficult if not impossible. The spiritual motive behind 'Sanyasa' is the attainment of the salvation of soul through meditation on God as well as self-purification by renouncing material goods, worldly relationship and attachment. But it is found that the characters in Narayan's novels choose this state with different motives.

When Chandran fails to marry Malathi only because their horoscopes do not match, he renounces his home and family and accepts 'Sanyasa'. But his renunciation or 'Sanyasa' is in protest against the traditional norms as also in frustration with life. As the novelist says, it is "a revenge on society, circumstances, and perhaps, too, on destiny" (108). Thus, his renunciation or 'Sanyasa' lacks the inherent spiritual motive. Moreover, he takes to 'Sanyasa' without passing through the prior stages of life and hence it is premature. This is why he fails as a 'sanyasi'.

Likewise, Raju's mother, Jagan and Raman's aunt leave their homes in opposition to the anti-traditional, unethical ways of life of Raju, Mali and Raman, respectively. But they don't appear to renounce the world willingly in order to attain the salvation of soul, which is the only spiritual aim of renunciation or 'Sanyasa'. But in *A Tiger for Malgudi*, a tiger and his Master, after passing through different 'ashramas' or stages of life, accept sanyasa at last in the usual, conventional manner of ancient Indian 'Sanyasis' (ascetics).

The tiger realizes that deep within him is not different from human beings. When the people of Malgudi are terror-struck at the sight of the tiger, a hermit tells them: "You need not fear; he has only the apperance of a tiger, but he is not one—inside he is not different from you and me" (126). Hence, there is nothing surprising that he accepts sanyasa later on. He has human understanding of life and its problems. Though he is fifteen, he is over seventy years in human terms. So the hermit advises him to give up his violent nature and start a new life in an altogether different manner. Subdued by the spiritual power of the hermit, the tiger comes out of the room and follows him wherever he goes. He baptizes the tiger as Raja and accepts him as his spiritual disciple while Raja accepts him as his Master. The Master initiates him into renunciation and asceticism. The spiritual teachings of the Master bring about a complete change in the life of Raja who renounces his wild life. Gradually, he begins to feel lighter at heart and his physical state becomes secondary. He finds this phase of life quite elevating. Thus, he becomes a real ascetic spending long hours in his quiet corner behind the shrub. He prefers to go without food. In course of time, Raja and his Master grow too old to do anything. The Master realizes that the time for his 'Samadhi' is near. This novel, thus, gives the traditional Indian philosophy of *sanyasa* (asceticism) leading to the salvation of soul from the bondage of body. Also Raja Rao in his novel, *The Cat and Shakespeare*, deals with this traditional philosophy of life in a symbolical way.

Thus, traditionalism, in its varied forms, pervades almost all of Narayan's novels. It promotes blind acceptance of the traditional values of life. Though, in a sense, it amounts to the philosophy of status quo, it gives a homogenous, systematic life. Moreover, Narayan does not appear to support passivity as it is found that his characters are actively engaged in their struggles for existence. His concept of *sanyasa*, slightly different from the *Upanishadic Sanyasa*, is conditioned by selfless duty (*Niskam-Karma-Yoga*). Religion, no doubt makes people orthodox, superstitious, fatalist, etc., but it gives moral strength to human being in miseries and enables them to take a calm view of life. The theory of *Karma*, which is supposed to mould human fate, makes people virtuous and conscientious by injecting moral scruples in them: "Abhor to that which is evil, cleave to that which is good" (*New Testament*).

Works Cited

AIR Interview on September 8, 1961. Published in *Miscellany*. Writer's Workshop No. 8 (1961).

Green, Graham. "Introduction". *The Financial Expert.* Mysore: Indian Thought Publications, 1989.

Holmstrom, Lakshmi. *The Novels of R.K. Narayan.* Calcutta: Writers Workshop, 1973.

Iyengar, K.R.S. *Indian Writing in English* (Oriental University Press, Printed in India).

Krishnaswami, Santha. *The Woman in Indian Fiction in English.* New Delhi: Ashish, 1984.

Naik, M.K. *The Ironic Vision.* New Delhi, Sterling, 1983.

Narayan, R.K. *A Tiger for Malgudi.* London: Penguin Books, 1983.

———. *The Bachelor of Arts.* Mysore: Indian Thought Publications, 1987.

———. *The Dark Room.* Mysore: Indian Thought Publications, 1988.

———. *The English Teacher.* Mysore: Indian Thought Publications, 1989.

———. *The Financial Expert.* Mysore: Indian Thought Publications, 1989.

———. *The Guide.* Mysore: Indian Thought Publications, 1985.

———. *The Man-Eater of Malgudi.* Mysore: Indian Thought Publications, 1988.

———. *The Painter of Signs*. Mysore: Indian Thought Publications, 1986.

———. *Mr. Sampath*. Mysore: Indian Thought Publications, 1986.

———. *My Days: A Memoir*. Mysore: Indian Thought Publications, 1975.

11

R.K. Narayan's *Swami and Friends* and *The World of Nagaraj*: A Re-Reading in Colonial and Postcolonial Contexts

Yakaiah Kathy

The word 'colony' offers a different meaning. The *Oxford English Dictionary* (*OED*) denotes that the fourteenth-century word, 'colony', derived from the Latin *'colonus'*, meaning farmer, cultivator, planter, or settler in a new country, was used to describe the Roman Settlements during the fourteenth century. It was used in the sense of farm and landed Estate. Roman colonia stands for the settlement of Roman citizens who obtained lands in the new place, and worked as soldiers in their period. Later, the term 'colonial', according to the *OED*, refers to the 'belonging to or relating to a colony, or particularly, the British colonies.' The present paper focuses on R.K. Narayan's *Swami and Friends* and *The World of Nagaraj* with special reference to the colonial and postcolonial contexts.

Narayan's *Swami and Friends* is written in the pre-independence India. He explores the events and experiences in the genre of autobiography: "The story of a person's life written by him or herself. Autobiographical writing embraces a number of forms including memoirs, Diaries, and Letters, but the form proper usually involves the interaction of character and external event over a substantial span of a personnel's life" (Quinn, 43). The genre of novel offers the strong perseverance of the novelist in the fictional writing in English. However, it is succinctly the persistence of the authorial shadow that imparts a special sounding to such writings as D.H. Lawrence's *Sons and Lovers* or James Joyce's *Portrait of the Artist as a Young Man*. *Swami and Friends*, in Narayan's own words, grew out of "the urchin days at Ammani" (Mehta, 74), the boyhood days spent in his grandmother's home. The impression would be conveyed by "the way the story is written, by the kind of details, by the value placed on certain events, very unimportant events often" (Rubin, 399). The novel, however, invites criticism for being an autobiographical one. This is a continuing mode of prevailing certain writings over others and expresses the hope for the eventual development of "form of a fiction which would not be limited by the figure of the author" (Foucault, 729).

Narayan explores the ill-effects of colonialism and racism. Thus, the postcolonial critique of colonialism, that we see in literature from the independent nations, is anticipated in Narayan's work. In *Swami and Friends*, the scripture teacher, Ebenezar is projected by Narayan as a 'fanatic,' who criticizes Hinduism: "Oh, wretched idiots! The teacher said...why do you worship, dirty wooden idols and stone images? What did your gods when Mohammed of Gazini smashed them to pieces trod upon them and construed out of them steps for his lavatory if those idols and images had life, why did they not party Muhammad's onslaughts" (4). Ebenezar further extols the virtues of Christianity and asks: "Did our Jesus go gadding about with dancing girls like your Krishna? Did our Jesus go about stealing butter like that arch scoundrel Krishna?" (4). All this proves too much for Swami, who, then asks why Jesus was crucified and "if he was god, why did he eat flesh and fish, and drink wine" (4). In response to the question, Ebenezar simply goes on wrenching his ear. The novelist presents the unbearable humiliation meted out to the student in the Indian classroom. Swami's father writes a letter to the headmaster:

> Sir,
>
> I beg to inform you that my son Swaminnathan of their first Form, A section, was assaulted by his scripture

> master yesterday in a fanatical rage. I hear that he is always most insulting and provoking in his references to the Hindu religion. It is bound to have a bad effect upon the boys. This is not the place for me to dwell upon the necessity for toleration in these matters. (5)

Narayan shows how colonialism suppresses the natives' belief system, as a preliminary moment to spread Christianity in the country.

The novel was published in 1930s. The novelist perpetuates the pre-independent incidents such as the Indian Freedom Movement, Quit India Moment, Non-Cooperation Moment, Salt Satyagraha, etc. The novelist also shows the colossal damage done to the Indian culture and tradition. All these inhuman activities lead the irrepressible rebellions against their rules by opposing the foreign clothes and caps. Some of the boys, wearing Gandhi caps, go around the places asking people to burn the foreign clothes and dressing. Swaminathan, the main character looks up cloth discreetly. Somebody asks him:

> "Young man do you want our country to remain in eternal slavery."
> "No, No", Swaminathan replied
> But you wearing foreign cap."
> "Oh I didn't notice he said and
> Removing his cap flung it into the fire with a feeling that
> He was saving the country." (112)

During the agitation, the group arrives near 'Board High School' where the classes are in progress. A spokesman of the crowd says to the headmaster: "Sir, we are not here to create a disturbance. We only want you to close the school. It is imperative. Our leader is in goal. Our motherland is in the throes of war" (115). The moment the headmaster denies, the mob intrudes into the school and damages the furniture of the missionary school. Later, they continue their procession towards the Market Road where the spokesperson addresses the gathering:

> We are three hundred and thirty six millions, and our land is as big as Europe mines Russian. England is no

> longer bigger than our Madras presidency and is inhibited by a handful of white rogues and is thousands of miles of away. Yet we bow in homage before the English man! Why are we become, through no fault of our own, docile and timid! Let every Indian spit on England, and the quality of saliva will be enough to drown England.... (95)

The police reach the square immediately so as to disperse the mob. The superintendent of police threatens the mob to leave the place. The mob ignores the order of superintendent and then the police rush into the crowd and starts beating up everybody inhumanly. The protagonist, Swaminathan shrieks: "Don't kill me I know nothing" (118). One of the policemen runs after Swami and catches him by his hair and asks, "What business have you here?" (118).

The following day, the headmaster surveys the class for a few minutes and asks: "Are you not ashamed to come and sit there after what you did yesterday" (121) and he goes on reading out the names of the students who participated in the protest by quitting the classes. However, each student comes up with something to escape from the situation. Swaminathan, however, has a different excuse: "No-no I was stoned. I tried to come but they took away my cap and burnt it. Many strong men held me down when I tried to come...when a great man is sent to goal.... I am surprised to see you a slave of the Englishmen. Didn't they cut off-Dacca Muslim slaves of slaves" (123). Narayan shows callous attitude of the English towards the Indian students in educational institutions:

> "Hello, blockhead, how are you going to waste your vacation?"
> "I am going to sleep, sir,"
> Mani said, winkling at his friends
> "Are you likely to improve your head by
> the time you return to the school?
> How it is possible, sir,
> Unless you cut off Sankar's head and present it to me? (73)

Narayan showcases the quintessential aspect with regard to the colonial controversies. The novelist pictures the series of events and incidents that are faced by the principal character. At the end of the novel, the protagonist's life remains in a nostalgic mode due to his friend Rajam who suddenly departs from him because of the promotion of his father who is a policeman. In the depiction of Swami's indulgence in the nationalist movement, "we are slaves of slaves..." (93); it is the narrative voice speaking; but next focus is on Swami's own reactions "the persons who cut off Dacca Muslim..." (105).

This section deals with the postcolonial aspect in *The World of Nagaraj*, written in the 1980s and published in 1990. It portrays the postcolonial counterpoint in response to his first novel. It examines the postcolonial influences on people in the city of Malgudi where things have changed in all realms: "We are about twenty unrelated families in Kabir street, each having inherited a huge rambling house stretching from the street to the river at the back. All that one did was to lounge on the pyol, watch the street, and wait for the harvest from our village lands and cash from the tenants" (14).

Narayan shows an archetypal south Indian village, Malgudi, where things are created and re-created in the novel. The protagonist, Nagaraj, calls upon Kanni's stall at the market corner in order to get the betel nut for his regular life. The journalist is a solicit advisor to Nagaraj who plays an important role in the novel. The painter of signs, Raman, Albert Mission School, Albert Mission College, Varma's Boardless Coffee House and Sambu, all of them extend their cooperation to create the familiar world of Malgudi. The eponymous Nagaraj lives in one of the "huge rambling houses", mentioned by Tim, with his parents and elder brother, Gopu, to be later joined by their spouses, Gopu's wife Charu and Nagaraj's wife Sita. The main character spends most of his life watching and wool gathering which were important activities in his scheme of living. Left to himself, he was prepared to sit on the pyol "the whole day, looking on the life and movement of Kabir street" (7). He is a foil to Gopu—while Gopu has a first class in B.A. degree, but "scraped though with a third class later" (49). After their father's demise, Gopu works hard in the fields, uses modern technology to improve yields and even constructs the gobar gas plant. Nagaraj's reaction to Gopu's agricultural feats is one of the contempt: "Gopu is a rustic who wears a tuft and dabbles in mud and manure on my mind" (55). Nagaraj is given the Kabir street house as his share of the property. But he does not need to do anything; he is content with his wife: "Worry had been a luxury unknown to Nagaraj" (16).

Narayan explores the erosion of Indian traditions and culture with the emergence of postcolonial modernity. It is found in the clothes of the younger generation who wears ubiquitous jeans and T-shirts and how girls cut their hair short and boys wear their long: "What are women coming to these days, ordering men about" (82). The changing time in the 1980s is shown to the reader. The shift is also depicted in the portrayal of Sita, Nagaraj's wife and Saroja, the main character's nephew's wife in connection with playing on the harmonium. Nagaraj contemplates: "No wonder Sita wants it to go on. She herself used to play the harmonium once but had to abandon the dreadful instrument when his mother, who had governed the family with a form hand, advised her that in a crowded family it was unseemly for a girl to isolate herself and practice music" (143). Sita stops playing music, but Saroja does not stop. She too plays and sings at the Kismet club, for which she is paid. Tim says: "Young people of these days are different" (113). The novelist has shown the endeavour of the main character to write about the 'Sage divine', Narada. The kind of two generations—colonial and postcolonial—have thus been shown between *Swami and Friends* and *The World of Nagaraj*.

The central figure experiences travails with the arrival of Nagaraj's nephew, Tim. Later Tim gets married to Saroja. Nagaraj "found his peace disturbed" (93) by Saroja's strong desire for the music practice sessions. The situation gets worse when Tim and Saroja move out to live with them in Kabir Street. The novel recreates the familiar characters, streets and locations and centers on the daily life of the protagonist:

"There is...a disturbance of order—followed by a return, a renewal, a restoration of normalcy" (Iyenger, 301). In this novel, Tim experiences mental agony in terms of pursuing daily duties. Saroja's final 'restoration of normalcy' is reached when Tim and Saroja return to Kabir Street.

Nagaraj's younger brother is not amicable. He is incapable of being a responsible adult. Yet he is a sensitive character. He puts clothes, an "ochre robe", for half an hour everyday and his father calls him a "dreamy" fellow. As the problems come to him, he dons his robe and "retreats into the Puja room, dead for the hour, away from all strife" (43). This is an excuse to escape from the regular disruption of life. But Nagaraj is usually undemanding, and "little anxious and nervous" (37). Nagaraj's family members confront Tim's reasons of reaching home late nights in a state of intoxication by staving off the college education. He is further advised to avoid all irregularities to take up family issues. Nagaraj rehearses his "tone of authority and firmness" (66). Yet he fails to reprimand Tim for his behaviour. He simply looks for excuses to avoid confrontations, either by being a loving and protective uncle who is unable to scold his nephew or by realizing the "unimportance of a direct answer and the peace that comes consequently" (69) during his conflicts with Gopu or Sita. He is, however, very conspicuous to show the kaleidoscopic colours and shapes of the objects of everyday life, like the vegetables in the market and the stationary at Bari's shop that the so-called 'active' and 'worldly' characters miss out on. He also seems to have read literature and is able to quote lines, although on many occasions, he adds humuor in the text. Like a rich aristocrat, Nagaraj's only 'occupation' is his effort to fulfil what he perceives as his mission in life, which is to write "the Magnum Opus":

> A writer's life is a subjective one, and it may not always be feasible for him to discharge his duties completely as a captain steering the ship of family in the ocean of existence (...). However realistic a writer he may be he is likely to prove to be the most dreamy of persons on earth, and the demands of practical life may prove

> bewildering if not actually distressing to him. (Narayan, 182)

Tim and the old librarian at the town hall library suggest that he should "invent stories of Narada" (19), but Nagaraj wants to write something which is authentic. He thinks that it might be a good idea because that is eventually "how the saint's biography grew and became authoritative literature over a range of a million years, each narrator is inventing and adding some stuff. The great stage himself inspiring every story teller in his own way" (117). Narayan contends that even the traditional literature, like the *Puranas*, has grown out of 'invented' stories. The main character wants it in English language to show the world in a significant way. Composing in English language suggests that postcolonial emulations have emerged in the novel.

Similarly, it is also observed that the protagonist has become postmodernist thinker in terms of writing in English to disseminate his ideas throughout the world. English discourse functions either ways. It provides a necessary induction of the Indian mythology for the English people and the Indian educated class. It is directed at the colonized to mitigate their disappointment over the neglect of native systems of knowledge and education. In fact, the main character reminds that where Raja Rao, in his oft quoted Foreword to *Kanthapura* (1938), writes:

> The telling has not been easy. One has to convey in a language that is not one's own the spirit that is one's own [...]. [Y]et English is not really an alien language to us. It is the language of our intellectual make up [...] but not of our emotional make up [...]. We cannot write like the English. We should not. We cannot. We cannot write only as Indians.

Narayan explores the use of classical language in the novel. The protagonist considers a large number of choices in terms of composing his "Magnum Opus". He has to do research to trace out the authentic source, like the *Narada Puran*, that Bari offers to translate for him or the four volumes in Sanskrit on the life of the sage that Kavu pundit gives him. But Nagaraj is not familiar with the Sanskrit language, and moreover, it is known as the 'Deva Bhasha' as Kavu pundit calls it. In "The Problem of the Indian Writer", Narayan points out that Sanskrit is a classical language that is now "often called a 'dead language' but dead only as a mountain could be dead" (97).

Nagaraj is forced to counter ironically Kavu pundit's unacceptable use of English language: "He wanted to blurt out that Sanskrit was a dead language and no one cared" (96), but he also wants to dispute the pundit's using of English as a "mlecha bhasha (outcaste language)" because he "love(s) the language" (97). The Pundit rebukes Nagaraj for being blind and deaf to Sanskrit and advises that Nagaraj should rather "write the fable of the inquisitive monkey who had his balls crushed when he sat on a split log and pulled out the wedge, in any bhasha you please, but leave grand subjects alone" (99). Nagaraj knows that the story of Narada is common: "The story of Narada is known to everyone in our country, even a child knows it. One does not have to be a pundit to talk about Narada. I can do it if sit down and collect all the stories my grandmother told me, while she held me down on her lap coaxing me to swallow the rice forced between my lips" (117).

By writing only in English, Nagaraj wants "to reach the wide world...(he also wants) Narada's personality to be understood universally, irrespective of caste, creed, nationality or religion" and the Talkative man adds "for this purpose English is the right language" (125), but Nagaraj does not accept to get it translated from Kavu pundit, who expects money from Nagaraj for his translation from the ancient classical language. It is an indication of how one has to depend on such crook and unhelpful characters. And the other option is to bank upon the unreliable translations of a person like stationary shop owner, Bari. Narayan remarks of the stories told and retold by a story teller: "The tales have such inexhaustible vitality in them that people like to hear them narrated again and again, and no one has ever been known to remark.... "stop! I've heard that one before.... They are heard or read and pondered over again and again, engendering in the listener an ever-deeping understanding of life, death, and destiny" (97). Nagaraj wants to reach out to the world in English. Narada's personality has to be understood ignoring caste, creed, nationality or religion. Kavu Pundit's dishonesty in accepting money from Nagaraj, without helping to read and translate the Sanskrit text for him, is an indication of how one has to depend on somebody who has no knowledge to read and understand ancient Indian texts written in the classical language.

The narrative technique of the text is connected to the theme of authorship and question of authority, which are self-referential strategy of metafiction. Linda Hutcheon shows that "metafiction today is recognized as a manifestation of postmodernism" (xiii). In his strive to search for authoritative sources on Narada's life, Nagaraj chances on the fact that a Narada temple and a Narada festival, which take place once a year, are to be found in Gotia in Aligarh, Bari's ancestral home. Bari informs Nagaraj that any pundit child in Gotia can give you information of Narada: "He [Sunil], the young attendant in Bari's shop can tell you more stories of Narada that any pundit can" (121). Nagaraj relies on Kavu Pundit to tell him about the details of Narada's life from the Sanskrit volumes that the pundit owns. Since he has not received the required help from the Pundit, Nagaraj changes his mind to take extensive notes from Bari's reading and translation in "broken Tamil and pidgin English" (125) from the *Narad Puran*. Thus, the entire exercise is based on oral information. But Nagaraj's denial of learning Sanskrit language and read the classical authoritative sources for himself and his self-confessed inability "to reduce them [the notes he has collected from Bari's reading] all to a cogent, relevant narrative" (129) eventually lead to his "whole life's aim" (113) being left. At first glance, it would seem only natural that a character like Nagaraj, who is incapable of any serious work, should fail to write on a subject that "had occupied his thoughts all his waking hours for years" (180). The novelist leaves the exact reason for this failure open. The question that arises here is— "why does Nagaraj give on his project?" Is it because of the essential lack in his nature to do anything constructive? Or is it because he chooses a subject that should remain "unchallenged"? Perhaps in his later years, Narayan himself was skeptical of his role as an author. This would very well explain the self-defeating end of the novel.

Narayan's essay titled "History is a Delicate Subject" questions the historical chronicles in a truthful way. He comments firmly in this essay: "I am happy that someone is taking a second look at all history" (183). Elsewhere, he comments: "At some point in one's writing career, one takes a fresh look at the so-called myths and legends and finds a new meaning in them" (Baghmar, 11). This obviously suggests the need to revisit the past. Nagaraj's various attempts to try to find the material on the sage Narada's history engineers Narayan's questioning of the authenticity and accessibility of such classical and mythological texts. They are different stories with regard to Narada's life and Nagaraj wants to 'dispute' the theory about Narada's History that Bari reads out from the *Narada Puran*. We recognize in this the postcolonial thoughts of the writer. The mythological stories of Narada, that are known to all are part of the generally accepted beliefs of the society, have been represented here.

In conclusion, Narayan's *Swami and Friends* and *The World of Nagaraj* are representatives of the colonial and postcolonial contexts. The colonial theme is projected through the colonial experiences of the protagonist who undergoes rapid changes in the process of the colonial life that turns them out metaphorical towards the colonial life from the fixed traditional life. In *The World of Nagaraj,* Nagaraj's great endeavour to write a book on the *Saint* has provided the postcolonial presentation with reference to the writing a book in *Authoritative* language of English.

Works Cited

Baghmar, G.P. "R.K. Narayan: Nagpur." New Delhi: Vishwa Bharti Prakashan, 1992.

Foucault, Michel. "What is an Author?" *Literary Criticism and Theory*. Ed. Robert Con Davis and Laurie Finke. New York: Longmans, 1991.

Hutcheon, Linda. *Narcissitic Narrative: The Metafictional Paradox*. London and New York: Methuen, 1984.

Iyenger, Srinivas. K.R. *Indian Writing in English*. Bombay: Asia Publishing House, 1962.

Mehta, Ved. "Profiles: The Train had Just Arrived at Malgudi Station." *New Yorker*, 38:30 (Sept. 1962).

Narayan, R.K. *A Writer's Nightmare: Selected Essays 1958-1988*. New Delhi: Penguin, 1988.

———. *Talkative Man*. Madras: Indian Thought Publications, 2002.

———. *The Story Tellers World*. New Delhi: Penguin Publications, 2000.

———. *Swami and Friends*. London: OUP, 1935, 1978.

———. *The World of Nagaraj*. London: Heinemann, 1990.

Quinn, Edward. *Literary and Thematic Terms*, New York: Facts on File, Inc. 1932.

Rubin, L.D. "The Self Re-captured." *Kenyan Review*, 25.3 Summer 1963.

Rao, Raja. *Kanthapura*. New Delhi: OUP, 1989.

12

R.K. Narayan and Sarat Chandra Chattopadhyay: A Study in Overlapping Landscapes of the Mind

Indrani Mukherji

Eschewing some basic differences in time and locale, the vision of R.K. Narayan and Sarat Chandra Chattopadhyay, two powerful writers, emerges as a unique amalgam of conservatism and modernity.

A comparative study of some of their significant writings promises to be both fascinating and revelatory. This paper seeks to explore the major thematic considerations of the two writers, vis-à-vis their art of story-telling, non-conformist attitudes, feministic concerns and an ironic over-view of love and marriage, notwithstanding the variance in the moral or purpose that lies behind their oeuvre.

R.K. Narayan (1906-2001), one of the most celebrated Indian novelists writing in English, is immortalized in the fictional South Indian town of Malgudi. This master story-teller managed to capture, in his writings, the essence of ordinary life. Human relationships, more particularly family relationships, constitute a major theme in Narayan's novels as well as his short stories.

Narayan's narratives highlight the social context which is sensitively portrayed through the travesties of everyday life. The subtlety and conviction, with which family relationships are treated, e.g. son and parents, brother and brother in *The Bachelor of Arts*, husband and wife and father and daughter in *The English Teacher*, father and son in *The Financial Expert* and grandmother and grandson in *Waiting for the Mahatma* and the conflicts emerging within the network of these many more complex relationships, make his works stand out as realistic works of art.

Time and again, Narayan has highlighted the problems related to accepted practices, for instance, the plight of students exposed to the rigorous punishment of caning and the associated ignominy focused in *Swami and Friends*; the concept of horoscope-matching in Hindu marriages and the devastating emotional toll on the bride and groom showcased in *The Bachelor of Arts*; the concept of a wife putting up with her husband's torture in *The Dark Room*.

However, though the centrality of Hindu traditionalism asserts itself in a big way in Narayan's work, it is often challenged by the characters who entertain somewhat 'modern' or overtly individualistic values. Interestingly, members of Narayan's prominent protagonists work to resist traditional religious and familial duties and expectations, and later, inadvertently or apparently fortuitously relapse into roles that exemplify the very values or lifestyles which they reject. Although these timeless codes and norms, that have resisted being supplanted by modernity and have retained their capacity to reassert themselves in the daily lives of the characters, seem to triumph in the author's world, what really transpires is a special kind of intervention of 'Indian modernity' into the traditional colonial mindset.

Since the notions of Western modernity and Indian tradition have multiple possibilities and implications, the self-constitution of India's modernity becomes a complex and diverse adventure rather than any simplistic supplanting of tradition with modernity or the revival of tradition at the expense of modernity. Indian modernity is thus neither anti-traditional nor necessarily pro-Western. It is, instead, a subtle interplay of multitudinous forces which are both complimentary and contradictory. Reform, revival, resistance, conflict, collusion, collaboration, capitulation, compromise, adoption, adaptation, synthesis, encapsulation, hybridity, and multiculturalism are all a part of the Indian's experiments in modernization.

Tradition thus reaffirms itself in an unusual, unexpected way; quietly, not stridently. In the struggle between tradition and modernity, tradition wins, not in a robust manner, but in an unassertive, almost inept way—in spite of itself, very reluctantly as it were. Narayan's critique and undermining of modernity are gentle and subtle. The claims and promises of the modern are neither rejected out of hand nor overtly condemned, instead they are often shown to be ineffectual and mistaken.

His take on love and marriage is equally ironic. In the poignant tale of *The Dark Room*, conservatism and reform are contrasted with the quiet irony and subtle humour which have become so characteristic of R.K. Narayan. The author has beautifully crafted the marital saga of a couple interspersed with conservatism along with the dawn of reformist ideas. The novel epitomizes Savitri's revolt against her husband's inhuman nature. She would always sulk there, sometimes for days, feeling helpless at her sordid state and for being treated like dirt by him. Her return to her family and her succumbing to the male-dominated society are viewed with an ironic perspective. At the experiential level, it is a clash of the traditional and the 'liberated' woman, but conceptually, it is a reflection on the age-old familial demands of the Indian society tightening its noose round the solitary rebellious woman.

The female protagonists in Narayan's novels voice his strong feminist concerns. From Savitri in *The Dark Room* (1938) to Bala in *Grandmother's Tale* (1992), the women in his works grow stronger, and gradually, evolve as independent, bold, assertive and self-reliant characters. Rosie, in *The Guide*, depicts a romantic and artistic spirit that is restless and thirsting for fulfillment. When Rosie confesses to Raju: "I'd have preferred any kind of mother-in-law, if it had meant one real live husband", she echoes the sentiments of an empowered woman, a unique combination of the values of tradition and modernity. The fact that Narayan could conceptualize the idea of a live-in relationship outside marriage in a conservative society is itself a bold projection of his unconventional and non-conformist ideas.

When Savitri laments for not being educated, she realizes the misery of her dependent position and rightly observes: "If I had gone to a college and studied, I might have become a teacher or something. It was very foolish of me not to have gone on with my education". She yearns to give her daughters the light of education so that they become self-reliant and independent. Savitri further aspires to make her daughters study up to B.A. so that they need not seek their salvation in marriage. Her aspiration does not stop here. She thinks resolutely: "Yes Kamala and Sumati must take their university course and become independent". Narayan has clearly voiced Savitri's predicament in these lines, where she thinks that her two daughters should receive not just graduation degrees but should also pursue their education further. In 1938, which incidentally was the year of publication of this novel, a woman aspiring to take up a postgraduate degree was a rare phenomenon. Very few elite women stepped out of their comfort zones to access higher education.

In his classic novel, *The Guide* (1958), too, Narayan presents Rosie as an educated and ambitious woman who is a postgraduate in Economics. Rosie's mother, who belongs to the devdasi family, does not want her daughter to suffer the same plight of illiteracy, and hence, strives her utmost to help her to gain education. Incidentally, Marco marries Rosie because she is an educated woman which, in turn, helps to elevate her status in the society.

Daisy is yet another female protagonist in the novel *The Painter of Signs* (1976), who aspires for education and a career. She is a Family Planning Officer and dedicates her life for the cause of population control. Sarasa, in *Talkative Man* (1986), is portrayed as an educated and career woman, who is bold and assertive. Bala, in *Grandmother's Tale*, thinks on the same lines as does Savitri. Narayan, in his fiction, starting from *The Dark Room* in 1938 to his last novel *Grandmother's Tale* in 1992, thus, presents women characters who yearn for education. Therefore, we find Narayan to be an advocate of women's education and he truly subscribes to this progressive outlook which is reflected in his fiction quite evidently. Time and again, Narayan shows that education is a prerequisite for a woman to become bold, assertive, strong and independent. His women characters are not just submissive and dependent women, who are merely appendages to men. Realizing that education helps to bring awareness among women about their rights and duties, which eventually leads to their empowerment, Narayan has, from the very beginning of his novelistic career, created strong characters like Savitri, Bharati, Rosie, Daisy, Sarasa and Bala, who recognize the importance of women's education and work doggedly in this direction to reach their goal in life. He uses these women protagonists as his mouthpieces to express his modernistic outlook.

The encounter between the holy man and the semi-Westernized family of the New Extension of Malgudi in *The Bachelor of Arts* is, in a way, an encounter between ancient and modern India. The modern has reverence for the ancient, the ancient cannot ignore the modern, but they hardly understand each other. The law protecting private property and the holy man with his belief in his right of access to others' houses and gardens exist side by side in Malgudi, an epitome of modern India, without coming into confrontation.

Teeming with as diverse a group as tragic shopkeepers, ethical pickpockets, mean beggars, storytellers, anxious college students and the Talkative Man, Narayan's world is peopled with characters, each with distinctive traits, making the situation as familiar to the reader as the immediate neighbourhood. Each of his short stories, be it "An Astrologer's Day" or the poignant "Forty-Five a Month", leaves an indelible impression on the readers' mind. By the delicate use of sympathetically observed details, the author establishes a world as real as his own.

Sarat Chandra Chattopadhyay (1876-1938) was arguably the most popular Bengali writer in the first half of the 20th century. Bengali novel originated from Bankim Chandra,

Tagore modernized it and Sarat Chandra set the trends of realism and protest in it. Some of Sarat Chandra's stories are very striking for their obvious sincerity and basic realism. These include "Bindur Chhele" (Bindu's Son, 1913), "Ramer Sumati" (Ram Returning to Sanity, 1914), "Araksanya" (The Girl Whose Marriage is Overdue, 1916), etc. His last complete novel *Ses Prasna* (*The Final Question*, 1931) is an attempt at the 'intellectual' novel where the meager theme is inflated by high brow talks on problems of the individual and of the society relating principally to love and marriage.

Sarat Chandra, who had woven magic with his words and some unputdownable series of writings, struck a chord with the basic human concerns. His simple, spontaneous and unsanskritized vocabulary came as refreshing change for the readers, from the tradition of that time. He breathed new life into the rural Bengal and gave it an identity of its own. His works have a rural essence as they are centred round simple day-to-day life-stories of the families, living far away from the humdrum of cities in the tranquility of nature.

His novels and short-stories appealed to people of all walks of life. His mastery on this branch of the Bengali literature was so complete that it is not at all surprising to note that remaining under the full glare of Tagore's creative genius, Sarat Chandra was never to be influenced by it. On the contrary, Tagore had been so moved by his stories that even he could not resist from the occasional forays into the latter's familiar territory. The novels of Sarat Chandra explore the varied, often slippery and treacherous, terrains that love takes people into. Steering clear of clichéd language and banal or maudlin situations, he could weave amazingly powerful themes into his stories. The strength of his imagination, the fusion of the story with the superb art of its telling, the structure and deeply drawn characters speak volumes of his creative skill. His novels not only deal with the different faces of love, but also the pain that comes with betrayal.

In *Charitraheen* (*Characterless*), Sarat Chandra treated the theme of love from an entirely new angle, showing supreme indifference to conventional morality, and the effect of this book on the Bengali public was shocking. The novel deals with a love-episode between an educated young man of middle-class family and a maid servant in a boarding house where the young man used to live. No other Bengali writer had up till then dared to portray the character of a 'low-class' woman from this standpoint. Bankim Chandra, in his famous novel *Krishnakanta's Will,* had dealt with the love of a handsome Zamindar youth for a beautiful widow, but the story ends in the murder of the woman in vindication of conventional morality. In this novel, Sarat Chandra portrayed Sabitri who, in the light of the then social prejudices, mental make-up and religion-oriented morality, would appear to be no better than a fallen woman and a mere degraded maid-servant. In fact, Sarat Chandra wanted to rouse a strong urge for social revolution by generating pain, anguish and a feeling of want in the minds of readers—leading to a yearning for higher values of life.

In his next novel, *Devadas*, a youth is found to be led astray by the failure of his early love, taking to wine and women. Parbati (who can easily be taken as the counterpart of Rosie in R.K. Narayan's *The Guide*), is the object of the love of Devadas, who did not forget him even after she had been married to another man. Such affairs exist in real life, but their portrayal in literature was forbidden until Sarat Chandra broke this law. It was impossible to find fault with his work simply on account of his attitude of all-pervading sympathy with the fallen, all social victims or rebels.

Sarat Chandra is at his best in his masterpiece, *Srikanta*. Many consider it to be his autobiography, but it is a peculiar combination of biography and fiction. In Part Four of *Srikanta*, Rajlakshmi once tells Srikanta: "Would I be having you for naught without paying a price—having no obligation to fulfil—am I not to reciprocate? That I came in your life truly—shall I not leave behind an imprint? When I depart, shall I go barren like this? No, never". These suggestive lines reveal the writer's superb artistic expression of love. In the Third Part of *Srikanta*, in which the construction of a railway track is described, the spontaneous indignation, with which Srikanta bursts out on observing the wretched condition of the workers with whom he had to spend a night in the slum, reflects not just humanist thinking, but something more—a higher thought and culture. For example, seeing the subhuman and distressed condition of the workers, Srikanta says: "But, you, the bearers of modern civilization, you are dying, you die! Forgive not, in the least, this cruel civilization that has made your life such. If you are to carry it, carry it down speedily to the abysmal depth of its grave".

His novel *Pallisamaj* (*Village Society*) attracted a great deal of notice. It gave a true and vivid account of life in the villages, with its petty jealousies and ignorance, superstitions and prejudices. With his narrative skill, Sarat Chandra spun a love-drama around two beautiful souls against the background of village cruelty. Ramesh, the hero, was a bachelor, but Rama, the heroine was a widow, although she had almost no memory of the man whom she was married to. But Hindu society has no solution for this apparent maladjustment, for widow-remarriage is not the general custom. Sarat Chandra attacked the fabric of this moribund Hindu society and attacked its rigid norms powerfully. This want of a solution for the Ramesh-Rama affair and its consequent loss to society of normal, orderly life, rich in every sense of human progress, moved all readers of the book to thinking. It was claimed to be one of the best productions in Bengali literature and, naturally, ran into many editions like most of his other works. He held women in high esteem and very realistically depicted their plight in a patriarchal society.

In Sarat's work, women are not just submissive and docile, despite being portrayed within the framework of traditional Indian values and depicted as reconciling to the inequities inherent in the tradition, e.g. Annada Didi and Rajalakshmi in *Srikanta,* Parvati and Chandramukhi in *Devdas,* Ma-Shoye in *The Picture* and Bijli Bai in *Light Out of Darkness.*

The powerful rebel female characters of Sarat Chandra realize the inner strength of women, and that how could they be instrumental in ushering in a new era, when women would not be dominated by men, but would be their equal, enjoying the same social status as men. Saratchandra's Parbati, Bijali,

Abhaya, Madhabi, Chandramukhi, Sabitri, Kiranmayi, Kamal, Bindu and Hemangini successfully revolt against the tradition. By depicting such female characters, he has established that in gaining their equal, respectable and dignified status in society, women do not require the help of men. By their inner strength, women are instinctively capable of frustrating all the evil designs of men to subdue them. In his short story "Adhare Alo", the heroine, Bijali is a dancing girl. She daily goes to the river Ganga for a dip, and there she happens to meet one Satyendra; and they fall in love. When Satyendra comes to know that she is a dancing girl, he turns his face away from her. At that time, she does not cry or create a scene, but tells him in a forceful language: "Go, but do not be guilty of not having faith in a fact, which I have, though I am supposed to be guilty. Have faith that God resides in the heart of every human being and He does not leave the body till his death. Might be that in every temple God is not worshipped, yet one cannot deny the fact that God is stationed there. You might not kneel before Him, but at the same time you cannot ignore Him". These extremely powerful words by Bijali set the readers rethinking about the social structure. Thus, in Sarat Chandra's novel, even a dancing girl has a message to give—a message of faith and piety. Bijali is not there to arouse our sympathy, as is usual for female characters in other novels, but to impart a new vision to the readers.

In his novel *Srikanta*, when the hero is in reflective mood, he feels that he has ill-treated Rajlaksmi. He says to himself:

> Man does not consist of his body alone. Piyari is no more. She is dead, but if she has soiled her body once, am I always to look at that black spot with a magnifying glass, and turn away my eyes from her, who stands in front of me with all her brightness and purity, having successfully come out of the fiery ordeal? Am I to evaluate a human being, by the fake standard of the animal residing in me, and not offer even a seat to the Divine in her, which has emerged from her after suffering all the humiliations and ill-treatment and tortures of society? Is it the correct method of evaluating

> a human being? My mind from within replied with all its force: No. No. No.

This view of Srikanta is shared by all the readers of the novel. Due to this spirit of revolt, the female characters defy the social norms and males, like Srikanta, ask for forgiveness for their behaviour. It is for such emancipated views about women that Sarat Chandra endeared himself to readers for freeing them from the age-old misconceptions about women.

Sarat Chandra also made revolutionary changes in the traditional conceptions of good and evil, of morality and immorality, of sin and piousness. He upgraded the women who were considered low and abominable, and he brought out the goodness in them. Analyzing the female characters of his novels, we find that Alaka has discarded all moral values; Parbati loves somebody who is other than her husband, and not only that, she considers her lover as her husband; Saudamini and Kiranmayi are 'unchaste' women who are disloyal to their husbands; Chandramukhi is a dancing girl; Rajlaksmi entertains people who are immoral; Kamal has abandoned her two husbands and is living illegally with a third person. She, like an existentialist, gives more importance to momentary things than to eternal things. Yet, Sarat Chandra has depicted these characters in such a manner that we actually sympathize with them. By highlighting the virtues of his female protagonists, he has elevated them. His male characters are also depicted in such a way that though by strict conventional standards they appear as immoral and low; they manage to evoke the reader's sympathy and compassion. Debdas, who is a drunkard and visits prostitutes, is depicted in such a way that all the readers love him and sympathize with him. Srikanta, who is a vagabond and loves a dancing girl, and also loves a woman like Kamal Lata who has renounced the world, is also depicted in such a manner that he endears himself to the readers. This is so because Sarat Chandra does not evaluate a human being with borrowed ethical standards.

Another remarkble contribution is that he has not limited the motherly love of women to her own children but has widened its horizon to take in others' children and love them as their own, and even more. In many of his novels, female characters come in clash with their kith and kin simply because they love others' children. In his *Ramer Sumati*, Narayani loves her brother-in-law, while all hate him because of his pranks. Because of Ram, she earns displeasure of her mother as well as husband. Hemahgini of "Mejdidi" loves an orphan, who is step brother of her sister-in-law, and when her husband resents, she leaves her husband and returns only on her own terms. Bindu of *Bindur Chhele* comes into conflict with all the members of her family for the sake of the son of her brother-in-law. Thus, Sarat Chandra has given us a glimpse of the vast resources of motherly love which is intrinsic in women.

Sarat Chandra opened new horizons for successive writers. He also showed our writers that there was enough of raw material for the fiction in the day-to-day happenings in the family, and even trifling and insignificant happenings have immense potentialities for a fiction writer. In most of his novels, the incidents are from day to day life of the family. In a way, we can say that his novels depict what happens in a family. *Parinita*, *Baradidi*, *Baikunther Will*, *Ramer Sumati*, *Bindur Chhele*, etc., are family stories. Yet from trifling incidents, he has erected artistic structures.

Like R.K. Narayan, Sarat Chandra shows an intimate knowledge of day-to-day life as lived in middle-class families and in the homes of peasants, boatmen and other village folk. He also shows a deep understanding of all kinds of rogues, mendicants, snake-charmers, wandering actors and singers, fishermen impersonators, astrologers and a host of other fascinating people. He penetrates to the core of social and economic relationships to acquire first-hand knowledge of their customs, rituals, beliefs and experiences.

Sarat Chandra strove to highlight the problems of life by evoking compassion and awakening a sense of deprivation leading to a deep yearning for something noble and great. He sought to inscribe in the minds of the people the loftiest ideas of life by arousing pathos and compassion, working upon the contradictions and conflicts that arise centring round life, the complexities that develop in human relationship and the waves and turmoils that grow in the feelings and emotions of the human mind. In *Pather Dabi*, Sabyasachi says: "There is nothing like realization of absolute or eternal truth in this ever-changing world. It comes into being and goes out of being. With passage of time, from one age to another, it undergoes changes and assumes newer and newer forms in conformity with the changing needs of human society. The truth of the past must be adhered to in the present—such a belief is erroneous, such a notion superstitious". He further remarks: "To me, truth or falsehood, good or bad, are determined only by the necessity of 'Pather Dabi'. This is the creed, the guiding principle of my life. This is my mode of existence, this is what I am, my candid realization. You speak of the ultimate truth, the eternal truth—to you these meaningless, hollow words are inestimably valuable, but there is no greater a trick to befool the ignorants. I never lie, but I create truth at the dictate of necessity".

In the novel *Sesh Prasna*, Sarat Chandra has very beautifully portrayed the concept of the freedom of love. In *Sesh Prasna*, Rajen tells Kamal that he would leave Harendra's 'ashram'. "Because", he says, "I have nothing in common with them, either in views or in method of work; affection and love are the only bonds". Kamal replies, "What could be greater than this, Rajen? When the minds have met, let there be difference of opinion. If views differ or methods of work vary, does it matter much? People can live together only when all would think alike, all would act alike—why should it be so? What is education worth if one cannot respect the views of others?" In reply, Rajen says to Kamal: "You were saying that the ability to respect different ideologies is a great virtue, but do you know who can respect all views and beliefs? Only he who has no belief of his own. Education enables one to silently ignore opposing views, but not to respect those". His contention, here, is that education may enable one to tolerate the opposite views.

Interestingly, we often meet Sarat's characters in very unusual situations. And yet they appear true to life because the author has the artistic skill and the emotional sensitivity to capture the unpredictable element in life and communicate it in a vivid and convincing manner. Similarly, the uncertainty, that Narayan's characters encounter while negotiating the crisis of spirit or circumstances, brings in the element of unpredictability. It is due to his predominant ironic vision that he springs a surprise in his narratives making way for unexpected turn of events. *The Astrologer*, *Engine Trouble* and *The Guide* are just a few examples.

Whether it is through the make-believe village of Malgudi in R.K. Nrayan's narratives or the real and pulsating Bengal in Sarat Chandra's novels, both the writers had the unique ability to connect with the mind of the reader. With their simple and unpretentious style, they could write about the intricacies of Indian society, unfolding at the same time the little ironies and paradoxes of life. The use of nuanced dialogic prose with gentle Tamil and Bengal overtones respectively, have enabled them to get a complete insight into the lives of their characters. The depth of compassionate humanism is unparalleled in their writings. The sacred and the profane blend harmoniously in their works.

Both have brilliantly captured the idiosyncrasies and absurdities of human character so much so that the characteristics of Malgudi and Bengal portrayed in their respective works transcend their geographical boundaries to become universal. Underlying these basic similarities, what comes in the way of distinguishing features is perhaps Narayan's all-pervasive humorous and ironic vision which may be contrasted with the predominantly tragic outlook of Sarat Chandra, who was more of a social reformer deeply committed to the cause of the underprivileged. He strongly wrote against social discrimination, superstitions and injustice that went on in the name of religion.

Works Cited

Devdas in Bengali Text.

Ganguly, Swagato. "Introduction." In Sharat Chandra Chattopadhyay's *Parineeta*. Translated from Bengali into English by Malobika Chaudhuri. New Delhi: Penguin Books, 2005.

Kain, Geoffrey. "Eternal, Insatiable Appetite: The Irony of R.K. Narayan's Baited Hero." *R.K. Narayan: Contemporary Critical Perspectives*. Ed. Geoffrey Kain. East Lansing: Michigan State University Press, 1993. pp. 101-13.

Naik, M.K. *The Ironic Vision: A Study of the Fiction of R.K. Narayan*. New Delhi: Sterling, 1982.

Narasimhaiah, C.D. "R.K. Narayan's *The Guide*." *Aspects of Indian Writing in English*. Ed. M.K. Naik. Delhi: Macmillan, 1979. pp. 172-98.

Naravane, V.S. *Devdas and Other Stories by Saratchandra Chatterji*. New Delhi: Lotus Collection, 1996.

Narayan, R.K. *Swami and Friends*. 1935. New Delhi: OUP, 1983.

———. *The Bachelor of Arts*. 1937. Mysore: Indian Thought Publications, 1985.

———. *The Dark Room*. 1938. New Delhi: Orient Paperbacks, 1982.

———. *The English Teacher*. 1945. Mysore: Indian Thought Publications, 1989.

———. *Waiting for the Mahatma*. 1955. Mysore: Indian Thought Publications, 1969.

Updike, John. Review of *My Days*. *New Yorker* 50 (September 2, 1974). 80-82. Reprinted as "R.K. Narayan: A Writer Immersed in His Material." *SPAN* April 1975. 38-39.

Walsh, William. "The Intricate Alliance: The Novels of R.K. Narayan." *A Review of English Literature*. 2.4 (1961). 91-99.

http://www.hinduonnet.com/thehindu/fr/2002/05/31/stories/2002053100950300.htm

www.penguinbooksindia.com

13

Spiritual Syndrome in the Fictional World of R.K. Narayan

Harcharan Singh Arora

R.K. Narayan (1906-2001) is regarded as one of the best-known Indian English writers who appeared on the Indian literary scene, along with two more stalwarts, namely Mulk Raj Anand and Raja Rao. The Trinity began writing during the freedom struggle soon after the Civil Disobedience Movement of early 1930s. A recipient of *Padma Bhushan* in 1964, the eminent Chennai-born writer of about 14 novels and 6 collections of short stories, R.K. Narayan was awarded *Sahitya Academy Award* in 1960 for his magnum opus *The Guide*. Malugdi, which is only an imaginary town in South India, is to Narayan what Eden Heath was to Thomas Hardy. It is the place where his mind, his heart and his soul lie. This great novelist is considered Anton Chekhov of India because like the great Russian writer, he understood well the weaknesses of his characters. He wrote, with utmost simplicity, about the lives and aspirations of lower-middle class Indians because he himself was a part of it and understood it well. In his fictional world, those who spring to life are—a peon, a vagabond, a teacher, a coolie, a loving father, a beggar, a rickshaw puller, a neglected worker, a pedlar, an astrologer, an attendant and several other homeless, hapless and helpless persons. To a newer generation, honed by trans-continental success of Salman Rushdie, Vikram Seth and Arundhati Rai, he may appear a back number but the fact is that it was R.K. Narayan who stormed the world of letters. The sizable body of work that Narayan has produced has a vivid, complete and graphic picture of the ancient Indian culture, traditions, customs, philosophy and spirituality. To accomplish his purpose, the great novelist, at many places in his fiction, refers to mythological scriptures like *The Bhagvada Gita*, *The Ramayana*, *Panchtantra*, Indian *Vedas* and *Puranas* mentioning gods and goddesses like Gayatri, Saraswati, Lakshmi and Shiva in his writings.

The Guide is the story of Raju, told partly by the omniscient author and partly by the protagonist himself. It deals with the rise and fall of his fortunes as guide, lover impresario and prisoner and then his end as a saint, who is neither born nor made but simply happens almost like the weather. On his release from the prison, Raju stops to rest near an abandoned temple, where a villager named Velan mistakes him for a holy man. He does not want to return in disgrace to his friends in Malgudi and reluctantly assumes the role of a sage—which has been thrust upon him, only to act as a 'Spiritual Advisor' to the innocent people of Mangla village, situated on the banks of the river Sarayu. He is transformed from his role as a tour guide to that of a 'Spiritual Guide', and from a sinner to a saint, though he is never truly a sinner, and never truly a saint. At this point in the novel, there is a role reversal—while the villagers believe that Raju is their Guru, Raju is their disciple; their faith and piety propel Raju to transform himself.

In the novel, we see that he is content with the arrangement until a terrible drought hits the area and, to save face, he is obliged to undertake a twelve-day fast. At this stage in the novel, Raju, hungry and frightened, undergoes a process of inner cleansing, a catharsis; 'morbid' and 'fantastic' thoughts give place to a peculiar Spiritual Strength—"If by avoiding food I should help the trees bloom, and the grass grow, why not do it thoroughly" (237-38)? The inner sea-change is imperceptible but unmistakable: "For the first time in his life he was making an earnest effort, for the first time he was learning the thrill of full application, outside money and love; for the first time he was doing a thing in which he was not personally interested" (237-38). He felt suddenly so enthusiastic that it gave him a new strength to go through the whole ordeal: "When the mirror of understanding is cleansed of the dust of desire, the life of pure consciousness is reflected on it. When all seems lost, light from heaven breaks, enriching our human life more than words can tell."

R.K. Narayan appears to have a message for mankind that from a simple tourist guide, how Raju transcends this life. The novel probably talks of a hope that a criminal, broken, used and depressed person can have, by looking life from another perspective, where all that is past can be reconciled by what is present. The moment Raju stops thinking about himself, he becomes free from all kinds of worldly attachment. He does become the 'Guide', but of a superior mould in the final analysis—the Spiritual Guide of the gullible villagers. He finds himself alienated as the vital links of tradition snap one after another. The moment of self-awareness comes when, after a protracted period of self-deception, Raju re-establishes his bonds with community and tradition. Like Conrad's Jim, he discovers himself in love and sacrifice for others. The painful realization, which Krishnan in *The English Teacher,* had after Susila's death—"a profound and unmitigated loneliness is the only truth of life" (Gilra)—is echoed in Raju's case when he finds himself lonely in the midst of a vast crowd. The great 'Spiritual Loneliness' is caused by an inner emptiness. Raju's scale of life's values had gone awry. He has to right the balance, and he does it by doing a thing in which he was not personally interested. The moment of his sacrifice is the moment of his triumph; the tourist guide ends as a 'Spiritual Guide'.

Raju plays the role of the Swamy to the best possible extent, but once again, he is overtaken by the inexplicable eventualities. Things take a dramatic turn when Velan's brother mistakenly reports that the Swamy will not eat, 'till rains come' instead of 'till they stop fighting' over a matter of selling and buying. Events that follow are beyond Raju's control. He had never imagined that there would arrive a time when the fake *Sanyasi* in him would transform into a genuine one. People take him as a 'holy one' with a Spiritual Power to bring rain to the drought stricken land. At such moments, one realizes that it is 'divinity that shapes our ends.' With the fast, Raju undergoes a Spiritual Transformation. As the fast goes on, his fame spreads. People, by the thousands, come to see him and take his blessings. An American journalist asks him whether he truly believes that his fast would bring rain; he smiles and says: "These people have faith in me, and I have faith in their faith." Upon hearing his fame, Rosie pays him a visit; so do his mother and his friend Gaffur, a Muslim. Bhola does not allow Gaffur to enter the temple because he is of a different religion. Then Raju comes out of the temple and asks Bhola what is his religion. He tells Bhola that humanity, love and helping others is the true religion of a man. Then Bhola begs excuse and sees Gaffoor and Raju hugging each other sentimentally and his eyes also become wet. Raju realizes that now he has everything that he had lost long ago. He transcends himself. His health starts deteriorating and he ponders over the real meaning of his life. Despite grave danger to his health, he continues to fast until he collapses. Amidst thunder, clapping and heavy downpour, his soul departs this earth while the crowd is rejoicing and the beloved ones are crying. The climax of the novel, here, teaches, Bhagvad Gita's principle: "Man does not die, it is only body which dies. Soul remains forever" (*The Gita*, 2.20).

He went down the steps of the river, halting for breath on each step, and finally reached his basin of water. He stepped into it, shut his eyes and turned towards the mountain, his lips muttering the prayer. Velan and another held him each by an arm. The morning sun was out by now; a great shaft of light illuminated the surroundings. It was difficult to hold Raju on his feet, as he had a tendency to flop down. They held him as if he were a baby. Raju opened his eyes, looked about, and said, "Velan, it's raining in the hills. I can feel it coming up under my feet, up my legs—and with that he sagged down".

The English Teacher has psychological insight, spiritual depth and practical wisdom of R.K. Narayan. It records the personal experiences of the novelist who is unable to come to terms with life after the death of his beloved wife, Rajam. The novel is psychic and mystic and also a spiritual study of human mind. It starts as an interesting novel of domestic fidelity but gets bogged down in spiritual things and philosophic discussions which, many a time, tax the patience of the reader. Not only had writer's own wife died under circumstances very similar to those in which the narrator's wife contracted typhoid and died in *The English Teacher,* but the eerie communication with her beyond the grave, Narayan affirmed, occurred in real life as well:

> More than any other book (of mine), *The English Teacher* is autobiographical in content, very little part of it being fiction.... Krishnan, is a fictional character in the fictional city of Malgudi; but he goes through the same experience I had gone through, and he calls his wife Susila (instead of Rajam) and the child is Leela instead of Hema. (*My Days*, 135)

No wonder, many Western readers and critics, and probably some Indians too, have special problems while going through the second half of the novel which takes us to unfamiliar regions and which is incredibly spiritualist with its supernatural elements. The whole book goes to show his steady spiritual faith and practice of those traditions that others may have wished to discard in the name of modernity. The novel is "an attempt to look steadily at death and see if there is anything beyond" (Gilra, 57). Krishnan's final contact with his wife's soul may appear as improbable and incredible to a critical mind. But it is surprisingly authentic in an occult-cum-spiritual sense. At least, with a willing suspension of disbelief, we are made aware of an unknown plane of being. As for Krishnan, "life has taught him a little, but death has taught him more, and he has reasons to be grateful to life and death" (Gilra, 60). Narayan writes about the reactions of his readers to the supernatural, the occult dimension of the second half of the novel: "That book falls into two parts, one is domestic and the other half is "spiritual"...psychic experience seemed to have become a part of my normal life and thought...for some years, almost every night,...gradually...the interest diminished when I began to feel satisfied that I had attained an understanding of life and death" (*My Days*, 146-47).

The central theme of the novel is obviously the 'death' of Susila in the first half and her 'resurrection' in the second half. Here we see resurrection greater than life itself—Paradise Lost being followed by Paradise Regained. Krishnan loses Susila in the flesh, but on the last page of the novel, she comes back to him, to be with him forever. He has resigned his post as lecturer in the college to become a teacher of children under the idealistic 'headmaster'. Albert Mission College arranges a farewell party, and Krishnan returns home with a jasmine garland. He reflects sadly on the way that there is no Susila at home to receive the garland. Back in his lonely room, he cries in an access of despair:

> I softly called "Susila! Susila, my wife..." I fell into a drowse, whispering, "My wife, wife." How long? How could I say? When I opened my eyes again she was sitting on my bed looking at me with an extraordinary smile in her eyes.
>
> "Susila! Susila!" I cried. "You here!" "Yes, I'm here, have always been here." I sat up leaning on my pillow. "Why do you disturb yourself?" she asked.
>
> "I am making a place for you," I said, I looked her up and down and said: "How well you look!"...her saree shimmered with blue interwoven with "light" as she had termed it...." How beautiful! I said looking at it. "Yes, I always wear this when I come to you. I know you like it very much," she said....
>
> "Oh wait," I said and got up. I picked up the garland from the nail and returned to bed. I held it to her "For you as ever. I somehow feared you wouldn't take it...." She received it with a smile, cut off a piece of it and stuck it in a curve on the back of her head. She turned her head and asked: "Is this all right?"
>
> "Wonderful," I said, smelling it....
>
> A cock crew..."Dawn!" she whispered and rose to her feet.... We stood at the window, gazing on a slender, red

> streak over the eastern rim of the earth. A cool breeze lapped our faces. The boundaries of our personalities suddenly dissolved. It was a moment of rare, immutable joy—a moment for which one feels grateful to Life and Death. (227-28)

The Vender of Sweets deals with the father-son relationship in a more analytical, searching and psychological manner. The most important part in the novel is spiritualism which we see when Jagan completely changes himself after experiencing the worst of life. He seems to be spiritually transformed when he goes, in the company of Chinna Dorai, to the garden with a pond in it, and sees a God rising from a stone. He is spiritually awakened and begins to think that he is no longer his former self. In his next life, he wants to be born anyone except a money-making sweet-maker with a spoilt son. An internal transformation has taken place in him for which he thanks God for taking pity on his miserable conditions by sending Chinna Dorai in his life. At this stage he reminds himself:

> I have probably outlived my purpose in this house. If I live for ten or fifteen years more, it will have to be on a different plane. At sixty, one is reborn and enters a new janma. That was the reason why people celebrated their sixtieth birthdays. He remembered his father and mother, his uncle and aunt and a score of other couples celebrated a man's sixtieth year like a wedding, with pipe, drum and feasting. (133)

R.K. Narayan presents all his characters with appealing human flaws. It is in the true tradition of all great writers like Kalidas and Shakespeare, gods give us defects to make us human. In one of his letters, when Mali advises his father and the nation to eat beef, as it would solve food problem and the problem of the useless cows in our country. Jagan feels outraged because the Sastras defined the five deadly sins and killing of a cow headed the list. Now, if we think about human flaw in Jagan, we should not ignore the fact that, without fail, he, very prudently takes his cheque book with him to his retreat. Nor does he forget Grace for whom he is willing to buy a ticket if she desires to return to America.

No one can deny the fact that a person becomes spiritually enlightened—a saint—the moment he gets rid of the worldly attachments. It is at this stage of life that he attains spiritual enlightenment. He realizes that he has come to a point where the struggle of life stands irrelevant. The conclusion of *The English Teacher* is profoundly philosophical; it is perhaps Narayan's own outlook on life wich is realized fully by Jagan:

> Wife, Children, parents, brother, friends—we come together only to go apart again. It is one continuous movement. They move away from us as we move away from them. The law of life cannot be avoided. The law comes into operation the moment we detach ourselves from our mother's womb. All struggle and misery in life are due to our attempt to arrest this law or get away from it or in allowing ourselves to be hurt by it. The fact must be recognized. A profound unmitigated loneliness is the only truth of life. All else is false. (218)

Before I pause, I won't hesitate to add that a significant part of Narayan's fictional world is that which borders around Sanyasis, recluses, sorcerers and Hindu Gods and Goddesses. It is psychic, mystic, spiritual and fathoms the mysteries of human nature. The actions of his characters are constantly guided by the Gita and the Purans, in which the protagonists learn some moral lessons and also receive some spiritual insight through personal experiences. Raju in *The Guide*, Jagan in *The Vendor of Sweets* and Krishnan in *The English Teacher* make us aware of a sadness that has its roots in separation and spiritualism. All the three novels start with domestic fidelity only to get bogged down in philosophic, spiritual and mystical discussions.

Works Cited

Conrad, Joseph. *Lord Jim*. Delhi: W.W. Norton & Company, 1983.

Cowasjee, Saros. *Studies in Indian and Anglo-Indian Fiction*. New Delhi: Harper Collins, 1993.

Gilra, Shiv K. *R.K. Narayan: His World and His Art*. Meerut: Saru Publishing House, 1984.

Iyengar, K.R. Srinivasa and Prema Nandakumar. *Indian Writing in English*. New Delhi: Sterling, 1987.

Moore, William Haydon. *Galaxy of Indian Writings in English*. Delhi: Akshat Publications, 1987.

Nagarajan, M.S. and Eakambaram, N., Natarajan A. *Essays in Criticism on Indian Literature in English*. New Delhi: S. Chand & Company, 1991.

Narayan, R.K. *The English Teacher*. Madras: C.L.S. PRESS. rpt. 1998.

———. My Days. New York: Viking Press, 1974.

———. *The Guide*. Mysore: Indian Thought Publications, 1958.

———. *The Vendor of Sweets*. rpt. King Penguin, 1983.

Rao, M. Subba. *Readings in Indo-Anglian Literature*. New Delhi: Kanishka Publishers, 1995.

14

Modern Version of Hindu Mythology: A Critical Analysis of R.K. Narayan's *The Man-Eater of Malgudi* and *The Painter of Signs*

Rashmi Gupta

R.K. Narayan is deeply rooted in his ancient culture. His fictional world 'Malgudi' has a firm creative base built on certain traditions, values, culture and ethos of life. Its inhabitants are men and women with their roots in family and religion. They cherish a heritage of faith and values, customs and rituals and even dogmas and superstitions. This constitutes Narayan's frame of reference to which he keeps returning continually for sustenance and inspiration. By attempting the English novel form, he brought into it a distinctly Indian flavour, as he once said: "The impact of life, the material and substance of our thought are the same everywhere, in any state. Traditionally, India is the Ramayana, the Mahabharata and the Puranas. The values remain the same in every village, town or city" (43). So, he used mythology as a means of reconciling Hindu tradition to the modern world. He always finds an ancient myth or legend to express his vision of modern life. His novels were a delicate sketch of a middle-class Indian, burdened with the weight of his heritage, constantly attempting to accommodate his traditional values to rapidly changing social codes and the innate irony of his conflicting ideologies.

As we all know, Hindu mythology occupies a singular position in today's world for possessing the ability of combining our glorious past with perpetual contemporaneity. The chief storehouses of the Hindu myths have been the two great epics Ramayana and Mahabharata, and the Puranas. The epics treat the legendary actions of heroes as mortal men whereas the Puranas celebrate the powers and works of gods; philosophical speculations and mythology, all combined together. Though the mythology and the philosophy are two distinct features of religion, the elements intermingle constantly in text after text within the Hindu tradition. Thus, on one side, we have pious philosophical systems, preoccupied with discovering the nature of life and on the other, we have its gods and demons, perpetually at odds with one-another with the hapless man placed at the centre of it all.

Narayan's interest in various facets of Hindu faith and mythology can be seen in his novels throughout his literary career. Due to this very fact, he attempted a retelling of Hindu myths in "Gods, Demons and Others" (1965) and also translated two great Indian epics, "The Ramayana" (1973) and "The Mahabharata" (1978). We can find innumerable examples of credulous superstitious side of Hindu religion and mythology in his novel, for example, in *Mr. Sampath* (1949) the myth about Shiva and Kama is incorporated. An interesting re-interpretation of Hindu myth in modern terms is beautifully portrayed through the legend of Bhasmasura in *The Man-Eater of Malgudi* (1961). *The Guide* (1958) is based on the traditional Hindu belief that gods can be propitiated and rains can be brought about to end a severe drought if somebody sacrifices his life through fasting and prayer. The mythological relationship of the Holy Ganga and the King Santhanu offers a parallel to Daisy-Raman relationship in *The Painter of Signs* (1977) and so on. In this respect, Narayan is in the line of old saints and prophets, interpreting the present-day human conditions in terms of ancient myths, legends and fables. In the words of Professor William Walsh: "The religious sense of Indian myth is a part of Narayan's grip of reality, of his particular view of human life and his individual way of placing and ordering human feeling and experience. What one says about Narayan without qualification is that he embodies the pure spirit of Hinduism" (166-67). For detailed discussion, in this paper, I have selected two novels: *The Man-Eater of Malgudi* and *The Painter of Signs*.

Throwing light on the germinal idea of *The Man-Eater of Malgudi*, once Narayan himself said: "At some point in one's writing career, one takes a fresh look at the so-called myths and legends and finds a new meaning in them. After writing a number of novels and short stories based on the society around me, some years ago I suddenly came across a theme which struck me as an excellent piece of mythology in modern dress. It was published under the title The Man-Eater of Malgudi...I based this story on a well-known mythological episode, the story of Mohini and Bhasmasura" (*The Literary Criterion*, 47-48). *The Man-Eater of Malgudi*, Narayan's magnum opus, narrates the story of the printer Nataraj and the disruption of his serene and well-ordered life, caused by an aggressive intruder, Vasu, a taxidermist hunter, who symbolizes not only the present as opposed to the past, but is also a darker influence opposed to light and grace. In sharp contrast to Vasu, Nataraj and his friends are products of history and mythic tradition. Thus, they exist in a world that is very real, but whose realism is very much dependent on acknowledging the presence of myth.

The main protagonist of the story, Nataraj, is portrayed as a person governed by ritual, ancient beliefs and traditions: "I hung up a framed picture of Goddess Laxmi poised on her lotus, holding aloft the bounties of earth in her four hands and through her grace, I did not do too badly" (7). The novel begins with Nataraj setting out to the river to perform his morning ablutions. All along the way, he has his well-defined encounters with milkman and his puny white cow, the old asthmatic at the end of the street and the watchman at the taluk office. His ordered life and his meticulous observance of rituals are all unfolded with care to establish the atmosphere of tradition and custom vital to the Hindu society of Malgudi. When Nataraj wakes up in the mornings, the first thing he does is to recite "a prayer to the sun to illumine my mind" (9). The prerogatives of Hindu rituals and religious ceremonies unquestionably predominate over the civil and professional aspects of life. After his morning routine, Nataraj goes to his office and spends a pleasant day doing his work and chatting with his various friends, specially the poet and Sen, a would be journalist, who constantly drop by. This shows a life where habits and traditions are so intrinsically a part of one's existence that no reasons are needed to justify it. This is very clear from the humorous description of curtain in Nataraj's press: "Between my parlor and the press, hung a blue curtain. No one tried to peer through it. When I shouted for the foreman, compositor, office-boy, binder or accountant, people imagined a lot of man working on the other side; if I had been challenged, I should have gone in and played the ventriloquist" (8).

This harmonious existence is shattered, however, with the arrival of Vasu. Relentlessly, he forces his entry in the attic of Nataraj's press much against his wishes: "He came forward, practically tearing aside the curtain, an act which violated the sacred traditions of my press" (15). We are alerted to the possibility that the sacred traditions of the society themselves may be under threat. Vasu's presence begins to affect the destiny of all those who came in contact with him directly or indirectly. His exceptionally well-built body, firmness of resolve and egotistic character make him stand out, from the very beginning, as an overpowering personality. Nataraj and his friends, with all their pretended boldness, find themselves helpless before him. He has all the characteristic traits of the typical rakshasa of ancient Hindu mythology and that is why he is nicknamed as 'man-eater'. Right from the moment he enters Nataraj's press, he sets himself up as an enemy of every established custom. He is the voice of present modern era which has no respect for the myths and traditions of the past. This is evident from his reply to horrified Nataraj who was bewildered on seeing the stuffed birds and especially sacred eagle:

> "Don't you see it is a garuda?"
>
> "What if it is?'
>
> "Don't you realize that it's sacred? That it's the messenger of God Vishnu?"
>
> "I want to try and make Vishnu use his feet now and then." (50)

He also explains that he is serving people in his own way by providing them with stuffed eagles that they can worship in the comfort of their own homes and this made Nataraj understand the very fact: "Nothing seemed to touch him. No creature was safe if it had the misfortune to catch his eye" (51). Vasu indeed seems to inhabit a universe where all the common human laws that bind a society together seem not to exist. He occupies Nataraj's attic without permission and when requested to leave, he makes a complaint to the rent controller for being harassed by the landlord. This sets a chain of events rolling and reveals only more strikingly the negative potentiality of Vasu as an evil force. When Vasu's behavior becomes intolerable and a foul smell of dead animals stinks up Nataraj's entire press, Sastri, Nataraj's printer, rightly appraises Vasu as a 'rakshasa' or a demoniac creature "who possessed enormous strength, strange powers and geniuses, but recognized no sort of restraints of man or God" (72).

We observe that Narayan has gently woven mythic pattern into this texture of the narrative with great artistry. Every little factor used to describe Vasu is carefully made to fit into the archetypal perspective being promoted. Vasu's entry in the narrative is strategic to this pattern for it follows after the traditional pattern of life has been carefully delineated. From the moment of his entry, his strong physique and his striking appearance are graphically described: "A tanned face, large powerful eyes under thick eyebrows, a large forehead and a shock of unkempt hair, like a dark halo" (15). His physical likening to a rakshasa is subtle but persistent. At the same time, Vasu's self-assurance, as described by Nataraj, cleverly raises him above mere human stature: "He was pleased to think that humanity could move only after securing a clearance from him. There was no use arguing with him as he was one of those strong men who have no doubt at all about their own conclusions" (98).

So, Vasu is presented as a supernatural being in the disguise of a powerful human, a pattern commonly found in Hindu myths, where a supernatural being assumes a human form for his own evil ends. Vasu has a physical likeness to *rakshasas*, but more crucially, he appears to share their less attractive moral attributes as well, he utterly lacks moral refinement. Sastri, very accurately, compares Vasu with Bhasmasura, who after getting the boon (from Lord Shiva) that he could burn to ashes anyone on whose head he placed his hand, immediately started to test his power by placing his hand over Shiva's head. Lord Shiva fled in terror and sought refuge with Lord Vishnu. Vishnu took the form of a beautiful woman, Mohini, to entice the demon, who became infatuated with her. She promised to yield to him only if he imitated all the gestures and movements of her dancing. And while dancing, demon followed Mohini's gesture of placing her palm on her head and was burnt to ashes.

The significant parallel between Vasu and Bhasmasura is that in a typical rakshasa fashion, the first person they try to destroy are their benefactors. The aggrieved Nataraj once said: "He should feel himself in debt to me and yet he doesn't hesitate to have me hanged" (62). In Hindu world, tradition always assumed paramount importance and in the novel, Vasu is quite frequently shown as adopting a derisive attitude to all traditional attitudes. In Hindu mythology, evil always, ultimately, turns on itself. Good, in the myths, does not always directly confront the evil but acts as a catalyst to speed up the process of evil destroying itself.

Vasu's identity as an evil force is established fully for the people of Malgudi with his contact with Rangi, the temple dancer, which contributes to his downfall. The daring plan of Vasu to kill Kumar, the temple elephant, which is communicated to Nataraj by Rangi, marks the point of climax in the novel. Nataraj is appalled at the thought that he is harbouring a murderer. He would have stopped the entire celebration if it was possible, but they had gone so far ahead that there was no coming back. He lets out a terrific cry to Lord Vishnu for saving the elephant and all innocent men and women who are going to pull the chariot. Needless to say, Vasu gets his just reward. Sitting at his window, waiting to shoot the elephant, unprotected by his mosquito net, he is plagued by mosquitoes, he "had evidently trapped a couple of mosquitoes which had settled on his forehead by bringing the flat of his palm with all his might on top of them.... It was also the end of Vasu.... That fist was meant to batter thick panels of teak and iron" (173). Like Bhasmasura, Vasu meets his end. Evil recoils on itself and digs its own grave. The inevitable self-destruction of evil man emphasizes the implicit moral of the novel: "Every demon appears in the world with a special boon of indestructibility. Yet the universe has survived all the rakshasas that were ever born. Every demon carries within him, unknown to himself, a tiny seed of self-destruction, and goes up in thin air at the most unexpected moment. Otherwise what is to happen to humanity?" (173-74). Sastri's remark at the end offers a word of hope about the possibility of human survival and also suggests that a balance and unity can be achieved in the world only by setting modern realism in a mythological context, by living in a social present that is well grounded in the mythical traditions of an authentic past. The world of tradition temporarily disrupted by the presence of Vasu, once again returns to its former state of peace and gently regains ascendancy.

For another illustration, we can turn to *The Painter of Signs*, where Narayan has aptly used one of the legends from *The Mahabharata*—of King Santhanu and Goddess Ganga in modern perspective. Raman, the main protagonist of the novel, is a painter by profession and believes in the age of logic and reason. His aunt belongs to the older generation who cherishes traditional beliefs in myths and rituals. Again, Narayan is seen at his best in portraying incongruity in human nature, social environment, traditions and the material advancement of the modern days. When Raman comes in contact with Daisy, a young lady, who has just started a family planning centre in

Malgudi, he falls passionately in love with her. Raman, a rationalist, who feels irritated at his aunt's traditional replies, begins to behave like a romantic fool. He starts to feel a bond with her that cannot be explained in rational terms, but rather calls for spiritual, mystical terms. He tells her: "I feel as if we had known each other from several janmas," to which he receives her cold rational response: "It is imagination, really" (73). Daisy approves of the relationship between a man and a woman on equal footing, but not the imperatives, liabilities and inter-dependence customarily attached to Hindu traditional marriage. Raman's decision to marry a girl of another community and religion creates an unprecedented crisis in the family. Since Raman cannot give up Daisy, the aunt has to give him up. The beloved nephew has to be sacrificed at the altar of Hindu tradition. In the clash between tradition and modernity, the latter wins. Raman's aunt decides to leave for her final pilgrimage to Kashi. A girl's (Daisy) running away from the family, her bringing up and education at a missionary organization, her acceptance of social work and her living, all by herself without male supervision and support—are some of those phenomena which would not be tolerated in an orthodox Hindu family.

Daisy proves to be a stronger character than Raman. Her encounter with Raman and their association for a few weeks in the propogation of the family planning programme arouse her dormant sexuality and she carries on an affair with him, without the intention of marriage. When Raman is insistent, she lays down two conditions for accepting his marriage proposal: "One, that they should have no children, and two, if by mischance one was born, she would give the child away and keep herself free to pursue her social work" (158), and still further, she declares: "If you want to marry me, you must leave me to my own plans even when I am a wife. On one day you question why or how, I will leave you...." There was a mad glimpse in her eyes when she spoke thus, but Raman said: "Whatever you say, I will never interfere, I won't question you. I will be like the ancient King Santhanu..." (159).

Now, let us revisit the legend from *The Mahabharata* to understand this relationship. It runs as follows—King Santhanu was hunting for a deer in the jungle when he separated from his group. He led the horse to the river Ganges to drink water. He saw a beautiful damsel by the banks of river. Santhanu was smitten by her beauty and decided right there that she would be his queen. "Marry me", the king said simply. The damsel replied, "You do not know anything about me and yet you want to marry me? I have one condition. You should not question what I do or stop me from doing what I want to do. If you can give me your word on it, I will marry you. However, if you ever break your vow, I will go away from your life forever," said the girl. "You have my word," said the King Santhanu. They got married. Eight children were born unto him. But those children, as soon as they were born, one after another were thrown into the river by the queen. But the king could not utter a word lest his wife should leave him. When the eighth child was born and his wife was about to throw him into the river, the king anxiously said, "Kill it not". Then the queen replied, "According to our agreement the period of my stay with you must now end...I leave you." She revealed her identity that she is Goddess Ganga and the eight sons that she bore were the eight Vasus. They were cursed by Rishi Vasishtha for playing a prank with him. On pleading, Rishi gave a way out, if Ganga were to be their mother on earth and take them into her when they were born, they will be liberated from their curse. So, she told clearly that she was doing a service to the Vasus and she disappeared. And that child of Vasu known as both Devavrata was left to him.

Like Goddess Ganga, Daisy in *The Painter of Signs*, does not drown her innocent children as she does not marry Raman. She had already understood that they both did not share same views and thinking. For Daisy, her work is her solemn and profound commitment to life. She attaches no sentiment to married life. Her fulfillment is not in having a personal life but in the pursuance of her social work. She, at first, agrees to marry Raman and it seems a balance can be struck between the old ways and the modern, between tradition and reason, between the mythic and the real. But, later on, she refuses saying: "Married life is not for me. I have thought it over. It frightens me. I am not cut out for the life you imagine. I can't live, except alone. It won't work" (178-79). She was busy with her trip to the district where birth-rate had increased over 30% for the year, when Raman asked her "Do you see an end to it?" (that is about the dilemma regarding their marriage) and he realized that, like Santhanu, he has made a mistake as Daisy refused and went to the village leaving behind Raman in Malgudi. So, *The Painter of Signs* is a modern interpretation of Mahabharata legend, where the result is an unhappy disunity and disharmony. The reason for this could be that Raman and Daisy are extreme modern rationalists, fundamentally cut off from their ancient, traditional roots. They don't believe in ancient myth or custom. As per Narayan, one can never achieve a balanced or complete life without connections to an authentic past and traditions. We can say that realism must be tempered by myth and tradition to achieve a unified whole. Narayan does not advocate the thrust towards ultra modernity in Indian life. His use of situations and characters of ancient epics and myths shows that he is not only faithful to his tradition and culture, "but also evinces that his questionings and solutions are firmly rooted in his own cultural ethics" (Asnani: 21).

Narayan revisits the ancient mythological plots and introduces a new creative element into it as is evident from the above discussions. He succeeded in presenting Indian myths in the way they would have been told by an old wise man. He has often been viewed as an unselfconscious and spontaneous teller of tales, a myth that he himself has perpetrated to a large extent. He once remarked: "I can't like any writing that's deliberate" (Mehta: 57), that is, he does not appreciate didactic or moralistic writings. So, in his inimitable style through his re-interpretation of Hindu myths, he provides a new vision to the readers, specially the modern generation sans a didactic tone. But it does not mean that his faith in his culture does not make him aware of the increasing need to come to terms with western culture. He skillfully presents the conflicts between tradition and modernity, eastern and western values depicting interesting perspectives of an ancient mythic-culture struggling to cope with the modern world. He explores deep into the psyche of the individual to render aspects of mind colored by myth. He recreates an authentic Indian past through the use of myths. The concrete particulars are so accurate and convincing and their motivations are psychologically so true that the presence of central mythical idea never dominates or obliterates the real life depicted by the author.

Works Cited

Asnani, Shyam M. "The Use of Myth in R.K. Narayan's Novels". *Literary Endeavour*. 3 January-June 1982.

Illustrated Weekly of India, 1963, June 9.

Mehta, Ved. "The Train had just Arrived at Malgudi Station". An Interview, *New Yorker*. 31(30), Sept. 15, 1962.

Narayan, R.K. "Gods, Demons and Modern Times", *The Literary Criterion*. X, 3, Winter 1972.

———. *The Man-Eater of Malgudi*. Middlesex: Penguin Books, 1985.

———. *The Painter of Signs*. Mysore: Indian Thought Publications, 1977.

Walsh, William, *R.K. Narayan: A Critical Appreciation*. New Delhi: Allied, 1983.

15

Portrayal of Children in the Works of R.K. Narayan

Riyaz Ahmad Kumar

> Childhood has its own ways of seeing, thinking and feeling: nothing is more foolish than to try to substitute our ways.
>
> —Rousseau

In arts and literature, there has always been a considerable influence of children upon adults. Poets have mourned the death of children, or worried about their future, and in prose, children have loomed large in the novels of all ages. They were symbols or icons, rather than protagonists in their own right, standing for innocence, emotion, and simplicity. Romanticism sought to recover for childhood a freedom of imagination which utilitarianism would have quashed. This meant access to the whole of literature, and there is much evidence that chapbook tales of magic, courage, cunning, strength and endurance, a literature which the polite world has consigned to oblivion, fed the imagination of many children in the eighteenth century. Rousseau's theory sustains that children are born innocent, and if they become bad citizens or bad 'men', it is because of what they are taught or, better, not taught, as a result of parenting and social impact. A teacher should not try to force a child to learn what is good and right; better to correct a wrong doing and explain the reasoning. Children should be allowed a free development, according to their needs, on their own rhythm. There are some other ideas in his writing that are far for being realistic, like how to educate girls, but Rousseau's theory about childhood development is considered the foundation of modern education. The image of the child in literature need not always be an authentic portrayal of childhood. It is often a functional metaphor. Fictional motifs serve as supplements to the central viewpoint. Apart from this, these motifs are also useful in supplementing our understanding of the child. The writers from India deal with children in fiction with Indian sensibility. The writers remain chiefly psycho-analytical in order to present the Indian childhood, frequently in autobiographical portrayals; and they present excellent understanding of the child psyche while creating a friendly rapport with the child reader also. In the writings of Anand and Narayan, we assume a large amount of familiarity with Indian childhood.

Rasipuram Krishnaswami Narayan belongs to the first generation of Indian Writers writing in English. Without doubt, Narayan's most significant contribution to Indian writing in English is his humour. The other equally significant, though not so well-explored contribution, is his portrayal of children and the depiction of childhood. He occupies a significant place in Indian English literature. His deep concern for children is reflected in his stories. His views about schooling, physical load on school children, freedom of children, their education, place of play and fun in the child's life are well reflected in his works. The reader gets an opportunity to see the world through the perspective of a child. He was interested in reconstructing the scenes of his boyhood as well as those of his children which had left a deep impression on his mind. In Saxena's words: "In his novels, his short stories, essays and even autobiography, one can hear the playing, giggling mischief making children itching to come out of his pages" (55).

Narayan's journey as a writer starts with his novel *Swami and Friends* (1935) which is a realistic portrayal of the children's world. It seems that Narayan is a psychologist who knows every nook and cranny of a child's mind. The world of children has been presented by him with minute details. It was of *Swami and Friends* that Graham Greene wrote: "It was Mr. Narayan with his *Swami and Friends* who first brought India, in the sense of the Indian population and Indian way of life, alive to me.... Swami is the story of a child written with complete objectivity, with humor strange to our fiction" (qtd. in Walsh, 28). Further, Greene hailed it as "a book in ten thousand". The novel is a pure escape into irresponsible boyhood. The novel has a bunch of juvenile characters rather than the individual round figures. *Swami and Friends* is more like a series of loosely strung episodes than a work structured around a particular theme. Its nineteen chapters recount various episodes in the life of Swaminathan, a young school boy, who seeks excitement in the company of friends, around whom revolves the whole of youth power. Narayan is able to trace the cure of ideals, aspirations and frustrations of the young as their sensitive mind and hearts encounter oppression, injustice and exploitation at various levels. The things that fascinate the eye of the young, enchant their soul and cast a spell on their vivid imagination are all described with a comic excitement and ironic detachment:

> The usual evening crowd was on the sand. Swaminathan and Mani sat aloof on a river step, with their legs dangling in water. The Peepul branches overhanging the river rustled pleasantly. A light breeze played about the boughs and scattered stray leaves on the gliding streams below. Birds filled the air with their cries. Far away, near Nallapa's Mango Grove, a little downstream, a herd of cattle was crossing the river. And the country cart man humming a low tune. It was some fifteen minutes past sunset and there was a soft red in the west. (13-14)

Swami's fascination for the hoop enchants his soul: "Swaminathan's one consuming passion in life now was to get a hoop. He dreamt of it day and night. He feasted on vision of an ex cycle wheel without spokes or tyre...he sometimes kept awake till ten thirty in the night, thinking of his hoop" (76-77). Children have aspirations; Swami, too, has one such of the hoops, he always saw it in his dreams:

> He dreamt one night that he crossed the Sarayu near Nallappa's Grove 'on' his wheel. It was a vivid dream: the steel wheel crunched on the sandy bed of the river as it struggled and heaved across. It become a sort of horse. When it reached the other bank. It went back home in one leap, took him to the kitchen, and then to his bed and lay down beside him. This was fantastic; but the early part of the dream was real enough. It nearly maddened him to wake to a hoopless morning. (77)

He continues to say: "My life depends on it. If you don't give it, I am undone" (83). Lakshmi Holmstrom Says: "It is linked here with Swami's vividness of imagination" (36).

The world of children is also the world of fears—the fear of parents, particularly of father, of teachers, of policemen, of ghosts and evil spirits, and even of other stronger children. The child is caught in all these fears in *Swami and Friends*. Swami and his friends live in the world that is very close to fantasies and spells, threats and tortures. Swaminathan is always afraid of his headmaster and even some of his friends: "He shuddered at the very thought of school: that yellow building; the fire eyed Vedanayagan, his class teacher; and the headmaster with his long cane..." (1). At home, he is afraid of his father's questions:

> "Where are you going?"
> "Nowhere"
> "Where were you yesterday at this time?"
> "Here"
> "You are lying. You were not here yesterday.
> And you are not going out now". (96)

The children in Narayan's fiction are quite intelligent and witty. Swaminathan shows his unwillingness to go to school on Monday morning which marks the termination of his playful activities: "It was Monday morning. Swaminathan was reluctant to open his eyes. He considered Monday specially unpleasant in the calendar. After the delicious freedom of Saturday and Sunday, it was difficult to get into the Monday mood of work and discipline" (1).

Children's world is the adult world in miniature. It is here that Wordsworth's concept of the child being father of man finds expressions in their daily activities. On the eve of his examinations, Swaminathan draws up a list of his needs as if it were some kind of a heavy annual budget. About the children of R.K. Narayan, Saxena observes: "Occasionally, Narayan's children smart up, and in their attempt to show off their cleverness reveal either their innocence and simplicity or their stupidity. For Swaminathan, the Indian climate is 'hot in summer and cold in winter' He goes to a physician, complains of delirium so that he could be freed from school at 4:30 and goes on to explain his delirium as "something of stomach ache" (58).

The novel presents a very important stage of man's life. Here, we get a vivid account of activities, thoughts and nature of school children. There is hardly anything about their life which has not been taken into account. While reading the book, one escapes to one's childhood and school days. Narayan shows us how children laugh at oddities of their teachers: "When the scripture Master pursed his lips and scratched his nose, Swaminathan had a wild impulse to stamp on the Pea's leg and laugh, for that was a joke that they had never failed to enjoy day after day for many years past" (37). In this connection, Gilra opines: "The adult characters are interesting in their grotesqueness and oddity as they are viewed through a child's eye" (171).

Narayan, in *Swami and Friends,* shows the child not only in school, but at different places. We feel we know him as we see Swaminathan in different situations with his set of friends, with the adult world of parents, grandmother and teachers, and in his world of fantasy and fears, gods, spirits and ghosts: "Swami's consciousness of the inimical quality of the adult world, his aversion to the rigors and discipline of school or study, his hero worship, his impulsive enthusiasm and yearnings (whether for the possession of hoops or joy of cricket and the companionship of kindred spirits) reflect the universal experience of boyhood" (McLeod, 170).

Narayan depicts the imaginative excesses of children's comprehension of life. A school boy has his own joys and sorrows, his own fears, hopes and expectations, which may seem small to us, but which are more exaggerated by a boy's imagination and seem more terrible or important to him than they would to a more mature person. The joys and heartbreaks of childhood are absolute bliss or the end of the world for the child. As Swami runs away from Malgudi, we are given his thoughts:

> He (Swami) dared not to take his eyes off it for fear that it might pounce upon him. He stood frozen to the ground and stared at the monster. Why did it cease its horrid whispers the moment he turned back? He stood staring. He might have spent about five minutes thus. And when the first thrill of fear subsided, he saw a little more clearly and found that the monster consisted of massive tree-trunks and their top branches. (188)

Before this incident, he was thinking to go home: "The only important thing now was home, and all the rest seemed trivial beside it" (185). And in this way, his fears and terrors, his deep anguish and his yearnings for home, are depicted with telling vividness. The adults may smile at his boyish terrors, but to the boy himself, they are real and intense. Narayan's delicate capturing of boys fleeting attention spans, and his understanding of the child's abstract notions are stated with masterly ease. William Walsh writes about the childish terrors of Swami: "The psychological quickness, the numbness of perception, the cool, and the untroubled scrutiny of the child's nature and mind which can issue into pure fun can also develop into a poetic sense of the intensities of the boy's experience and the depth of his personality" (Walsh, 34).

It is Narayan's insight into the rhythms of boyish consciousness that makes *Swami and Friends* a classic of school boy fiction. The school boys in the novel have childish qualities because of their rash and impulsive nature. A child's actions are impulsive, spontaneous and unpredictable. Swami, in particular, is basically a child, and yet he has a more individual and spontaneous existence than a school boy. He has the attractiveness as that of a child; he is still undistracted by worldly ambitions of money or career. He has begun to look at the adult world around him; he tries to understand it and come to terms with it, but still his responses to it are his own, rash and impulsive. That is why he is again and again involved in trouble: "What a boy you are!" exclaimed Rajam "You are always in some trouble or other where ever you go. Always, Always" (177). In Graham Greene's words: "A boy is a recognized figure in a given pattern obeying certain conventions. A child is an individual human creature, unprophesiable, unlegislated for, enjoying spontaneously an unrehearsed autonomy" (qtd. in Walsh, 28). Swami absents himself from class and indulges in a spree of smashing window panes. The result is that he is in trouble and when the headmaster canes him, he acts rashly, snatches away his hand and runs away from school. The next time again in school: "When another whack came on his back, he ejaculated, "Don't beat me, sir. It pains".... He had a sudden flood of courage, the courage that comes of desperation. He restrained the tears that were threatening to rush out, jumped down, and, grasping his books, rushed out muttering, "I don't care for your dirty school" (124-25).

Swami and Friends is filled with a sense of the comic, of school boys, and the experiences of the class room. We get a clear cut evidence of the comic in the opening pages of the novel. Swami is standing in front of his teacher Vedanayagam. His criticism of his teacher's face is very humorous: "His eyes were too near each other that there was more hair on his chin than one saw from the bench, and he was very very bad looking" (3). "Somu, the monitor is more or less the uncle of the class." Mani, "the Mighty Good-For-Nothing...seldom brought any books to the class...wearing his cap at an angle, with a Tamil novel under his arm, he had been coming to the school ever since the old school peon could remember" (7). About Shanker, the most brilliant and a somewhat, controversial figure, "there was belief among a section of the boys that if only he started cross-examining the teachers, the teachers would be nowhere.... He was said to receive his ninety percent as a result of washing clothes for his masters.... He could repeat history in his sleep" (8). Samuel is humorously called the "Pea" on account of his size. The boys serve as adequate reminders of our innocent boyhood at school. Swaminathan's response, when asked by the teacher to stand on a chair, is typical of the understated humorous depiction that is characteristic Narayan style: "And Swaminathan stood up without a protest. He was glad that he was given this supposedly degrading punishment instead of cane" (17). Consequently, he paid no attention to the rest of the lessons. His mind began to wander. Standing on the bench, he stood well over the whole class, he could see many heads, and he classified them according to the caps. There were four red caps, twenty five Ghandhi caps, ten fur caps and so on (18). Here, we can see Narayan's comic vision reflected in the children's simple ways of interaction with a world of serious dimensions. The children's participation in the freedom movement, without any mature understanding of the problem, is manifested in the burning of clothes and breaking of glass in the schools: "Swaminathan was an unobserved atom in the crowd. Another unobserved atom was busily piling up small stones before him, and dinging them with admirable aim at the panes in the front part of the school building" (114-15). This shows the inappropriate balance resulting from an interaction between the real world of serious business and the children's world of unadulterated pleasures. For a moment, the seriousness of the freedom struggle gives place to the play of children's impulses. Similarly the endless debate over the formation of a cricket club, the M.C.C. (Malgudi Cricket Club) and the letter to Messrs Binns speaks of the children's innocent attempts to enact roles of an adult world. In a way, the children, quite unwittingly, make a parody of the adult world.

About the relationship between child and adult in Narayan's novels, writes Jayant K. Biswal: "Childhood impulses and instincts are juxtaposed in a spirit of jubilant conciliation against the world of grave business, the specter of which hangs large in Narayan's other novels. Blissfully oblivions, the innocent children alter the reality of a complex world into their own simple and peculiar terms and strive for a full celebration of their urges" (61). It is in the children's simplicity, gullibility and idiocy that their nature is represented. Swaminathan believes that by praying to gods, a cardboard box, full of pebbles, could be converted into coins, but he gets disappointed when nothing happens: "As he gazed at the cardboard box, the scattered leaves, sand, and the unconverted pebbles, he was filled with rage. The indifference of the gods infuriated him and brought tears to his eyes. He wanted to abuse the gods, but was afraid to" (80). Here, we are reminded of Mark Twain's Huckelberry Finn who rubs an old tin lamp believing the djinn belongs to the person who rubs the lamp so that the djinn could be asked "to build a palace forty miles long, out of diamonds, and fill it full of chewing gum, or whatever you want, and fetch an emperor's daughter from China for you to marry" (Twain, 23).

Children want to live in the world of elves and fairies, Alladin's lamp and flying carpets, and their wild unrestrained imagination is unfettered by logic, reason and knowledge and is uncircumscribed by the age old questions of possibility and probability. Swami, too, is caught in such imagination: "He dreamt one night.... It was a vivid dream: the steel wheel crunched on the sandy bed of the river as it struggled and heaved across. It becomes a sort of horse when it reached the other bank...took him to the kitchen, and then to his bed and lay down beside him. This was fantastic; but early part of the dream was real enough" (77). Like Swami, a child in Narayan's story 'Uncle', shows a rich imaginative potential in his reflections on a series of pictures:

> As I watched the pictures my mind went off into fantastic speculations while my tongue recited holy verse "was the eagle a sort of aeroplane for Vishnu? Laxmi stands on lotus! How can anyone stand on a lotus flower without crushing it"? ....No I would turn to the picture of Sarasvati, the goddess of learning, as she sat on a rock with her peacock beside a cool shrubbery, and wonder at her ability to play the veena with one hand while turning the rosary with the other, still leaving two

> hands free, perhaps to pat the peacock. (Krishnan, 489-90)

'Uncle' presents a contrast between the world of innocence and that of the experience of a child. Before experiencing the outside world, the child lives a happy life with his only attachment in his world, namely his uncle: "My world was circumscribed by the boundaries of our house in Vinayak Street and peopled by uncle and aunt mainly. I had no existence separately from my uncle. I clung to him all through the day" (Krishnan, 484). The child has not been conscious of the outside world of experience till one day he was alone in a crowded market place: "This was my first day out, exciting and frightening at the same time. The world looked entirely different—the crowd at the market, which had seemed so entertaining before, was now terrifying. I feared that I might be engulfed and swept off, and never see my home again. As twilight came on and the street lamps were lit, I grew apprehensive" (Krishnan, 511).

The novel presents the child's world in contrast to the world of adults who have no concern for children's feelings. Narayan himself says about the contrast between adults and children:

> (Children) prefer to be treated as normal living creatures, as fellow citizens on earth, subject to the same impulse good and bad, as adults and expect the same amount of toleration that they see practiced among adults. They see that adults do practically all that they forbid the young fellow to do and never correct each other...thus children naturally resent that there should be two laws in the world, one for adults and one for them. (qtd. in Dhawan, 123)

In the novel, Narayan narrates:

> Swaminathan realized that the doctor had deceived him: he remembered the genial smile with which the doctor had said that he would see the headmaster. Swaminathan shuddered as he realized what a deep dyed villain Dr. Kesavan was behind the genial smile. (170)

Through *Swami and Friends*, Narayan strongly underscores the need for incorporating psychological approaches in the education of small children. A teacher must be well aware of child psychology which emphasizes a humane approach to the child's problems. The teacher's ignorance of the children's sentiments and their significance in the later life only widen the rift between him and the pupils. Often the confrontation compels the young ones to shun school at a premature age. Most children, on account of their daily burden, as Narayan asserts in his essay "Cruelty to Children", "develop a stoop and hang their arms forward like a chimpanzee while walking, and I know cases of serious spinal injuries in some children too" (Krishnan, 131-32). Had the Albert Mission School Headmaster been a little more affectionate and amiable, Swami would not have been forced to leave the school without completing his studies.

In "Spare the Rod and You won't Spoil the Child", which recently appeared in *The Hindu*, Malathi Mohan says: "What is important in our family relationship is: Love, trust and respect, whatever the age or gender of the children. Even toddlers have to be taught to respect and they should be given respect. Children should not be unnecessary shouted at, punished, beaten, starved, locked up or sent out of the house... I feel sad to read about corporal punishment being given in schools and homes, even today" (16). Patently, the inhuman methods of corporal punishment, callous and indifferent attitude of teacher in dealing with their students remind one of the barbaric age when people knew nothing about child psychology and freely resorted to flogging and caning. Such evil practices are, in a great measure, responsible for the loss of respect for the teacher among his students and for the decline of students' faith in teacher. Students like Swaminathan develop a feeling of alienation and distance from their teacher because the teacher never tries to come closer to them mentally and psychologically. That is the reason that Swaminathan 'was reluctant to open his eyes' and "considers Monday specially unpleasant in the calendar, after the delicious freedom of Saturday and Sunday" (1). On the contrary, D. Pillai is a favorite teacher of his students because of his cordiality. He has "earned a name in the school for his kindness and good humour. He was reputed to have never frowned or sworn at the boys at any time" (3). The mental faculties of a child should be allowed to develop in an atmosphere of freedom and friendliness.

The novel is full of innocence. Narayan portrays the simple joys and sorrows of children. The innocent little ones are not free from the fascination of glamour. One encounters several kinds of delineation of children in Narayan, like in the *Financial Expert* and *The Vendor of Sweets,* but *Swami and Friends* can be considered the full-fledged study of innocence. Ramesh Dnyate says: "It may be pointed out that although all the boys in the novella seem to be dramatizing the innocence, it is basically Swaminathan, the central consciousness in it, probably inspired by the child-God Balasubramanium Swami through whom it is chiefly realized" (35). Narayan seems to be skilfully equipped with a minutely observant eye and the reportorial gift to underline the preadolescent psychology of Swaminathan and his mates. He projects, as Dnyate writes, the boy's "innocence through his overall psychology exemplified mostly in his misadventures. This treatment of innocence, on the face of it, may indeed appear plain and straight forward. It is only when one takes a closer look at the young hero's milky innocence with it's equally naïve shades, that one realizes how convincingly and deftly doe. Narayan delineates the boy's characters, telescoping his imagination at every conceivable instance" (35-36).

R.K. Narayan also shows the relation between childhood and second childhood by portraying the grandmother of Swaminathan, Granny. Granny is passionately attached to Swaminathan, as every grandmother is towards the grandchild, especially in the traditional Indian family set up. "As regards her nature of innocence, it seems to have been realized through her association with her grandson. Their relation epitomizes the old proverb: Birds of a feather flock together'. Therefore to understand the nature of Granny's innocence is to read her story in relation to Swami" (Dnyate, 51). Granny herself says:

"Don't tease the boy. The child is so fond of me. Poor thing. He has been trying to tell me all sorts of things. You are not in the habit of explaining the things to me. You are all big men..." (152).

Swami is the proverbial schoolboy, and once the child reader is drawn to the book, there begins some degree of identification with the protagonist, which is further emphasized by the child's point of view that the writer has adopted. The experience, the author portrays, comes within the reach of the reader. In an interview, when asked why she chose *Swami and Friends* for theatre, Aruna Ganesh, the director of theatre play *Swami and Friends*, replied: "*Swami and Friends* was a book that had something for everybody. For children they can relate with the escapades of the three friends, for a young person it is reminiscent of their growing years; and for an older person they can relate it to their children" (*Hindu,* 1).

In conclusion, children should be allowed to talk about their problems openly, meet other kids who have actually experienced such issues. However, nobody takes their words seriously irrespective of age. Only when you are hit on the head, you know the pain. Children are not "lesser" humans; they are just at a different stage of life experience. They have the same ability to feel things, some times more intensely, and to have whole consciousness, albeit not a particularly verbal one. Narayan portrays the child as an outsider to the adult world with a twinkle of mischief in his eyes, focusing his camera, as it were, from a vantage point and zooming the lenses over them at an angle so to give a humorous-ironical tinge to the entire picture. The writer wishes to convey the message to the readers that the child is a model of raw and pure humanity. The child is not to be seen as the replica of adult aspirations. The child sees the world from an unaffected, unbiased, unbribable and unafraid innocent perspective. He is unaffected, because he has not had time to be inundated with cares of the world. He is unbiased because he has not yet had time to feed upon the opinions of those around him. He is unbribable because there is nothing that interests him outside of his own endeavors. His innocence is unafraid because he knows no need for fear.

Works Cited

Biswal, Jayant K. *A Critical Study of the Novels of R.K. Narayan: The Malgudi Comedy*. New Delhi: Nirmal, 1987.

Dhawan, R.K. (ed.). *The Novels of Mulk Raj Anand*. New Delhi: Prestige, 1992.

Dnyate, Ramesh. *The Novels of R.K. Narayan: Typological Study of Characters*. New Delhi: Prestige, 1996.

Gilra, Shiv K. *R.K. Narayan His World and Art*. Meerut: Saru Publications House, 1984.

Holmstrom, Lakshmi. *The Novels of R.K. Narayan*. Culcutta: A Writer Workshop Publications, 1973.

Krishnan, S. (ed.). *A Town Called Malgudi: The Finest Fiction of R.K. Narayan*. Viking Penguin Books, 1999.

McLeod, A.L. (ed.). *R.K. Narayan Critical Perspectives*. New Delhi: Sterling, 1994.

Narayan, R.K. *Swami and Friends*. Chennai: Indian Thought Publications, 1935.

Saxena, O.P. *Glimpses of Indo-English Fiction*. Vol. I. New Delhi: Jainsons, 1985.

Twain, Mark. *The Adventures of Hucklberry Finn*. London: Penguin Popular Classics, 1994.

Walsh, William. *R.K. Narayan: A Critical Appreciation*. London: Heinemann, 1982.

Newspapers

Ganesh, Aruna. "Universal Appeal". *The Hindu,* 14 Dec. 2010, Hyderabad ed. Metroplus.

Mohan, Malathi. "Spare the Rod, You Won't Spoil the Child". *The Hindu,* 24 Oct. 2010, Hyderabad.

Varma, Anuradha. "Make Your Kid Worldly-Wise". *Times of India,* 6 March 2011, Hyderabad ed. *Times Life*.

16

Re-"visioning" Intertextualities in R.K. Narayan's Novels: Comparative-Cultural Critique

Anand Balwant Patil

> Time for a pause, right there, I'm beginning to do exactly what I've always criticized the Naipauls for doing: drawing grand, sweeping conclusions from the flimsiest of anecdotal evidence. After all, one cannot be unaware that in trying to paint even an impressionistic portrait of contemporary Indian society and culture, one is recalling a concept to undefinable that T.S. Eliot was curious enough to call his book on the subject: *Notes Toward the Definition of Culture* and George Steiner, two and half decades later, could do no better that subtitle *In Blue-beard's Castle* as Notes Toward the Redefinition of Culture. I have neither the desire nor the ability to attempt to define or redefine this slippery term; one cannot entirely forget the pro-Nazi poet Hanns Johst's declaration, "When I hear the word 'culture', I reach for my gun."
>
> —Shashi Tharoor

Much water has flown under the bridge than what Tharoor means by "Indian society as culture" in terms of "the social heritage and contemporary life of Indians". Tharoor's title exhibits the echoes of intertextuality of Salman Rushdie's controversial *The Midnight's Children.* Moreover, revisiting any colonial text, from the postcolonial comparative cultural perspectives, would reveal a number of unexplored contradictory aspects than what is seen through the elitist "blue" eyes of Tharoor in *Midnight to Millennium*, R.K. Narayan in *The English Teacher*, Meenakshi Mukhergee in *Realism and Reality: Novel and Society in India* or M.K. Naik in a host of articles and books on Indian writings in English. Tharoor's sibling relationship and family romance, in Sigmund Freud's famous terms, with Naipaul's *The Area of Darkness* or *A Wounded Civilization* and Rushdie's *The Midnight's Children,* are apparent in this essay. Similarly, the fiction of the first famous trio, i.e. Raja Rao, Mulk Raj Anand and R.K. Narayan needs to be "revisited" with not only new strategies of reading their texts as a symbolic political unconscious act but also as products of Western, in Edward Said's phrase, "culture and imperialism". Stepping back and looking comparatively with postcolonial and postmodern perspectives at R.K. Narayan's, fiction and contemporary reality after nearly seventy years is more or less similar to what Chinua Achebe did in his "An Image of Africa: Racism in Conrad's *Heart of Darkness* (1972) and *Henry Louis Gates in his Race*, *Writing and Difference* (1995). Elsewhere, I (2011) have coined the term "castealization" based on Western "racialization" of literature to study national and international affiliations of intertextualities in Indian literature.

So concepts of revisiting, redoing, rethinking, re-imagining, re-visioning, re-reading, re-interpreting, re-writing, etc. imply improvisations or new dimensions added to the earlier knowledge. In Harold Bloom's terms, all reading is misreading and revisions lead to new creations. Intertextual relations are determined by the anxiety of influence and in Sigmund Freud's concept, "the family romance of writers". The pre-text makes the post-text possible. The author child is the father of stalwart "writerly" writer. Which R.K. Narayan do we want to revisit and from which perspectives? Does he represent the rich, in Bakhtinian terms, "carnivalization and heteroglossia", of diverse Indian cultures and languages? For whom did he write? In order to answer such pertinent questions, we have to take the descriptive term "revisiting" to the deeper analytical conceptual level. For the intellectuals, undernourished by colonized traditional curriculum of mono-literary studies, it is still a greater challenge to reinterpret colonized texts with pseudo-secularism and cultural illiteracy without Reymond William's vision and commitment to challenge Leavisian Great Tradition of critical thought. In the new millennium of internationalization, literature demands postmodern interdisciplinary approaches; but our criticism is stuck in the mire of Anglo-American modernity. See the simple dictionary meanings of the word "revisit" in the title of the theme of the Seminar. The dictionary meanings are many—to visit again; a second or repeated visit; go or come back to place, condition, or activity wheie one has been before; return to your native; and also to re-examine (a topic or theme) after an interval, with a view to making a fresh appraisal. Our "revisit" to the fictional world of R.K. Nayayan, with the ideology of Namwar Singh's preaching to decolonize Indian mind and prior to him, Ngugi wa Thing'O's 'battle cry' for decolonizing African mind, would certainly bring new revelations and rewards. Ngugi's "homecoming" (1972) and the agenda of "abolishing Departments of English" (1976) might help us more than our too subjective and impressionistic Indian criticism. It should be noted at the outset that the wavering loyalties of the colonized reader are not yet theorized in India (see Nancy Hogley). The "re-examination" of Narayan's *The English Teacher,* sixty-six years after its birth, by the post-independent Indian readers, fed on Anglomerican postcolonial theories and affected by our indigenous, or in Edward Said's word, "affiliations" of regions, religions, class and caste, needs new cultural approach today. For example, reading *A Passage to India* or *The English Teacher* in the light of postcolonial or cultural theories again enriches our understanding. But for this, we have to read Harold Bloom's "introduction" to the first and compare the latter with Naipaul's *A House for Mr. Biswas* in Fanonian terms. Such revision is bound to deconstruct and discard hegemonic intra-colonial judgments of Indian comprador class of imitators of Anglo-American New Critics and also takes us to their resistant counterparts in Black aesthetics. In fact, R.K. Narayan's oeuvre is the cultural product of Anglo-American "regional modernism", British colonialism and indigenous elitism. In this sense, Meenakshi Mukherjee's Brahmanical concept of "twice born" fiction falls short in contrapuntal analysis of cultural hybridity in any Indian English novel. It is confined to, in Edward Said's term, the "worldliness" of the earliest sociological twin process, namely Anglicization (modernization) and Sanskritization (Brahmanization) used for analyzing the process of acculturation after the elitist cultural contact with Europe. But why only "twice born"? Has it not projected the monolithic Brahminical image of Indian literature to the Western world? What about indigenous "native" cultural transformations? Why are they excluded both from *Kantapura* and *The English Teacher,* albeit both are set in the villages? Hence, the cultural representation of "the Other's double" in Indian English fiction is yet to become the subject of discussion. We may be able to trace how old wine in new bottle may be more poisonous, if we understand why Americans always condemn the French theories of structuralism, deconstruction and intertextuality as "poisonous".

Moreover, in our literary image building cultural industry, to use Fanonian theory, "the battle for reciprocal recognition" is determined by hierarchical cultural capital and degree of illiteracy. Consequently, this dominant Orientalist (British-Brahmanical) image of earlier Anglo-Indian, later Indo-Anglian-Commonwealth and the latest Indian writing in English by the Indian elitist writers with traditional, in Pierre Bourdeu's sociological concept, "cultural capital" must have led the German scholar Hyacinth Cynthia Wyatt to undertake the research topic for his doctoral degree "R.K. Narayan as a Brahman Novelist" submitted to Universitat Rovira I Virgili in 1997. We hardly find such cultural materialism and semiotic approach in our double colonized Indian critical thought. No one can dare to think of such inflammatory cultural area of research where devils fear to tread in a pseudo-secular environment. This shows how and why the term "culture" is considered not only the most difficult word among three English terms but also the most inflammatory of all as demonstrated by George Huntington in *Cultural Clash*. It is necessary to study any Indian literary text as a Walmikian as well as Homerian cultural battlefield. In the tsunamis of globalization, it is a right time to rethink of not only the relevance of true contributions of our stalwarts but also devise new strategies of rereading colonialisms of various kinds and replacing literary theories for survival in the new competitive literary market of the global village. I hope, this Seminar is a welcome beginning in this direction. But we should think of its concrete returns in terms of marketing new knowledge by producing books to be sold all over the world. Of course, there is the ending in the beginning itself. As a creative writer and comparatist-culturalist, I limit this discourse only to the intercultural and international intertextualities in two novels.

It is necessary to demonstrate comparatively, with the help of theory of intertextuality, how literature, in all formerly colonized countries, is Eurocentric, two-toned, multi-faced, and multi-layered. Owing to the, in Michael Echeuro's words, "culture conditioned imagination" in a peculiar Indian systemic way, a researcher is the victim of Anglo-American critical theories, and local structures of culture and imperialism. Let us juxtapose two samples of the titles and conclusions of the Doctoral theses, carried out in the same year in India and Germany. Ramesh Dnyate's *The Novels of R.K. Narayan: A Typological Study of Characters* (1996) was completed in University of Pune under the guidance of "a reputed Marxist interpreter of literature" and published with a bibliography which includes only eighty books but any periodical. The contents do not show least awareness of interdisciplinarity and the conclusions remain at very superficial levels. The final paragraph runs as follows:

> In short, the typological approach may be regarded as a strategy to focus on the essentials in the craft of Narayan's novel. The essentials seem to have been reflected (a) in Narayan's presentment of the epic of the ordinary conceived on the stage of the middle-class Malgudi; (b) in his bifocal vision of comic irony perceiving the essentially illusory nature of the life and

(c) in his positive vision of life despite its predestinate or karmic conception (170).

This title seems to be a misnomer and we do not know how Narayan's characters are "cultural products", which are determined by double binds of imperialism. The majority of Indian doctoral works on Rao and Narayan, excluding Anand, exhibit salient features of "culture and imperialism" and project the image of their novels as "prose epics of India" (see M.K. Naik). Elsewhere, I (1997) have demonstrated how *Kantapura* is "a bogus prose epic" of anglicized elitist India. What is consciously or ignorantly ignored by Indians is objectively analyzed by the foreigners. For example, we are first shocked by mere title of the English Doctoral thesis by Hyacinth Cynthia Wyatt: "R.K. Narayan as a Brahman Novelist" approved by Universitat Rovira I Virgili (1997) in Germany. It is a simple cultural study, which demonstrates once again how foreigners have studied Indian languages and literatures better than Indians. We cannot imagine of the first paragraph of the conclusions in this work in any caste and culture conditioned Indian criticism. The first paragraph runs as follows:

> Throughout this study, it has been shown that Hindu culture and Narayan's Brahmanical beliefs and preparation constitutes the substratum of his novelistic work. This study has also called attention to the strong presence of Narayan's Brahmanical heritage and erudition as revealed by the recurrence of cultural symbols and allegorical tendencies that appear at different levels of understanding in all his novels. It has been demonstrated that the myths and teachings continually influence the psychology and behavior of Narayan's protagonists, many living out roles similar to the mythological, some even with the same names, such as Chandran in *The Bachelor of Arts* (the myth of the King Chandran), Savitri in *The Dark Room* (the myth of Savitri), Vasu in *The Man Eater of Malgudi* (Vasu, the King of the Sudras), and Nagaraj in *The Wounded Nagraj* (another name for Shiva when he is the King of

> Dance). Others have similar names such as Krishnan in *The English Teacher* for Krishna, the avatar of Vishnu, Bharati in *Waiting for the Mahatma* for Bharat (another name for India) and Raman in *The Painter of Signs* for Rama the hero of Ramayana. (172)

Now, crossing the boundaries of one language and literature is inevitable in anglobalization. Let us study Narayan's *The English Teacher* and Naipaul's A *House for Mr. Biswas* to illustrate interculturalism and both poetics and politics of culture in fiction. What structures of literary feelings did go in making of Narayan's and his counterpart immigrant Naipaul's novels? Naipaul's *A House for Mr. Biswas* is a fine example of continuation of "distant nativism" of a different kind by the immigrants, especially diaspora writers of the original Brahman caste in majority. The names of his characters such as Mr Mohun Biswas, Shama, Tulsi, Ganesh, Jairam, Govind, Leela, etc., have distinct myths and legends associated with them and they are deeply rooted in Indian ethos. Even the names of houses, places and stores such as a Hanuman House, a Tulsi store, a Tulsi shop, etc., remind us of, in Derek Walcott's compliments used in his Nobel lecture, "the fragments of the great epic culture" on that distant island in the British colony. William Walsh has cited Gordon Rohlchr's to show how "the book can bc interpreted on several levels. There is the obvious surface level where Biswas can be seen as a second generation Indian who, although rebelling against his own decaying Hindu world, cannot compromise with the Creole world of Trinadad" (65). Walsh has not commented on the impact of British "high" culture and literature on Mr. Biswas. As an outsider, Walsh cannot claim adequate cultural literacy of India also, but recommends it Naipaul's masterpiece and further points out:

> The members of the community in *A House for Mr. Biswas*, even those like the Indians who were exempt from formal, historical slavery, carry about with them in their attitude and posture, in their management of life and feeling, the indelible mark of the slave, who is supremely the unnecessary man...Mr. Biswas constructs

> the proof of his necessity...that he becomes a model of man, just as the history and situation which formed him are seen to be a metaphor of the process which constitutes any man. (30-31)

It is not the coincidence that Narayan's protagonist is constituted in the same mould of the Brahmanical Vedic culture with very few local differences. I (2005) have demonstrated how a single "sign" like "bell" plays a significant semiotic role in the cultural structure of a novel. Wyatt has analyzed Narayan's protagonists in terms of four *ashramas*. Like his Raju (*The Guide*) and Raman (*The Painter of Signs*), Mr Biswas acquires knowledge through books and learns to help people as well *sarvadharma*. Mr Biswas represents *griastha* also. But he is the product of more hybridized culture which is reflected in a ritual meal described by Ganesh: 'Open a tin of salmon', Ramlogan ordered, 'and get some bread and butter and peppersauce and some avocado pears'. And he went himself to look after the preparations, saying, "We have a author in a family, a man, girl...". After quoting these lines, Theorux writes: "In the first year of their marriage Ganesh beats Leela considerably. No brutality is attached to beating; on the contrary, they are a source of pride for traditional Hindus. Mr. Biswas, not a wife-beater reflects..." (58). The interdisciplinary exploration of such Hindu culture specific structures in both the novels and the degree of westernization illustrate the significance of comparative culture studies. The problem of creative tension in representation of the colonized needs to be studied with reference to theories expounded by Frantz Fanon, Edward Said, Homi K. Bhabha and others. For example, Said argues:

> Think the narratives through together within the context provided by history of imperialism, a history whose underlying contest between white and non-white has emerged lyrically in the new and more inclusive counternarrative of liberation. This, I would say, is the full situation of postmodernism, for which Lyotard's amnesiac vision has been insufficiently wide. Once again *representation* becomes significant, not just as an

> academic or theoretical quandary but a political choice. How the anthropologist represents his or her disciplinary situation is on one level, of course, a matter of local, personal, or professional moment. But it is in fact part of a totality, one's society, whose shape and tendency depend on the cumulatively alternative or deterrent and oppositional weight made up by a whole series of such choices.... The main point is that anthropological representations bear much on the presenter's world as on who, or what is represented. (224)

The sources of this interculturalism and internationalism should be traced to the Anglo-American project of high modernism and aestheticism. The Joycian trend of modernization of myth had reached the Gate Way of India as well as shores of West Indies along with other western, to use Edward Said's term, "traveling theories" of novel. The Anglo-American "Project of Modernity and Aesthetic Experience" was designed in the 1920s immediately after the First World War. Narayan wrote his fiction in the next decade. Of course, he amalgamated Indian reality and "cultural heritage" in Western technique. Apart from Narayan's alien technical devices, Wyatt's mastery of deconstructing "Indian" myths from Vedas to modern "Bharata" can hardly be found in the corpus of Indian criticism on Narayan's novels. So his objective semiotic cultural interpretation of Narayan's novels is a novel intervention in Indian critical thought. Albeit not comparative, his cultural materialistic approach is so neutral and scientific that there is not a single casteist tinge that spoils the image of any caste. It is a very illuminating thesis of less that two hundred pages and not voluminous duplicate compilation like Indian "A Critical Study of R.K. Narayan's Life, and Works." If similar myth making is traced to in V.S. Naipaul's *A House for Mr. Biswas* set in a village in the West Indies, it will be more revealing and rewarding comparative cultural study. The semiotics of names of persons and places carries with it not only their religion, markers of identity; but also history, politics and what not. Perhaps Shakespeare wanted to ignore them when he said "What is there in a name?" His characters and plots of the plays were structured by the Western culture and society. It matters most as to how the creative writer uses or misuses/subverts these classical texts in his own fiction. Walsh has explored several "personal matters" in Narayan's life which reveals the texture of hybridity of Indian and Western elements of culture. He observes:

> An Indian child of this class and caste was introduced to the classical Indian tales, myths, and Vedic poetry very early in life. (11)
>
> He went first to the Lutherian Mission School (Madras) where he was one of the few non-Christians and the only Brahmin boy in his class. Scripture classes were devoted to lampooning the Hindu gods and ridicule was poured on the Brahmins, who, it was said, while claiming to be vegetarians sneakily ate fish and meat in secret and were probably responsible for the soaring prices of those commodities. (12-13)
>
> In addition, a priceless privilege for someone like Narayan were the amenities he enjoyed both in his father's library crammed with Carlyle, Ruskin, Walter Peter, Wordsworth, Browning. Byron and Shakespeare, and in the school library, particularly during the summer vacations. He read any book that he liked and all the magazines, of which there seemed to be copious supply, from *Little Folks* to *The Nineteenth Century and After: A Monthly Review* and *The Cornhill Magazine*. Through *The Strand* he became familiar with Conan Doyle, P.G. Wodehouse, W.W. Jacobs, and Arnold Bennett, and *The Bookman* introduced him to the library figures of those days, Shaw, Hardy, Ibsen, Chesterton and Belloc. He loved the literary gossip in *Johnson's London Weekly*, *The Spectator* and the *Times Literary Supplement*. He was another library cormorant, and certainly a fiction and romantic poetry cormorant, and he developed some extraordinary enthusiasm at this time, in particular, for example, for Marie Corelli and Mrs Henry Wood's East Lynne. (13-14)

All such auto/biographical references helped the earlier comparatists in traditional studies of literary influences, imitation, mutation, echo, adaptation, translation, offshoots, echoes, plagiarism, and so on. But in new comparative cultural study, it is more important to analyze the structures of writer's literary feelings in terms of the interculturalness, interliterariness, internationalness and intertextualities at the microscopic levels. It gives equal importance to the study of both poetics as well as politics of cultural productions. In the age of information, traditional umbrella term "autobiographical approach" has taken a new avatar of "literary biography". In the introduction to a recent book, aptly titled as *Built of Books: How Reading Defined the Life of Oscar Wilde*, Thomas Wright observes:

> Wilde's reading was the chief inspiration for his writings. He was essentially a pre-modern author who adapted and conflated the books he read, rather than a Romantic writer concerned with originality and self-expression. His works are saturated with allusions from his vast and miscellaneous reading: they form a little library of exquisite echoes.... Wilde knew how to use books—the traditional symbols of authorship and learning in Western iconography—to convey his culture and his literary achievements. (6-7)
>
> Wilde talked of books and often talked like books; he talked so well that he seemed to talk books away. He told stories based on books and countless anecdotes and jokes about them; in his writings, his characters are frequently compared to kooks.... (7)

Narayan (and also by 'heritage of loss' Naipaul) belonged to the priestly class and culture traditionally known for monopolized classical learning. He was a son of the Headmaster of the Secondary School, and William Walsh, like Wright, has used Coleridge's famous phrase, a true 'library cormorant' to show how was fed off a varied diet of books in the school.

Certainly, the above-cited references, albeit exclude any reference to Indian books, have contributed to the shaping of the spirit of *The English Teacher* (1945) which we will consider later. In addition, a comparitist, like monoliterary critic, should not believe the authorial confession cited by Walsh as follows:

> After Scott I picked up a whole row of Dickens and developed his London and the queer personalities therein. Rider Haggard, Marie Corelli, Moliere and Pope and Marlowe, Tolosti, Thomas Hardy- an indiscriminate jumble; I read everything with the utmost enjoyment. (14)

It is very interesting to compare literary intertextuality in these sample texts. Narayan's protagonist is a teacher of English in the pre-independence phase of the freedom struggle, which gives rise to the resistant literature of, to use Fanon's phrase, "fighting phase". It is neither the product of Fanonian violence nor of Gandhian non-violence but rather of a priestly ideological "return to the village", especially Malgudi, coloured by American aesthetics of regionalism. Krishnan is a college teacher, but the literary intertextuality is neither exhaustive nor illusive in Wildean sense. The absence of Indian texts, both *deshi* and *margi*, shows how Western cultural imperialism had been alienating our intellectuals from their own roots. It is the first person narrative which reflects the dialemma of Krishnan caught between two pulls: indigenous rustic and alien modern. His family is in the village and he stays in the college Hostel and engages four lectures per day. The colonized life is full of paradoxes. Krishnan, who once "devoured" English books and hopes to write poetry and later fiction by following British models and by reading books on creative writing in English, now begins to hate the white master's language and literature. This Prospero-Cannibal Complex needs to be illustrated in detail. The monotony of this exercise in, to use a strong term in Black aesthetics, "daffodilization' of minds and dislike of teaching profession strikes the reader in the opening paragraph itself: "some sort of vague dissatisfaction, a self rebellion" (5). Like Mr Biswas, the dominant presence of British texts in his consciousness is noticed in the next paragraph. The married teacher tells: "I took stock of my daily life. I got up at eight every day, read for the fiftieth time Milton, Carlyle and Shakespeare, looked through compositions, swallowed a meal" (5). He teaches *King Lear* to B.A. Junior students. Four lines from the stormy scene are quoted. The teaching of grammar and composition provides another but for a mild satire. He writes further:

> I spent the rest of the period giving a general analysis of the mistakes I had encountered in this batch of composition—rather very, as such for hence, split infinitives, collective nouns, and all the rest of the traps that the English language sets for foreigners.... Then I set men on Exercise in essay writing on the epigram 'Man is the master of his destiny'. "An idiotic theme," I felt, "this abstract and confounded metaphysics'" but I could not help it." I had been ordered to set this subject to the class (5-6). Further there is a pun on' Kant' and 'can't', American spelling and domination. The father in law of the protagonist provides one more model for him to rise up in arms against the British education system and tender the resignation to return to the village. He bring out the contradiction in the life of his father-in-law: "He was a B.A. of the olden days brought on Pater, Carlyle and Scott and Browning; personally looked after by Dr. William Miller, Mark Hunter, and other eminent professors in Madras...refused to enter Government service, settled in village. (19)

Two theoretical aspects might explain some aspects of intra- and inter-national colonialism and imperialism. The love and hate relationship with the ruler's culture and education takes us to the sources of comparisons in *Miseducation of Negroes, The Pedagogy of the Oppressed, Masks of Conquest: Literary Study* and *British Rule in India.*

Unlike Rao in *Kantapura*, Narayan has not mentioned M.K. Gandhi's name, which was the fountainhead of nationalism in those days. Here steps in the intra-cultural clash in India. So the resistant elements in this novel need to be studied at two levels: national and international. The latter is illustrated by the following intertextuality: "I picked up *Taine's*

History of Literature and leaned the glass against it." 'Taine every time' I muttered (22). But it is a very meek resistance which fits well into the pattern of the flexibility of the comprador class. Later, Jane Austen's *Pride and Prejudice* is mentioned as a text for non-detailed study. However, nowhere there is a deeper psychoanalysis of such literary responses. It seems that Narayan consciously guarded himself against British stream of consciousness techniques which had penetrated into Rao's novels. For locating such elements in a text, we have to take into consideration several factors such as place of writing, implied readers, publishers, critics, local creative tensions, etc. Krishna's creative urge is the only oasis in this desert. When he becomes introspective, he thinks loudly: "Nothing to do, Why not write poetry? Ages since I wrote anything?" My conscience had the habit of asserting itself once in six months—some pieces written in English and some in Tamil..." (He hopes to publish them). Wordsworth's "She was the phantom of delight and Keats'. "A thing of Beauty"...are cited. 'The Ode to the West Wind' gives the ironic touch to the letter of resignation submitted dramatically to Mr. Brown. The intertextuality of *Golden Treasury* (47) opens the Pandora's Box of pre-independence plagiarisms in Indian poetry. Finally, before protagonist's declaration in the resignation that "I am up against system...the whole system of education", "Insensible Shakespeare's sonnets or the ode" are referred to in passing.

Although the similar name of both protagonists invoke cultural signs associated with Lord Krishna, the degree of their literary acculturation differs in few ways. But similarities are many. Hindi texts and Jairam's teaching influence Mr. Biswas less, but British texts play vital role in making him a journalist of *Trinidad Sentinei. Bell's Standard Education, Volumes of Comprehensive Knowledge, Collin's Clear-Type Shakespeare*, other Western, especially British, texts mentioned by Naipaul, speak volumes for his more dialogic imagination and richer cultural hybridity in his novel. Paul Therous writes:

> His marriage is not a secret in Oagotes, he is welcomed tearfully by his mother, pestered for details by his relatives, who have the same awe for Mrs Tulsi that Joe

> Gargery has for Havisham in *Great Expectations.* Mr. Biswas's confusion (how to explain to these simple people the ways of those in that great house?) is similar to Pip's, but he must admit to himself that what he has done cannot be undone: "He was married. Nothing, now, except death, could change that". (62)
>
> Mr. Biswas, reading the *Meditations* of Marqcus Aurclius and Samuel Smiles, is trying to be different from the Tulsis, from the people he knows, from his own parents. He is trying to escape from tedium. (64)

In this way, both the protagonists "rise up against" two distinct systems in two different regions of the British colonies. Yet, the structures of their literary feelings are not much different like those in the French or Portuguese colonies.

What changed Krishna's love of European literature into hate of Western education and dislike to enter into the machine of otherness and made him resign the post of the teacher of English in a college in the nineteen thirties? Narayan graduated in 1930 and after his M.A. in literature, made "half-hearted effort to teach". This "love and hate" relationship needs to be studied in terms of Albert Memmi's *The Colonizer and The Colonized* (1957). He has theorized how the slave slowly internalizes the master's model and becomes Europe-America-centric. His resistance to the colonized wears different masks. For example, the colonizers always create the class of bourgeois 'of their own color, taste and culture' from among natives. Frantz Fanon, in his revolutionary *The Wretched of the Earth* and *White Skin, Black Mask*, presented the psycho-analysis of their violence which led to the apartheid movement in Africa as well as the Black Panthers' movement in the States of America. We cannot see the violence of that kind in the Gandhian era of non-co-operation and non-violence in which Narayan conceived *The English Teacher* and other novels. Thus, the major theme of resistance and nationalism, which is much hyped by formalist critics, needs to be reconsidered. "The white man's Burden" was shifted to the "whitish/wheatish" highest class/caste among browns in India. Narayan's writings represent that bourgeois class/caste which must have provoked "leftist students at Madras", as Walsh reports. Narayan's as well as Raja Rao's elitist nationalism in their novels needs to be reinterpreted in terms of the literary representation of the subaltern. Ranajt Guha opens his article, "On some aspects of the Historiography of Colonial India" as follows:

> The historiography of Indian colonialism has for a long time been dominated by elitism-colonialist elitism and bourgeois-nationalist elitism. Both originated in the ideological product of British rule in India, but have survived the transfer of power and been assimilated to neo-colonialist and neo-nationalist forms of discourse in Britain and India respectively. Elitist historiography of the colonialist or neo-colonialist type counts British writers and institutions among its protagonists, but has its imitators in India and other countries too. Elitist historiography of the colonialist type or neo-colonialist type is primarily an Indian practice but not without imitators in the ranks of liberal historians in Britain and elsewhere. (1)

According to Alpana Sharma Knippling, the period of the 1930s and 1940s shows that "the alliance of nationalism and colonialism produced India's modern 'moment' and now the writing of a certain kind of fiction participated in this inauguration of modernity" (170). Further she observes:

> R.K. Narayan (b. 1906) and Raja Rao (b. 1908), two early Indian writers in English, productively demonstrate how the literary project participated in the modern 'moment' inaugurated by the complicitous embrace of the discourse of the discourses of nationalism and colonialism. Narayan's *The English Teacher* (1945) and Rao's *Kantapura* (1936) are novels produced at a time when the most volatile political imperative concerned the need for Indian subjects to position themselves vis-à-vis British colonialism and Indian nationalism. But with the exception of *Waiting for Mahatma,* neither colonialism nor nationalism occupies a central position in Narayan's novels of this or for that matter any later

> period. Conversely, questions regarding colonialism and nationalism do occupy a large part of Raja Rao's *Kantapura*, but they are treated in such a way that they are deterred rather than addressed in both Narayan's *The English Teacher* and Rao's *Kantapura*, the aspects of colonialism and nationalism are engaged in a sidewise fashion, indirectly and obliquely. (170-71)

She has pointed out how *Kantapura* does a lip service to Gandhism, it fails to explain: why did it happen? Why did M.K. Naik laud *Kantapura* as "a prose epic of India"? How to decolonize such extensions of Anglomerican projects of modernism and aesthetics which demand, in Immanuel Kant's words, production of "ignorance" for retaining hegemony of "forms and culture". Our colonized curriculum produces much ignorance. It is necessary to take into consideration the second part of Kantian aphorism for gaining better comparative perspectives on all "Indian Writing in English" and the big process of internationalization of literature. My (1999) works have brought out some hidden aspects of this intra as well inter-colonialism. The different nature of colonialism and imperialism in Portuguese Goa still await explorations.

In order to understand this complex creative process, we have not only to master Blooming aesthetics of influence, Venetian theories of intertextuality, recent medical concepts of "textual intercourse" and K.K. Ruthven's long list of terms such as faking, remaking, retailoring, prefabricating, etc., but in addition to this, it is also necessary to define double colonized Indian reader as Nancy Hogley had done in case of Irish reader. From the new historicist perspectives, it is necessary to trace the significance of the relationship between culture and imperialism in Indian fiction.

Since this talk focuses on intertextualities in a novel on the English teacher is befitting to cite some lines from Ngugi wa Thingo's' "The Writer in a changing Society" (1969). He himself is a committed writer and a teacher of English. He writes:

> I too must have changed since I started writing in 1960. I was then a student at Makerere University College...I

> had read a number of writers, African and West Indian, and I knew that what they told, the song they sang, was different from what I had heard from the British writers who had been crammed down my throat in schools and at the University.... I grew up in a small village.... One day I heard a song. That song I heard as a child then spoke of things past and things to come. I was living in a colonial situation but I did not know.... I believe that African intellectuals must align themselves with the struggle of African masses for meaningful national ideal.... Perhaps, in a small way; the African writer can help in articulating the feelings behind this struggle. (7-50)

I believe our revisit to RKN and his Malgudi threatened by the Special economic Zone in Americanization "can help in articulating the feelings behind this struggle". Keep it up.

Works Cited

Achebe, Chinua. *Hopes and Impedements: Selected Essays 1945-1987*. London: Heinemann International, 1988.

Adiga, Aravind. *Between the Assassinations*. London: Picador, 2008.

Bhabha, Homi, K. (ed.). *Nation and Narration*. London: Routledge, 1995.

Guha Ranajt (ed.). "On Some Aspects of the Historiography of Colonial India". *Subaltern Studies I: Writings on South Asian History and Society*. Delhi: OUP, 1982: 1-8.

Memmi, Albert. *The Colonizer and The Colonized*. 1957, trans. Howard Greenfield. New York: The Orion Press, 1965.

Naipaul, V.S. *A House for Mr Biswas*. London: Russell Edition, 1961.

Narayan, R.K. *The English Teacher*. Great Britain: Eyre and Sportiswoode, 1945, reissued by William Heinemann, 1978.

Patil, Anand. "A Comparative Study of Nativistic Intertextuality in Indian Fiction", in Paranjape, Makarand. ed. *Nativism: Essays in Criticism*. New Delhi: Sahitya Akademi, 1997: 177-210. Reprinted in *The Whirligig of Taste: Essays in Comparative Literature*, New Delhi: Creative Books, 1999.

Patil, Anand. The Bells in "Post-Colonial Indian Novels: A Semiotic Comparative Study", *Perspectives and Progression: Essays in Comparative Literature*. New Delhi: Creative Books Publication, 2005: 15-30.

———. "The Literature in British Bombay and Portuguese Goa". *The Whirligig... Op. cit.*, 160-78. The English translation of the original Marathi book is to appear online: Amazon, and hard copy to be released by Lap Lambert Academic Publication, Germany.

———. *Literary into Comparative Culture Criticism*. Ambala: Associate Publishers, 2011.

Said, Edward W. "Representing the Colonized: Anthropology's Interlocutors." *Critical Inquiry*, winter 15:2 (1989): 205-26.

———. *Culture and Imperialism*. London: Vintage, 1993.

Sharma, Knippling, Alpana. "Fiction of the Indian subcontinent". *Modern Fiction Studies*, 39:1, (Spring 1993): 169-86.

Tharoor, Shashi. "India at Forty-nine: Notes Toward an Impression of Indian Society and Culture Today". *Midnight to the Millennium and Beyond*. New Delhi: Penguin Books, 1997: 278.

Theroux, Paul. *V.S. Naipaul: An Introduction to His Works*. London: Hienemann, 1972.

Thing'O, wa Ngugi. *Homecoming: Essays on African and Caribbean Literature, Culture and Politics*. London: Heinemann Educational Books, 1872.

Walsh, William. *V.S. Naipaul*. Edinburgh: Oliver and Boyed, 1973.

———. *Narayan: A Critical Appreciation*. New Delhi: Allied Publishers, 1982.

Wright, Thomas. *Built of Books: How Reading Defined the Life of Oscar Wilde*. New York: Henry Holt and Co., 2009.

Wyatt, Hyacinth Cynthia. "R.K. Narayan as a Brahman Novelist" Thesis Doctoral, Universitat Rovira, I Virgili (1997).

List of Contributors

Rana Nayar. Chairman, Department of English, Panjab University, Chandigarh.

Raju Parghi. Assistant Professor, Department of English and Modern European Languages, University of Allahabad, Allahabad (UP).

Arun Kumar Mukhopapadhyay. Assistant Professor, K.M. Institution, Bankura (West Bangal).

Kishwar Zafir. Assistant Professor, Department of English, Aligarh Muslim University, Aligarh (UP).

Javaid Ahmad Lone. Research Scholar, Department of English, Aligarh Muslim University, Aligarh (UP).

Kavitha Gopalakrishnan. Assistant Professor, Viswajyothi College of Engineering & Technology, Vazhakulam, Kerala.

Bina Biswas. TRR Engineering College for Women, Jawaharlal Nehru Technological University, Hyderabad.

C.L. Khatri. Editor: Cyber Literature, Associate Professor of English, T.P.S. College, Patna (Bihar).

Dhananjay Tripathi. Research Scholar, Department of English and Modern European Languages, University of Allahabad, Allahabad (UP).

Shyam Bihari Tiwary. Retd. Professor, B.S College, Lohardagga, Jharkhand.

Yakaiah Kathy. Assistant Professor, Thushara Degree & PG College, Kakatiya University, Warangal (AP).

Indrani Mukherji. Professor, Department of English and Modern European Languages, University of Allahabad, Allahabad (UP).

Harcharan Singh Arora. Head, Department of English, D.A.V. College, Bathinda (Punjab).

Rashmi Gupta. Associate Professor, Department of Applied Science & Humanities, I.T.S Engineering College, Greater Noida (UP).

Riyaz Ahmad Kumar. Research Scholar, Department of English, Maulana Azad National Urdu University, Gachibowli, Hyderabad (AP).

Anand Balwant Patil. Retd. Chairman, Department of English, University of Goa, Goa.